THE GREAT
Bicycle
ADVENTURE

Nicholas Crane

 The Oxford Illustrated Press

© 1987, Nicholas Crane

Printed in England by J.H. Haynes and Co. Limited,
Sparkford, Nr. Yeovil, Somerset.

ISBN 0 946609 34 9

Published by:
The Oxford Illustrated Press, Sparkford, Nr. Yeovil, Somerset.

Haynes Publications Inc., 861 Lawrence Drive, Newbury Park,
California 91320, USA.

British Library Cataloguing in Publication Data
    Crane, Nicholas
    The great bicycle adventure.—(The Great
adventure series).
    1. Voyages around the world — 1951-
    2. Cycling
    I. Title II. Series
    910.4'1 G369

ISBN 0–946609–34–9

Library of Congress Catalog Card Number 87-80505

Front cover photo © David Higgs

CONTENTS

For Ruth Dingley

I

Should Be Easy

NORWICH TO GREECE

It has been a disappointment to me that real men, like Sherpa Tenzing and Biggles, haven't worn spectacles. I have found only two good things about spectacle-wearing: they can create an impression of high intelligence, and by tying them with string to your head they act as goggles when travelling at high speed on a bicycle. It befits us all to make the best of what we've got.

Most of my boyhood friends had perfect vision, and nearly all of them rode bicycles. Fresh from school, one of my first moves on starting a three-year stint at the Cambridgeshire College of Arts and Technology was to buy a bicycle. It cost £4.50 and was a 28-inch-wheeled ladies' Raleigh, with a 'loop' frame and a saddle so high that I could look down on cars. It was useful for raising laughs and turning heads; facilities I had long found to be a good way of meeting people, especially policemen. Since Cora — as the bicycle was known — had no brakes, I also bought a pair of heavy leather boots with nailed soles. A favourite after-dark performance was to accelerate past Parker's Piece, hitting 20 mph at the lights in the High Street, where I would jump off the saddle and skid past the queue outside the Arts Cinema with fountains of sparks shooting from my heels. The noise was similar to a car travelling on its roof, and it would send the queuers diving for shop doorways.

I joined the college running team, and made a speciality of getting lost on cross-country runs. So I signed up for the rugby team. Obliged to play without my spectacles, myopia limited me to leaning on people, and chasing after the biggest moving object on the field. The wing-forward was a Scotsman called Douglas Rennie Whyte and together we re-launched the college mountaineering club. Most of its members were ardent bicycle riders. When I met Doug, he had just written off his landlady's bicycle in an unfortunate incident following a successful score at a home match. Doug was evicted, and seeing an opportunity to share the rent, we moved into a room full of furniture and mice, that fronted on Mill Road. Doug is a solid Scotsman and doesn't enjoy spending money. His choice foods were oats, swede and tripe, though he seldom ate tripe because it required turning on the gas.

Towards the end of the academic year I began scouring my atlas. I had ten weeks; enough time for a real journey. Going by bicycle would be cheap and challenging. It was also a mode of adventure-travel that ran in the family. In the late forties, my father Hol had twice set off on a bicycle across Europe, reaching the Auvergne on his first trip, and Naples on the second. In 1950 he pedalled to the edge of the freshly-erected Iron Curtain, in Austria. I had never tired of hearing his tales of crossing Germany with his foot wired to a broken crank, or of the wily thief who stole his passport and money from the saddlebag he was using as a pillow on an Italian beach. For as long as I could remember, Hol had kept a bright red Raleigh Record Ace in the driest part of the garage. It always seemed to shine, despite the dust. On the handlebars were two trigger levers that operated the five-speed hub-gear, a unique gear system my father had created by taking a cog from a Sturmey-Archer four-speed, heating it in Aunt Ella's coke stove to soften the metal enough to file off the slope of a castellation, then re-hardening the steel with another 'cooking'. It was many years before Sturmey Archer got round to marketing a five-speed of their own. The bike he used most of the time was a sturdy black Raleigh roadster that he'd bought in 1938 with pocket money saved over the years. It's still in use now and features in gold lettering on the tubing 'The All-Steel Bicycle'. It also had four gears.

Two weeks before the end of term, on page 25 of the atlas I located the goal: the tip of a remote peninsula projecting from southern Greece. Cape Matapan is the most south-easterly point of mainland Europe. I showed Doug the atlas, tracing a finger along the page. 'How far is it:' he asked. I measured it: Three thumb-lengths, plus a bit for wiggles . . . 3,000 kilometres. 150 a day. That's 20 days. Should be easy.'

'I've never ridden a bike abroad' said Doug through a raw swede. He sounded doubtful. Then: 'I haven't even *got* a

bike!' 'Buy one', I said. 'Paul Hunt's got one going spare.'
Paul Hunt had a beautiful hand-built touring machine made from Reynolds 531 tubing. It was painted cream, and had many Campagnolo parts. He sold it to Doug for £20, the parting from which left Doug nauseous for several days. We assembled our 'expedition' at my home in Norwich. Hol was chief advisor. 'You won't need a jersey so long as you've a windproof layer' he told us. 'Take as little as possible. Save weight.'

Every bearing on the bikes was dismantled and greased. Before we left, Hol put each loaded bike on the bathroom scales. Mine weighed 75 lb. We left Norwich at 6 am, hoping to catch the midday boat from Harwich. The distance was 60 miles. It was a hot July day. Neither of us had thought to fill our water bottles. I found out about dehydration five and a half hours later on the outskirts of Harwich.

'You go on!' I called weakly to Doug as he pedalled into the waving heat haze that danced on that interminable grey road. I had tried my best, indeed persevered far beyond my greatest expectations. But the heat and the miles had won. I hadn't drunk anything. Released at last from the excruciating effort, my mind became pleasantly light; eyes unfocussed. I was leaning over the handlebars, steering idly with one hand. My mouth hung open. The front wheel bumped onto the verge, ran along the grass for a few feet, then tipped down into the ditch. I passed out.

I was woken by a Greenline bus grumbling by. Passengers' faces turned. I mounted the bike and wobbled towards Harwich. I had eight minutes before the boat sailed. In rising panic I took two wrong turns before pedalling into the ticket office shouting 'one-way to the Hook!' While I rummaged furiously for money an avalanche of bread rolls — mother's last-minute donation — cascaded from a split carrier bag. The bike fell over. I rounded up the rolls. A uniformed man nonchalantly remarked that the '1200 hours service to Holland departs in two minutes.'

I leapt onto the bike. A truant coffee jar went into a jacket pocket, the torn carrier bag into one hand, and the passport between my teeth. Head-wobbling and frantic grunts were interpreted correctly as indicating that any interruption to my dash through the customs' shed was likely to make me miss the boat. A man waved me on. I made a final sprint across the quayside. All but one of the loading ramps had been lifted. A two-foot wide steel bridge remained.

With a last lung-bursting effort I surged forward. Someone shouted. The rubber of the front tyre bounced. Blackness flashed beneath me. I was in the hold. I spat out the passport and folded over, gasping for air. I looked around. Where was Doug? He was not there.

Suddenly starving, I snatched a roll through the side of the carrier bag, and using my sharp new camping knife sawed through the roll and half way through my hand. I looked at the blood and nearly fainted. 'Must find a sink' I said to my hand, and staggered towards a stairway beyond the close-packed cars. Dripping blood, I ran along a corridor till I reached a door which had a sign showing a man modelling a suit. At that moment cramp locked both my legs and I pitched forward, tripping over the high sill on the doorway to career across the cloakroom and crash into a sink. There was a smashing of glass. I stabbed at the tap. It was one of those sprung-lever designs common in public conveniences that either releases a derisory trickle or explodes with the force of a water-cannon. Water sprayed in all directions, filling my pockets, blasting my hands and hair and soaking everyone in the cloakroom with a fine wet mist. Worse still, I'd hit the tap so hard that it wouldn't turn off. Crouched, damp men were throwing themselves out into the corridor. The floor was flooding. Desperate, I yanked the handle of the tap upwards with all the strength I had. The spray gently subsided, and the tap gurgled, choked and ceased to flow. A calming, immense relief coursed through me as I stood ankle deep, proud that for the first time that day I had taken control of events. Remembering the cut, I uncurled my stinging hand. In it was the tap handle. I had snapped it off.

It took some time to pick the pieces of broken coffee jar from my pocket. The coffee itself had hydrated into a sticky strong-smelling syrup, like molasses, that could only be removed by my undressing and washing my jacket and trousers in the sink. Looking like a shipwreck survivor, I made my way to the ship's medical room where a part-time doctor applied a bandage and said that he hoped my holiday would take a smoother turn.

A renewed search through the gloomy depths of the ship's hold established that Doug was definitely not on board. I

4

asked to see the captain. He, I was informed, was busy, but I could if I liked make a formal address in writing. I did so, and was taken to a telephone, where I made a ship-to-shore call. Hol answered. I explained that since leaving them seven hours earlier the trip had been going well, except that I'd collapsed with heatstroke, nearly missed the boat, half cut my hand off, broken the coffee jar, snapped a tap and lost Doug.

'If Doug phones you' I rambled in a moment of rare foresight, 'tell him I'll wait at the Hook of Holland.' Hol, who was trained as a signaller during his National Service, repeated my instruction word-by-word, said 'Message received and understood', and put down the phone.

That night, feeling very alone, I set off in search of a camp-site. I found one on the edge of the Hook of Holland. There, a polite Dutchman told me that I could not stay because I didn't have a tent. Baffled by the logic of this, and too naïve to argue, I cycled to the sand-dunes that surround the port area. It was very dark, and each time I laid down my sleeping bag, shadows and whispers seemed to emerge from the blackness. For two hours I braved it as a bold first-time adventurer, then decided that it would be much less stressful behaving as a bandaged nervous wreck, so went to sit on the steps of the railway station for the rest of the night.

Doug arrived in the morning and we studied our map. It was one of those free Tourist Information handouts that shows motorways and the bigger oceans. Rotterdam seemed the next large town inland, and a woman in the currency exchange office pointed us towards a red-brick cyclepath.

Relaxing into the adventure, we pedalled side-by-side, marvelling at the facilities for cyclists: there were special traffic lights to help us cross busy roads, dainty little loops to carry us behind petrol stations and lots of signposts painted with little red bicycles. Frequently, we came to paths marked by stern black signs bearing the word 'Fietspad' — which we understood to mean 'footpath'. Rather than anger the locals by riding bicycles on their footpaths we rode long detours — often of several kilometres — to avoid them. In a country so well known for its sympathy towards the cyclist, we did begin to wonder after one particularly long diversion, why it was that pedestrians were being treated so preferentially.

We talked excitedly of our journey. Not having had time to research the route or the countries we'd be travelling through, my perceptions were largely drawn from paperback thrillers and illustrated school text books: sleeping outside in the open air with no tent meant silent knifings and poisonous snakes, and it went without saying that we would be robbed in Italy. Fourth-form geography had taught me about salt extraction in Alsace Lorraine, but I knew less about bicycle route-finding than a dinosaur does about cooking *coq-au-vin*. It turned out that neither of us spoke any foreign languages.

Near Schiedam, on a path running below a tall grass-sloped dyke, we met with a moped. The driver had a trilby-style hat jammed low over his forehead and the thick arms of his sizeable wife wrapped around his own ample waist. Being used to riding on the left-hand side of the road, our instinct was to swerve out of the way — to our left. The Dutchman's instinct was to swerve to his right. It was immediately understood by all parties to the impending collision that this was the moment to resort to an emergency manoeuvre. Doug went over the side of the dyke. I closed my eyes. The Flying Trilby and his wife, still aboard their moped, shot in an arc of churning turf up the banking of the dyke. They descended to the red-brick path with a hearty mechanical 'clump' as shock absorbers and springs flattened their end-stops, then proceeded away from us with the unflappability of high-wire performers.

'You'd think they'd want to stop and hit us, wouldn't you' said a disappointed Doug, looking at the dissolving blue exhaust as he pulled his bike out of the dyke.

Dusk on that first day on foreign soil found us in 's Hertogenbosch confronting a breakdown. Probably the most complicated part of a bicycle is the freewheel — the cluster of small cogs attached to the hub of the rear wheel. Inside this assemblage are many small ball-bearings, and some sprung metal flaps called 'pawls' that act as ratchets. When the pedals are at rest the ratchets click round allowing the bike to freewheel, and when you push on the pedals the ratchets engage and drive the rear wheel. On Doug's bike however, the pedals were freewheeling in both directions.

Hol had encouraged us to carry certain precautionary spares: one of these was a length of galvanised wire, which he had stowed inside our handlebar tubes. Using pliers, we cut the wire into lengths and tied the freewheel to the spokes of the wheel, thus locking the pedals to the wheel. This meant that the bike would now move forward when pedalled, but also that there was no way of stopping pedalling. All Doug had to do was revolve his legs, without resting, for the next 3,000 kilometres.

'Whatever you do, keep pedalling' I said as he edged warily from the curb 'If you stop, you'll tear all the spokes from the wheel!'

It was, we agreed later, a clever idea, but one which required a degree of mental application far beyond our own. Too quickly we found ourselves going down a hill.

'Don't stop, don't stop!' I shouted as we picked up speed. By the time we reached the bottom of the hill, Doug's legs were revolving so fast that his knees had started to glow. Just when I thought he was going to dislocate at the hips a car pretended to pull out from a side road in front of us. For a fraction of a second Doug stopped pedalling. There was a sound like a school ruler being scraped fast along a corrugated-iron fence, followed by Gaelic curses and a loud pinging and whizzing as pieces of bent wire flew past our ears.

On the pavement, we dismantled bit-by-bit the free-wheel. Several pedestrians paused to ask if we needed any help, and one of them, an elderly man with smiling watery eyes, took us into his home and let us wash the oil from our hands and arms. He brought us orange squash and sandwiches. We asked him why it was that there were so many *fietspads* for pedestrians, and why cyclists had to make such big detours to avoid using these footpaths. His jaw hung for a moment in disbelief, and then he creased over in compassionate laughter.

'*Fietspad*, boys, is not the footpath, it is the *cyclepath!*'

Over the following seven days we rolled southwards through Limburg, Belgium, Luxembourg, France, Germany and into Switzerland. We slept in woods and fields, creeping to cover in the last light of day. Since neither of us owned a lightweight tent, we had bought from a hardware shop in Lower Goat Lane, Norwich, two 6 x 7 foot sheets of polythene, which we used as groundsheets. We had a sleeping bag each which we had borrowed from the college mountaineering club.

Tied to the back of each bicycle was an army-issue canvas

knapsack containing trousers, a jacket, a spare pair of socks, a compass, string, a penknife, matches, a medical kit and dehydrated food. Convinced that foreign food would be inedible and would anyway cripple us with dysentery, we had brought with us dried vegetables, instant mashed potato, soya-bean meat substitute, 12 packs of tea and vast quantities of custard. Little of this food got eaten because in our caution we thought it best saved in case we came across a particularly barren part of Europe where we would be out of touch with habitation for several weeks. It was several days before we dared to eat locally-bought food that wasn't wrapped in plastic or tin.

We also had a stove that we rarely used because we didn't have the money to buy new gas cartridges. For cooking, we would light a small fire of twigs and dead wood and balance across a hearth of stones the small 'D' shaped canteen that my grandfather had used in the First World War. It was made of steel, so its inside would acquire a new patina of rust each day.

Like spectres we would creep into a field or wood at nightfall and depart just after dawn, leaving on the ground as our calling card two flattened strips of grass and a small black circle of ashes. We learned each day. One morning, on a dewy hillside outside the city of Luxembourg, Doug discovered that the best sort of firewood was the dead branches still hanging in the trees. Dead wood that has fallen is always damp. We also learned to avoid the dew by sleeping under trees, and that east-facing hillsides catch the early sun which dries sleeping bags.

The Alps of my dreams didn't reveal themselves as icy peaks sparkling like diamonds in the sun, but as a cold and soggy khaki mess spoiled by concrete dams and motorway construction sites. Because it was the only road on our map that crossed the strip of dark brown running from Yugoslavia round to southern France, we found ourselves climbing the St Gotthard pass, one of the main routes between Switzerland and Italy. It rained so much in the night that we had to wring out the bread before we could eat breakfast.

The beauty of the Italian Lakes is legendary. Here, the velvety lower folds of the Alps meet with the crystal waters of lakes whose shores are lined with villas, magnolia, lotus, oleanders, pomegranates and palms, cedars and lilies. Even the impoverished traveller cannot help but wonder at the bright canvas of this historical landscape. To celebrate our arrival in southern Europe we treated ourselves to a special meal. Sheltering from the rain in a concrete subway in Lugano, we used some of our precious gas to cook double portions of porridge.

The weather could only improve. 'It's the rain shadow' said Doug, cleaning the lid of the cooking-pot with a piece of bread. 'Once we're clear of the Alps and into Italy we'll get more than enough sun.' He put the bread in his mouth.

Leaving Como's early morning drizzle, we pushed on south past rhyming signposts. Hilltop towns like Solzago, Lurago and Barzago, Olgiate, Merate and Agrate slid by, and at Gorgonzola we turned left into the flat pan of the Po Valley — a place in Hol's stories that had assumed the heat and vastness of the Sahara. In Como, we had added to our possessions a road map of previously unimagined detail. That map changed our lives; it was the key to freedom. Between the main roads we found a maze of byways and villages. Suddenly we were released from the diesel and noise of heavy traffic. By lunchtime we had cycled clear of the mountain rains. Steam lifted in wraiths from the tarmac in front of us, and our layers of sodden clothing were blow-dried by the valley's toasting air. Instead of looking for ways of keeping warm, now we were experimenting with methods of keeping cool. Doug's fair Scottish skin burnt and bubbled till he looked like an overdone omelette. In a ditch, I found a hat with half a brim to shade my eyes. It got hotter and hotter. The people looked poorer. The Po Valley simmered. We passed peeling wooden signs announcing the region a disaster area. Mirages lay as puddles in the road. We began to wonder how we'd make it to the far side of the valley. In a soothing dusk we rode into Cremona, home of Stradivarius, Guarnerius, Amati, Monteverdi and of the woman who polished Galileo's balls. It was quite dark when we left, and our road from the town took us headlong into clouds of waiting mosquitoes. The road undulated, chilly pockets of air collecting in the low hollows. We spent the night gyrating in a knobbly field while squadrons of mosquitoes tried to eat us through some foul-smelling slime that we had bought from a chemist in Norwich. It attracted insects, and if it strayed to more sensitive parts of the body it had the sting of a thousand scorpions.

We were up at 5.30 am, intending to ride some miles before the day became too hot. As an enormous red sun pushed its way through the mist and trees we rolled through Cingia de Botti and onto the N343. We arrived in Casalmaggiore at eight o'clock to find the spacious main square bustling already. Eggs, plums, tomatoes and bread rolls were stuffed into our packs. We pressed on through Viadana and at last rode over the tea-coloured Po on a sagging Bailey bridge.

The next day we crossed the Rubicon. Doug marked this by buying from an international book-stall in Rimini his last British newspaper — for the Test scores. Also in Rimini, we met an Italian airline pilot. He had been looking at our parked bicycles, and was wondering where we had cycled from. 'You do not look like Italian cyclists,' he observed courteously. This was true. Italian cyclists like to wear tight, sleekly efficient, brightly-coloured apparel, and they like to be seen on machines pared down to the lightest, shiniest essentials. Doug and I looked as if we had crashed into the back of a garbage truck. We wore baggy Post Office dungarees, torn T-shirts and scuffed hiking boots. Our grimy bicycles were loaded with ex-WD equipment and an assortment of plastic carrier-bags suspended by string picked up at the roadside. We had cycled 1,200 kilometres, sleeping in the open air and cooking on wood fires. A large part of us had gone back to the Stone Age. Washing was not relevant. We were obsessed with food. If Doug had been shown a bar of soap, he would have eaten it. The pilot bought us an ice-cream each.

That night we slept on a headland overlooking the Adriatic sea then rose early, before the shadows shortened. We were riding a road marked on our map as a 'Strada Panoramico'. Along the way were small villages with lumpy cobbled streets, their houses decorated with wall paintings and divided by graceful little arches. But once we'd freewheeled down the hairpins into Pesaro, we joined the main coast road again, and the scenery became unremarkable. The road ran beside the railway, which ran beside the beach, for mile upon mile.

Two more days of pedalling brought us to the sprawling southern city of Foggia. We arrived at night, tired and hungry. Stopping outside an *alimentari* to buy some food, we were quickly engulfed by grubby, fingering children who entertained themselves by trying to dismantle the bikes. In rising ire Doug politely insisted that the little children leave his bicycle alone, and when they wouldn't, he bellowed in Gorbals vernacular loud enough to clear the street and make his nose bleed.

We tried to find the way from Foggia but soon became lost and, desperate to find a way out of the maze of dark, claustrophobic streets, asked two boys if they would show us. They rode their bicycles with the slapstick agility of circus clowns. We took lefts and rights beyond count, nipped through narrow alleys, cycled the wrong way up one-way streets, skittered over pavements and crossed streams of hooting traffic, and, twenty minutes later, when we were dizzy with tiredness, they brought us back to the place from whence we had started. The two boys hooted with laughter. Doug, haemorrhaging profusely, didn't. Realising that their latest prank was about to become their last, our two friends had a change of heart. This time, they promised to show us the right way out of town. We followed. My stomach rumbled. Doug spluttered in the darkness.

The boys left us, shouting 'Borgo mezzanone!' and pointing, which, with eager salivations I took to mean that there was a burger bar just down the road. But Borgo Mezzanone turned out to be a farmhouse and barn. Too tired to go any further, we lifted the bicycles over a high wire fence and crawled beneath a low canopy of vines. Doug looked as if he had sneezed into a bucket of tomato ketchup. Lying lengthways along one of the ditches between the rows, we wriggled into our sleeping bags and had just begun to drift away from the awfulness of the evening when the sound of a slow-moving vehicle snapped us awake. The lights of a pick-up truck were moving intermittently along the end of the row of vines. Every second or third row, the truck would stop and a powerful beam would fire down the tunnel between the vines.

'Don't move!' I whispered.

'Be quiet!' came the response. I was trying not to hear my heart thumping.

'Must be the farmer' I whispered, 'looking for grape thieves.'

SSSSssshhhhhh!' Doug hissed back, piercing the dark with a sound louder than a steam valve.

'For Chrissake shut up, he'll hear us!' I blurted, even louder.

'Get down!'

We sank into the earth. Was it the Mafia, I wondered. Would the farmer shoot on sight? If he did, would my bicycle tyres get punctured? Please, please do the row *next* to ours. We're only on holiday after all. The engine picked up, then stopped. A white beam lifted and glanced off the bushes two rows away.

'Bloody hell. We're next!' The engine rose and fell and the truck blocked the end of our row. There was a light metallic clunk. The spotlight flicked on, splashing the row beyond us in daggers of brightness.

In the morning, it just seemed like a bad dream.

The two main ports on Italy's heel are Bari and Brindisi. In 1807 local sailors stole from the Turks the bones of the benevolent bishop Nicholas, one of whose exploits it is said was to have reconstituted the bodies of three children who had been cut up and pickled in brine by a miscreant butcher. The story goes that the Dutch turned St Nicholas into 'Sint Niklaas', and then children 'babytalked' the saint into 'Sinter Klaas'. Thus Santa Klaus hails not from the frozen Pole but from the basilica at Bari. We cycled through Bari one evening, completely unaware of this interesting fact.

Brindisi was the jumping-off point for the second part of our adventure. From here a ferry slides across the smooth blue Adriatic to the Greek port of Igoumenitsa. From here too, Phileas Fogg boarded the *India Mail* in his fantasy journey *Round the World in 80 Days*. We had made our journey across Europe from Norwich to Brindisi in 18¹/₂ days.

At three o'clock on a roasting August afternoon, we sailed for Greece.

The pulse of life drops by half as you cross the Adriatic eastwards. The spaghetti complexities of Italy give way to the benignly slumberous airs of the Peloponnese and its myriad islands. Greek passion is buried deep. We slept the first night on a beach; the second in an olive grove on a hillside. As we lay back watching for shooting stars the darkened valley was filled with a medley of night noises: donkeys braying, cicadas buzzing, dogs barking, the whistle of goatherds, odd calls from the nearby village and the tinkle of animal bells. We woke in the morning to find that grasshoppers had helped themselves to half our loaf of bread.

Our unhurried plan was to ride south along the coast then cross the Sea of Corinth into Arcadia. At first, we were following sandy donkey tracks that linked the coastal villages. In one of these, a little place before Margarition, we ate squid beneath the trees, and a little further on, near Loutsa, paused to mend a puncture. It was hot. Doug fell asleep. People wandered past us on the dusty track. Riding on donkeys or small horses, the older men would clop past with a salute; the women would avert their eyes, pretending not to see us. Most of the little boys would stop for a chat. One of the boys disappeared up the rocky slope, to return minutes later with his pockets bulging with pears. Doug woke up. The pears were sweet and juicy and the boy wouldn't let us rest till every one was eaten.

I was still busy kneading an errant inner tube into the tyre when a young man sat down beside us. He was a teacher on holiday, and together we walked to the village cafe, where he insisted on buying us lemonade. Many of the people of his village worked in Germany, sending money home, saving for the day when they could return to retire. Once, this was part of Albania.

Continuing towards Loutsa, our track wound a narrow and steep course through the foothills, lifting us above the broad fertile plain that ran to the coast. Above this plain rose higher islands of rock on which had been built the villages. At Himadion — too small to be marked on the map — we slept on the edge of a small patch of vines.

At Riza, the next day, we asked in the cafe if we could buy a honey melon. A young man told us to wait. He returned clutching a huge melon. When we tried to give him money for the fruit he just shook his head and smiled.

Outside the village at the start of a long and very steep hill, the pack fell off my bike. I was busy tying pieces of string together when a man came by riding a donkey. He slid from his animal and stood watching till I was finished, then grabbed Doug's bike and started pushing it up the hill for him. We followed with the other bike and the donkey — an amiable animal better adapted to the rough tracks than our machines. By the time we reached the hilltop the young Greek was pouring with sweat from the effort of pushing the heavy bicycle. He pointed us at the shade of a spreading tree, and did the now familiar disappearing act. It must have been some way to the pear trees because it was twenty minutes before he bounded round the hillside with a shirt full of fruit.

Disappointingly, the road improved as we cycled southwards. We emerged from this garden of plenty later that day, to find ourselves riding beside the overgrown walls of the ancient city of Nikopolis. We left the bikes and hacked a path through a jungle of thorns till we came to the crumbling masonry — large square stones alternating with layers of flat red tiles. In one of the towers could be seen the socket holes for the floor-beams. Augustus built the city to commemorate his victory over the navies of Antony and Cleopatra at the nearby sea battle of Actium, fought on 2 September 31 BC. The civic amenities included a theatre, stadium and baths. Without cars, you can build quite a pleasant city.

The island of Levkas is separated from the mainland by a narrow sea canal cut across a flat isthmus. In the town, we bought a map of the island, and pedalled across the low-lying olive groves to the hairpin climb that winds up into the mountains that form the island's central spine. In the softness of early evening we arrived tired at the hill village of Lazarata. We paused to fill our water bottles, but were soon surrounded by a cheerful crowd. While the village policeman deputised some small boys to rinse and fill our bottles, we were led by the arms to a *taverna*. Glasses of water were brought, then small tumblers filled with a clear viscous liquid were rapped onto the wooden table.

'Drink!' they shouted.

'What is it?' I asked Doug.

'Haven't a clue.'

Our hosts were waiting expectantly, miming by throwing back their elbows that this was a drink that should be tipped down in one. I looked at Doug; sniffed the tumbler. Together we tipped. Doug's eyes crossed while they recorded a sequence of incendiary sensations. It began with a scorching of the thorax, was quickly followed by a kick to the base of the spine then reversed to rise in an eye-watering vapour that occasioned smiling faces round the table. My hand collided with Doug's as we groped desperately for water to extinguish the fires.

'What was *that!*' I mouthed.

'Ouzo! Ouzo!' all the delighted faces shouted, and the tumblers were re-filled. Anxious not to displease we repeated the theatricals twice more before being led crookedly across the square to another *taverna*. A large Greek with a curly grey moustache and a huge grin brought us bread and kebabs, and a medical student on holiday from Athens University brought us bottles of 'Fix' beer. More people joined the table till we had a merry throng that included two students, the policeman, a couple of Greek solicitors, a riot of small boys and some shepherds leaning on their sticks.

With each new beer our coordination suffered a little more. Manoeuvring a kebab skewer into the mouth required the dextrous concentration of an astronaut docking a space-station. The bench on which I was perched grew less stable. Doug said he had so many skewer holes in his cheeks all his beer was pouring through the perforations. We stayed all evening. When finally it was time for us to leave, the road was crowded from side to side with waving villagers.

We had no lights on the bikes, and were stoked up on enough ouzo to fuel a power station for a week. Round the hill from Lazararta we flew, laughing, with our legs and heads spinning in the clear mountain air until we met the pile of gravel that had been left in the road, ready for hole-filling at some distant future date. The bicycles decelerated from 30 mph to stationary in less than a second and, side-by-side, we flew over the handlebars to land in a confusion of arms and legs on the far side of the gravel pile. Helpless with laughter we crawled back to see the two bicycles standing upright with their front wheels firmly wedged into the pile of stones, regarding us with the expressions of long-suffering mules.

At a small village on the island's coast we settled down to several days of idling. On the third day we walked along the cliff paths and over the hill to Levkas town, where, at 11 am outside the post office, we met with the battered grey family Land Rover. Hol, my mother Naomi and sisters Liz and Fiona, had driven across Europe in a fifth of the time it took Doug and me to ride the same distance. A couple of days later, Paul Hunt arrived, on his way around the continent by thumb. One night there was a small earthquake and we were woken by rocks rattling down the hillside. After a week of swimming, eating, and watching the moon rise over coffee, we went our separate ways. The pedal-adventure resumed. Our goal was close. The southern part of the Peloponnese spreads in three fingers into the Mediterranean. The middle finger is the longest, and its tip is the most south-easterly point of mainland Europe: Cape Tainaron, Cape Matapan, Hades — the classical gateway to hell. From Levkas we cycled south to Mesolongi, a steamy mosquito-ridden place sitting on salt flats beyond the mouth of the Gulf of Corinth. In a scrubby park we ate bread and tomatoes at the foot of a statue of Lord Byron. Beneath the statue is buried his heart. He died here of fever in 1824 after months of inspiring its defenders against the Turks during the Greek War of Independence. A ferry took us across the Gulf and we began riding into the heart of Arcadia.

The road climbed above green-bottomed valleys and through mountains whose hazy peaks rise to 2,500 metres. Then we dropped down into the dusty valley that leads to Tripolis. Twice I managed to puncture my tyres. The second time it happened, Doug muttered 'Why don't you look where you're going?' I didn't know it at the time, but he was being driven as mad by my carelessness as I was by the noise he made when swallowing. We were both becoming affected by each other's irritating habits. If there was broken glass, a fish hook or a sharp stone to ride over, I could be guaranteed to hit it fair and square. Since leaving Norwich I had notched up an impressive total of 13 punctures, to Doug's four. On the rolling hills south of Tripolis my back tyre exploded violently enough to send two drifting hoopoes into a power dive.

Beyond the hills, Sparta revealed itself as a splash of white in the floor of a broad basin set against a backdrop of the grey Taygetus Mountains. Outside the town's museum Doug dropped our rubbish in a wastepaper bin, together with his wallet. Five minutes later we were on the road to Ancient Sparta when my travelling companion clutched his pocket, uttered a sound like a strangled haggis and turned his bike round so fast his tyres rubbed off on the road. Pleased not to be the careless one for a change, I occupied myself while Doug was gone by tightening my brakes with our adjustable spanner. He returned looking sheepish. Two days later, Doug asked for the spanner so that he could fix his brakes too. I rummaged through the torn plastic bag in which I kept my tools. The spanner had gone. I thought back in rising panic. With awful clarity I could see the spanner lying under the tree outside Sparta where I'd thrown it down after using it last. Doug, who *always* counted his tools back into the special cloth bag he'd sewn from a roadside scrap, said nothing.

We spent the day visiting antiquities. From a wrinkled septuagenarian we bought tickets to look at Ancient Sparta, then went up the hill to look at the Byzantine ruins of Mistras. Some of the churches had frescoes; others were locked and ageing into the creeping brambles. Eight days later, after a side-trip to the decaying Byzantine town of Monemvasia, we were poised to finish our journey, down the 'middle finger' to Cape Matapan. We rode into Gythion, a town of pale stone dwellings clinging to a scrubby hillside above the placid waters of a sheltered bay. The town guards the neck of the peninsula. We were excited and travel stained. On a steep hill above the harbour the pedals on my bicycle suddenly slipped round and spun uselessly. The freewheel had broken.

'Nick, I've got an idea. Let's use pieces of wire to tie the cogs to the spokes . . .' offered Doug.

We retired to the town square, a tranquil spot. The piercing chirrup of billions of cicadas was all but drowned by the discordant strains of *bouzouki* music which echoed from the battered face of a wooden loudspeaker bolted to the doorpost of the *taverna*. Inside, the shadowy outlines of broad backs and flat hats could just be glimpsed, bent over backgammon and glasses of retsina.

Outside, it was hot. Very hot. White walls surrounding the dusty square bounced heat onto anyone who dared wander into the furnace. A eucalyptus tree offered token shade; a temporary respite from the noon-day heat of the Peloponnese in high summer.

Beneath the tree, Doug sat writing in his notebook, while in front of him, on all fours, I was groping in the dust for a number of tiny ball-bearings that had dribbled out from the freewheel of my bicycle. I had taken the freewheel apart, to find the little metal 'pawls' mashed and the delicate springs bent into ringlets. Tripolis, 120 miles away, seemed the nearest town likely to have a shop which stocked these parts. We discussed the options. I could hitch-hike to Tripolis and try and buy a new freewheel. I could take a bus, which would cost more. Or I could sell the bike to one of the boys leaning against the eucalyptus. Or I could try and mend the pawls and springs. We voted for the last option.

By unwinding a strand from a wire brake cable, we ended up with strands of steel of roughly the same diameter as the damaged pawl springs, and it wasn't too hard to bend them to shape, then insert them into the anchor holes in the freewheel block. But mending the pawls was a different story. An hour of filing reduced by half the diameter of my thumb and fore-finger but made little impression on the hardened steel of the pawls. Disconsolate, I dropped the file in the dust. This proved the most productive move of the afternoon, for it prompted a small boy to walk forward, grab me by the arm and lead Doug and me up a side street to a weatherbeaten wooden door. Inside was the most comprehensive collection of miscellaneous junk ever assembled in the western hemisphere, including, we noticed with fluttering hearts, a rusty bicycle frame. The boy talked quietly to an old man in dungarees, who occasionally glanced over towards us.

We pointed at the rusty bike frame, and the old man nodded enthusiastically, turning to scribble a figure on the back of an envelope. But we didn't want to buy his bike — just acquire a very small part of it, which, judging by the bike's advanced state of decomposition, had long since gone. How could we convey to him our need? We tried miming the action of a freewheel, Doug using his hands to indicate the flapping of the pawls and springs, myself pedalling and clicking alternately. The crowd clapped appreciatively. The old man looked on with blank amazement. We incorporated gear changes into the pantomine, flew down a hairpin so fast out tongues ached from the clicking then tackled a steep hill. Our gyrations were interrupted by the arrival of one of Gythion's officers of the law. I thought he might arrest us.

But fate proved kinder: the policeman hauled a serious-faced lad from the cluster of grinning onlookers. He could speak English and delivered our enquiry to the old man, whose face slowly brightened with enlightenment. Fishing behind a heap of ropes he produced a small tin box which he opened with a solemn reverence normally reserved for coronation ceremonies. As the lid lifted, heads craned forwards and an audible gasp whispered around the shadowy room. It was *full* of freewheel pawls.

There must have been several hundred of them. We chose

a couple, and took some for spares, and asked the price. Everyone laughed. There was no price. It was much colder in the square now. The reassembling took place before an interested audience. Replacing the parts of a freewheel requires delicate surgery. First the multitude of tiny ball-bearings must be balanced on the narrow curved race. They can be made to stick there by smears of grease, or soap. Then the pawls are slipped into their sockets on the block, and the little springs slipped in behind them. Next a piece of cotton is wound round to hug the pawls in to the block. At this point you need a friend. Doug held the ends of the cotton while I slipped the cogs over the top and tightened the locking ring. Doug then gingerly pulled out the cotton, and, to much applause, the freewheel was flicked to sing a smooth rhythm of clicks. It was just an hour or so before dark. I managed to collect two more punctures before the sun set.

We left town the next morning on a road which first crossed a green and fertile valley whose juicy scents reminded me of England in the spring, then climbed into an impressive gorge guarded by the castle of Passava. This is the entrance to the Mani peninsula — an arid sump of mystery and historical intrigue.

Since the beginning of time the Mani has been a receptacle for refugees. The Mani's history was one with that of Sparta until the monarchy ended at the turn of the third century BC. Fleeing before the tyrant Nabis, the Spartans found refuge beyond the Taygetus Mountains, on this 30-mile long peninsula. The Spartans merged with the Laconians, already established in the Mani, to form a Republic, which survived till AD 297. Life continued under the Byzantines, with new waves of Spartan refugees driven south by the Visigoths of Alaric. Fresh waves followed, escaping the Slavs, then the Bulgars. The thirteenth-century Frankish conquest of the Morea precipitated another swarm of refugees from Byzantine Sparta, and the falls of Constantinople, Mistras and Trebizond yet more. By now the once peaceful Maniots, hardened by contact with the warlike Franks, had turned into implacable warriors. Guerrilla leaders such as Korkodeilos Klades, and the swords and guns of the Mani kept the peninsula free while the rest of the Peloponnese was overrun by Turks.

Still more contingents arrived from other parts of the occupied world such as Asia Minor and Crete.

The continual influx of strangers, and the hard struggle for existence among the rocks and cacti, created a tribal system fraught with vendettas and feuds between rival villages, families and clans. The Maniots became mercenaries and pirates, while the Turks stood back rather than burn their fingers by getting involved. In the mid-seventeenth century the Turks created the first Bey of the Mani, a part-time pirate called Liberakis Yerakis. But Yerakis went on the rampage through Greece, fighting sometimes for the Venetians, at others for the Turks, and finally married a princess of Wallachia. The Turks were not impressed and it was a hundred years before a second Bey was appointed.

The revival of the rank of Bey in 1776 sparked off another spate of intrigues. Seven more candidates were deposed or executed in the ensuing 32 years. In 1808 the last and greatest of the Beys — Petrobey Mavromichalis — came to power in the Mani. Having played a leading part in ousting the Turks from Greece, Mavromichalis was imprisoned by the new leader of the state, Capodistra, for which indiscretion Capodistra was assassinated by a couple of Mavromichalis' nephews.

The castle at Passavá was built in 1254 by the Franks to keep the warlike Maniots on the peninsula. We scrambled up through clutching briars to the massive walls which sit in a great rectangle overlooking the narrow defile. Below the other three walls of the fort, the mountainside dropped steeply. Both the pass above Aeropolis and the sea near Gythion could be seen from this high point. Nobody passing beneath would have been safe from the watching ramparts. The Mani tapers into the sea twenty miles south of Passava.

Higher the road climbed, to cross a col flanked by high buff peaks, before descending to little Aeropolis — the Maniot 'capital'. The villages of the Mani look like Stone Age versions of Manhattan. Instead of conventional houses, the Maniots live in square-based towers that often rise seventy or eighty feet. These towers cluster together above shady alleys and steps. It's probable that the towers derive from the Nyklians, who arrived from Arcadia in the fourteenth century. Struggles for living space, grazing rights, use of tiny terraces where corn or olives could take root, and for salt-gathering rights along the shore, led to quarrels — often violent. Winners of feuds would be called 'Nyklians', and grant themselves rights over the subjugated. The Nyklians had their own hierarchy, calling the village elder a 'kapetan', while the chief kapetan over all was — appropriately — the 'bashkapetan'.

The first towers went up in around 1600, when the Nyklians began to compete among themselves. Often, several Nyklian families would establish themselves in a single village. Dominance could be achieved by bombarding any luckless neighbour whose tower happened to be lower than your own. Boulders would crash through the marble roofs, cannon crashed in the alleys. At night, and during truces, towers would sprout a few feet, thus gaining a height advantage ready for the next battle. The height of the tower was also a symbol of local status. The feuding continued into the nineteenth century.

A police jeep blocked our way as we entered Gerolimin. One policeman pointed his machine-gun at us, while the other demanded our passports. Our journey by now had removed any similarities between our real appearance and the photographic image in our passports. We said that we were tourists; that we had cycled from England. They didn't believe a word. The man with our passports said we were under arrest, and confined to Gerolimin for the night. We were allowed to sleep in a field at the water's edge.

Nearby was a tent containing a French couple. They told us that a big yacht had been stolen from Kalamata by two German men, and that the fugitives had landed at Gerolimin and fled into the olive groves. Every fair-haired foreigner was under suspicion. The Germans were said to be dangerous.

That night, lying in the open, I was woken by a sucking and gurgling among the rocks. 'Aqualung!' I thought. The Germans had escaped from the yacht by swimming underwater using breathing apparatus, and were now lurking in the rocks waiting for their chance to make a run for it. My heart raced. I woke Doug.

'They're down there. The Germans!' I whispered. This was a chance to prove our innocence to the police. We picked up a large stone each, and crept to the water, stalking the gurgles. On a pre-arranged signal, we leapt from cover.

But no rubber-suited, armed-to-the-teeth pirates fell at our feet. Thinking the aqualungs must have submerged, we peered into the heaving crannies. The watery breaths continued. 'Pretty odd', I said. Doug looked dubious. My credibility was on a knife edge. 'Let's wait till light.' I lay awake. The sucks and blows grew fainter. At dawn, I crept back. There was not a frogman to be seen, though I did find a hole in the rock through which each wave passed with a sound not dissimilar to that of an aqualung.

The police caught the Germans in the hills later that day.

Southwards from Gerolimin we cycled. At Vathia the road stopped. We carried the bikes up a flight of steps between the tower houses. Dogs yapped and shutters slammed. Eyes peered at us from high sills. In the shade of a doorway we passed an old woman who hadn't time to slip indoors. On her lap were some tiny birds and prickly pears, being plucked and peeled. Many of the tower houses seemed derelict, and on some of them we could clearly see the stratified layers of masonry that marked each new upward surge of building. We followed a small rocky track beneath an overhanging cliff. Across the sun-blasted hillside wandered broken walls hinging on a neglected terrace whose walls were tumbling back to the ground.

We pushed the bicycles, having to lift them frequently as the path deteriorated. On the thinnest part of the peninsula, at a place where it bottlenecks to a narrow ridge topped by the path, the back tyre of my bicycle exploded with a bang. I used the last of our large patches. Doug thought it was crazy to take the bikes further. We had no puncture patches left, and we wouldn't be able to ride along the rough tracks anyway. 'That doesn't matter. We can carry them!' I reasoned. He didn't see my point of view. It was, in any case, my fault for using up our stock of patches with my endless punctures.

We left the bicycles behind. I was disappointed, peeved that Doug hadn't wanted to carry the bikes with us to the Cape. Carrying a plastic carrier bag containing a tin of mackerel, sultanas and some water, we continued on foot. High above 'Kidney Bay' we walked while the village of Ahilla slid round behind us. At a well by a large church we drank from a rusty tin someone had thoughtfully left. Several barren brown fingers sloped down to the sea, with Tainaron clearly the one marked with a white lighthouse. In the shade of the lighthouse we sat looking southwards over the Mediterranean.

'Well we did it. Sort of' I said.

'Aye, we did.'

'Pity about the bikes. Someone else will go and do it with bikes now.'

'Probably.'

Six years later, a man came bumping down the track from Vathia. He was riding a Raleigh 'All-Steel' bicycle tied to the back of which was a pack containing a large quantity of puncture patches. It was Hol.

2

A Tandem Called Terence

FRANCE

The handlebars had a mind of their own. I over-corrected and the front wheel swerved right. 'More power' I shouted. At stalling speed, we zig-zagged towards a line of parked cars. I couldn't see what was happening behind me. 'I can't get my feet on the pedals' came Elaine's plaintive cry. Suddenly she did. It was like throwing the turbo-charge switch. Like a rogue missile the tandem careered across the road, missing a dim-looking Maths student by inches to snake between a Renault 4 and a Vauxhall Viva van, mount the pavement, rear up onto a rockery and crash down into a thicket of ornamental bullrushes. In less time that it takes to say 'I'm getting the hang of this at last' the front door of 128 Myrtle Road exploded and Mrs Szechepanski erupted onto the scene. Without even looking at the bullrushes, she moved towards us. She looked *very* cross.

We left for France a fortnight later. This was an odyssey that began with an advertisement in the back of the *Cambridge Evening News,* under the 'Miscellaneous For Sale' column. Nearly lost among the smudgy invitations to buy second-hand aquariums and old Hoovers were two lines which read: 'Tandem', it read in bold. 'In need of renovation. £10 o.v.n.o.' It was followed by a telephone number.

The tandem was beneath some sacking in the spider-infested garage of one of the posh houses off Grange Road. 'In need of renovation' was a piece of misinformation akin to Fred Flintstone calling his car an executive saloon. Beneath the sacks were three parts. There was a frame entirely stripped of components, and two wheels that looked as if they had fallen off Stephenson's Rocket.

But it was a start. All I had to do was to find the little bits and pieces to fill in the gaps. I made a list: handlebars, pedals, stems, brakes, cables, gears, chains, tyres, tubes ...

Then I hitch-hiked to London, spent a small fortune in a shop specialising in imported tandems and returned, grinning, with a bag full of booty. Not a single piece fitted the tandem. It was unbelievable. All the threads on the machine were 'oversize'. I consulted Doug: ' 'sright,' he said, 'Makes it stronger you see. The forces on tandems are much greater than those on a normal bicycle. Go and try whatsisname up Mill Road.'

It was one of those nearly-dark bike shops festooned in wheels and tyres, with a wall of brown varnished drawers whose brass label-windows were occupied by bits of paper saying 'Trivelox springs' or 'Lucas wicks'. Behind a counter covered in spanners and oil-cans was a man with a pump-connector tucked behind his left ear. I explained my problem. Before I finished, he cut in: 'Y'want half-eighth not three-thirty-second, an' y'want an eccentric bottom bracket, an' y'want 11 five-sixteenth balls, an' y'want one-eighth rings, an' y'want a number 16 axle or is it an offside drive?' he asked, looking up for the first time. 'Not too sure' I replied. He regarded me as if I was a complete dunce. 'Better join the Tandem Club' he said. 'They help people like you.'

I joined the Tandem Club and embarked on what amounted to a correspondence course in tandem reconstruction. The Technical Secretary, Mr Bob Tinley, wrote me long and detailed letters explaining the pros and cons of crossover drive, and how to clean the linings on hub brakes. I also learnt from Bob that my tandem was a 'Sun', a Fifties brand well-known for its sturdiness and immense weight. With each day's work, the tandem became longer, until it stretched from wall to wall of my tiny bed-sit. When it was finished, I found that it was too long to fit round the corner by the door. I had to take it all to bits again.

Re-assembled outdoors, Terence looked a magnificent beast. Every component was solid steel — even the mudguards. The frame was hand-painted the colour of nineteenth-century beer bottles, the mudguards were maroon and handlebars flaked-chrome. The braking system was of agricultural dimension: on front and back were two massive hub-brakes built by the British Hub Company and operated either by levers on the handlebars or by a large foot pedal. By the time he was rolling, I had spent ten times the original outlay. As a road vehicle, Terence was of Titanic scale and weight. Two years had elapsed since Doug and I reached Cape Malapan. We'd made another bike journey together in the meantime – to Africa – and then I met Elaine. In true romantic fashion the picture of a bicycle made-for-two rolling south towards the sun and who-knew-what captured our minds. But neither of us had ridden a tandem before. The key to mastering Terence, we learnt, was synchronicity of mind and body: under the coordinated application and easing of leg-power, Terence behaved with a modicum of smoothness. It was also great fun.

The idea was to ride across France to its most central town — a place called Nevers — and there meet up with Doug and three others from the mountaineering club. The year before, two of them, Mark Hampson and Peter Inglis, had cycled from England to Greece, while Doug and I were trying to pedal to Africa. The early miles through the easy 'B' roads of East Anglia served as a running-in prelude to the harder country. Most of our luggage was contained in two ex-Army canvas knapsacks hung over the rear carrier. An old plastic saddlebag tied up with string rested on the carrier, together with a vast barrel of polythene sheeting which contained the sleeping bags. Over the handlebars was hung a small canvas gas-mask case that I found in the garage at home. Terence had three speeds, the lowest of which would only just carry him over a shallow-angled railway bridge. At slow speeds he was virtually unmanoeuvrable. Only the springs of the front saddle existed, and a top had been fabricated out of a strip of carpet.

We bowled across Normandy and down through the woods to Duclair, where we waited beneath the limes on Liberation Quay for the small roll-on roll-off ferry. If a bicycle journey can be measured in rivers crossed, then it is always the first that brings the greatest surge of excitement.

The first good hill is also something worth looking forward to. This came on the way out of a town called Dreux. Inexorably gathering speed, like a runaway train, Terence rolled faster and faster. It seemed a pity to use the brakes. The wind rushed over the bags and bike tubes with the disturbed gusting of a falling biplane and with every added kilometre per hour, Terence became less inclined to turn the corners. By the bottom of the hill he was making use of both sides of the road. We rolled to a halt with smoke trailing from the brakes. The spires and flying buttresses of Chartres Cathedral grew, like the masts and rigging of a ship, from the open fields above the Eure Valley. At Orleans we came to the Loire along whose banks stand châteaux of a romantic fantasy. Outside ivory-walled Chateau de Sully, we lay above the water of the moat, munching our way through crunchy *baguettes* with pâté and Camembert. Joan of Arc came here more than once, and later Voltaire too. But it is the roof timbers of the Chateau du Sully that tell the best story. These were put in place in 1363, having been cut from chestnut trees that had been stripped of their bark while standing, then squared, soaked in water for several years, dried for several further years, then disinfected before being used in a geometry that allowed the best circulation of air. Six hundred years on, there is no rot or worm in them. We followed the Loire upstream, on little roads that loved to nudge the easy river on one side, or the wooded slopes of its valley on the other. Sometimes castles would catch us by surprise: hidden by a topographical fold or stand of trees.

With Elaine's encouragement – she was fluent in French – I learnt more of the language. Early attempts to communicate with a French person had not been promising. Returning with Doug from Africa the previous year, we had found ourselves stranded in Paris for the afternoon. Unable to take the bikes from the train, we had set out on foot to explore the sights. I wanted to see the Arc du Triomphe and Champs Elysees. Outside the Gare du Sud I walked boldly up to a newspaper vendor. 'Oo ay lez chomps elleesays' I said. When she didn't appear to grasp what I was asking, I repeated it a little louder, which drew the attention of several passers-by. They stopped and leaned enquiringly into my face as if I needed urgent medical attention. I said it again, splitting the syllables to make it easier for them:

'Oo-ay-lez-chomps-el-ee-says.' At this point Doug uttered a few French words in an accent that sounded as if his tongue had got creased and all the passers-by broke into nodding and pointing. It was a hideous moment.

About 750 kilometres after leaving home, Terence rolled into Nevers, and, at 1 pm on the prescribed day, Elaine and I met with our four itinerant friends. For a few days we rode together through choppy, mixed countryside of forest and field, heading approximately south wards. This was the direction most likely to bring drier weather. It rained a lot, and we slept beneath trees in shelters made from our sheets of polythene, cooking over fires whose flames roasted our faces and whose red embers dried the soaking earth. We widened the necks of our water-bottle holders to the diameter of wine bottles. The average daily mileage dropped. Short of time, Doug and Robin departed for Brittany, leaving four of us to continue. With Mark and Pete, we dawdled through byways burgeoning with leaf and fruit.

We lived on blackberries and plums and apples and on 'mealies' — the chewy cobs of maize that the French farmers feed to their cattle. Having left Nevers with no particular goal in mind, we found ourselves being drawn towards the highest part of central France: into the mysterious volcanic heartland of the Auvergne. It was as if a good view over the big green hills of the Masif Centrale would provide a clue to our future direction.

We were using roads so small that we had to stop at farms to ask the way. This was not an area any tourist would think to visit; a kind of transition zone between the fertile pastures of the upper Loire and the scenic focus of the Auvergne. For two days we rode beside the River Sioule, sometimes in its gorge. When the road ran out, we pushed the bikes along a stony forest track while the river churned below and an eagle wheeled above. Presently the roads lifted us from the deep valleys onto the higher plateau. To the east we could see the perfect pyramid of the Puy de Dôme, up whose spiral road has raced the Tour de France. Eddy Merckx was punched by a spectator on the Puy de Dôme. From the top, you can look at the line of shattered old volcanoes stretching across the wooded Auvergne heights. As the hills became steeper, Terence spent more time being pushed than pedalled till he came to be seen more as a lopsided wheelbarrow than as a bicycle.

We walked up a hill from Rochefort-Montagne, passing through a volcano which had been cut in half by a glacier. The slow grinding ice had exposed the hexagonal columns caused by the contracting of the solidifying basalt, so that the inside of the mountain now rose in gigantic organ pipes. At the heart of the Auvergne, at 1,885 metres, is the highest mountain in central France. On a wild and windy morning we climbed the Puy de Sancy. It was disappointing. The fragile skin of vegetation is ripped by tracked vehicles and there is a *telecabin* station on the top. It would be hard to find a more desecrated mountain and a biting wind turned us quickly back. West from here, the next piece of higher land is the Absaroka Range in the Rocky Mountains. The roads were empty; the hills blowing with washed air. We arrived in the Vallée de Chaudefour at 80 kph shrieking with laughter as each machine tried to go faster than the next. Fully loaded, our tandem was so heavy he needed two people to lift him, but given a run-up of several kilometres Terence's dead weight could descend a mountain pass with the sureness of a falling meteorite. Pete and Mark were on lighter solo bikes. With plastic carrier bags, billy cans and kettles hanging from every corner, they could only achieve the same speed as Terence by revolving their legs at the speed of catherine wheels.

Once, we came unstuck. We were coming down a hill into a village near Riom. Under some effort, a battered Citroen 2CV began to overtake. When the driver thought he had passed us he began to draw back to the kerb, unaware that by now Terence had accumulated yet more speed and was creeping level with the passenger window. The driver's eyes popped. The narrowing vector of road in front of Terence disappeared. The 2CV swerved. Terence flew over grass and into a garage forecourt. He struck a petrol pump a glancing blow before skidding to a halt in a tangle of legs.

The Frenchman had brought his car to a standstill and, through the spokes of the front wheel, I watched him walk towards us.

'Monsieur, peut être vous eplique l'accident', I spluttered.

'Il est possible le tandem que nom, Terence, est très, très cassé.' Elaine was hopping round on one foot and holding the other. It occurred to me that we had narrowly missed being projected headfirst through the face of a 97-octane Shell Super Plus petrol pump. I raved on: 'Je pense il est necessaire a telephone les gendarmes, parce qu'il nous sommes nearly mort.' The man shook his head.

I wasn't making contact. Elaine hopped over and intervened, speaking quickly and calmly in French. I watched in amazement as the man flipped open his wallet and handed her a note. When he had gone I asked

'How much?' 'Ten francs' replied Elaine grinning. A fortune! Enough to live on for several days.

Straightening the handlebars and collecting the bits and pieces that had been broken loose by the impact, we patched our shins and rode westwards. Over the following days it continued to rain and we slept in hay-lofts, cow byres, burnt-out houses and once, in a ruined church. Pete's heart had stopped when he saw the eyes of a black-cowled woman watching him over a gravestone.

We pushed Terence over the Puy Mary in cloud so thick it soaked us, then hurtled down through the Cele and Cere valleys to the limestone-walled Lot. Here Pete and Mark departed for the Pyrenees, while Elaine and I continued westwards. We were running low on money, and began asking at farms for work. It was September, the vines were heavy and the *vendange* about to begin. When Terence's freewheel broke for the third time, we walked to the next village, a little place called Verdelais. It was on a hill, looking over the valley of the Garonne. The first door we knocked on was opened by M. Fonteyraud. His uncle, he thought, could give us work, and in the nearby town, Langon, there was a good bicycle shop for Terence's freewheel.

M. Fonteyraud's uncle was fair but grumpy. He was called M. Bernard, and lived in the next village, Sainte Croix du Mont, in a large and very old house called Château Lamarque. His wine was bottled under the same label. M. Bernard gave us a single-roomed cottage to live in. In one corner was a wooden stand bearing a porcelain wash bowl and jug. We worked six days a week. On Sundays shot rattled on the tiled roof. The woods were dead, every bird blasted away by Sunday sportsmen.

Hardly could a product of such romantic association seem so distanced from the ugly reality of its origins. It was a small farm, employing during the vendange maybe 20 or so casual workers, mostly Spaniards who had crossed the Pyrenees for the season. Some of them would stay all winter, moving northwards with the ripening grapes, finishing the year picking up potatoes in Pas-de-Calais. On hands and knees in sticky mud, or in a back-breaking stoop, we cut the bunches of moulding grapes from the vines. We would be given one row each, and everyone would be expected to keep up with the fastest picker. It was cold, dirty work. After a couple of days I was told to work as a 'carrier' — the person who collects the full baskets of grapes from the pickers. Attached to my back with leather straps was a big metal bin. The call of 'Panier!' would tell me which muddy gully to slither along next. Compared to picking, it was a holiday. When it wasn't raining, M. Bernard would stand at the end of the rows, watching. He had a silhouette not dissimilar to that of Mussolini.

The more unpleasant the occupation, the more hilarious become the moments of relief. There was a boy called Patrick who could not stop himself from whistling a catchy but sickly tune called 'Viva Espana'. This mindless song became so appalling to hear that just the first three notes would bring a rain of rotten grapes down on the head of the hapless Patrick. After lunch, when we had consumed our statutory litre of wine each, the pickers would entertain themselves by throwing the buckets of grapes into the bin on my back with as much force as possible, to see if my wine-weakened knees would give way. On the last day I tripped over my own feet, and 60 lb of slushy, very mouldy grapes poured over my head.

When the vines were stripped and the last bucket had been filled, we all crammed onto the trailer amid the brimming bins and drove to the *cave*, where M. Bernard, smiling at last, poured us glasses of fizzy, sweet red wine straight from the bubbling presses.

The frosts had already arrived when we oiled Terence for a final time and began the long autumnal ride back to England.

It took us five days to reach the English Channel. Through the deserted pine forests of Les Landes, we came to the mouth of the Gironde. A small, empty ferry took us from Point de Grave to Royan and we pedalled northwards through the chilly mists of Normandy. Elaine cut up a jersey and stitched the wool into gloves.

★ ★ ★

We had been away nearly three months. The days of endless travel were over. Now it had to be 9-to-5 jobs and 2-week holidays. Life revolved around advertisements. Reading *Cycling* magazine in the public library one day, I saw a small ad inviting applications to join a cycling expedition across the Sahara Desert. That sounded my kind of job. The man organising the expedition was called Ian Hibell. I wrote off, but got no reply. I took a job in the Lake District, working in a youth hostel. Years later, when I eventually met Ian, he was able to tell me what I'd missed: he'd suffered burning sun, sand and flies; he'd got lost in the middle of the desert and one of his critical water-dumps turned out not to exist.

Poor Terence met a sad end on the North Downs. One Sunday afternoon he collided with a milestone hidden in long grass.

3

The Corsican Connection

CORSICA

The slightly shorter of the two raised a fist the size of a pineapple and advanced. His eyes were unusually close together. I quickly lifted the camera from around my neck. In doing so I accidently hit the man in the mouth. His cigarette was knocked upwards. He stopped. Ash smeared his stubble, where it smoked like a slow-burning defoliant. Death (mine) seemed imminent. The bigger man spoke. In a mixture of French and German he said he would like to throw us over the cliff. Then he changed his mind. I deflated in relief. He pointed to a rifle in the car. He would shoot us first and *then* throw us over the cliff.

Watching us all the time, the two walked slowly backwards towards their car. They climbed in. Then they drove off.

We had come to Corsica for a fortnight of mild adventure. On a hill above Cape Paolo the adventure got out of hand. We had been cruising contentedly down the tight bends high above the sea, when a car hurtled around the corner, nearly knocking Elaine over the cliff edge. In the best tradition of cyclists wronged, we shouted our feelings at the car. It stopped. Two men expanded from the doors. They were not so much tall, as wide and thick. Their legs appeared to move only from the knees downwards.

For the rest of that day, every shadow in the forest hid a murderous bandit.

I liked the idea of cycling round an island; the limitations of the island's size reduced the number of route decisions to be made. The edge of an island is its public face: here is usually found the capital, the ports, the bigger roads, the people. But its soul lies inland, in the air and rocks of the hidden plains and high mountains.

Of all the islands scattered across the Mediterranean, the most potent is Corsica. The 'mountain in the sea' rises sheer from the Mediterranean, its unapproachable slopes heavy with the fragrance of herbs and pines, its impenetrable *maquis* scrub a haven in days gone by for fugitives and rebels, among them, Napoleon Bonaparte.

We had travelled out from England the hard way. Having left work early on a Friday lunchtime, it was raining so heavily that we walked from Waterloo to Victoria, rather than risk London's rush-hour in the wet. At Victoria, we registered the bicycles through to Paris. The rain intensified. At Newhaven a ferry was waiting, and we crossed the English Channel in a Force Seven gale. Most of the passengers, including Elaine, became quite ill. The storm added an hour to the crossing.

It was 5 am when we reached Dieppe. On a train memorable for its hard seats, we travelled to Paris, where we reclaimed the bicycles from the baggage office. Now two hours behind schedule, we raced through the city to Gare St Lazare only to miss the connection to Marseilles by four minutes. Five hours later we boarded the next train to Marseilles. We drew into the port after dark, to find that our bikes would not be arriving until the next morning. We tried to sleep on some marble seats in Marseilles station, but were disturbed every few minutes by a mad tramp with a beard that reached his waistcoat buttons. He was keen that we admire some colour pictures of ice-skating he had found in an old copy of *Paris Match*.

The bicycles arrived at six the next morning. With some relief we rode to the harbour, where we were told that the seamen on the passenger ferry to Corsica had just announced that they were on strike. This was a blow. On another quay we found a cargo ship sailing for Ajaccio. We paid one of the stevedores to put our bikes in the ship. Then, with a German tourist and two Belgians we took a taxi to Marseilles airport. It was still raining. In a small plane we flew southwards through a storm cloud which made the plane fall like a stone for hundreds of feet. Several people were ill.

The plane landed at Ajaccio in the middle of a thunderstorm. After all the other passengers had collected their baggage, Elaine and I were left standing on our own watching an empty carousel. We asked where our bags were, and were told that there had been a mistake. They had been flown back to Marseilles. This was an unexpected setback.

Later in the day, the bags arrived, and we spent the night sleeping on a hillside outside the town, beneath a sheet of polythene. It rained a lot and we became very wet. In the morning, we walked to the harbour and watched the cargo ship arrive with our bikes. 'Great!' I said, 'I'm ready for a bit of biking.' Elaine was not so sure.

The bicycles were brought across the quay piled on top of oil-drums being moved by a fork-lift truck. A kind Frenchman lifted the bikes down for us. We, our bags and our bicycles had finally been united in Corsica. The only problem was that the back wheel on Elaine's bicycle had been bent into a banana shape. While I was jumping on it to bend it straight, there was a muffled boom. Later, we heard that a plane had been bombed at the airport.

⋆   ⋆   ⋆

'Let's go to the hills. It'll be quieter there' I said to Elaine from the safety of a concrete culvert. We left Ajaccio at a healthy lick and didn't stop until we were 15 kilometres down the road. We ran into the sea and floated around watching the island for bandits.

Even for the southern Mediterranean, the Corsicans have high blood pressure. Added to the centuries of clan feuding, the Corsicans have not quite decided whether to be French or Italian — or independent. There are modest explosions now and again, and any vacant stretch of rock or concrete is plastered with political slogans. In some mountain villages the black and white flag of independence hangs in the sultry air. Back in 1768 the Republic of Genoa sold Corsica to the French who were kind enough to grant the islanders equal rights 21 years later. France controlled the island until its own monarchy collapsed, at which point the Corsican nationalist hero Pascal Paoli offered the island to the British. They keenly accepted, and later buried Paoli in Westminster Abbey. The tail then wagged the dog: Corsica exported to the mainland a stubby hellraiser called Napoleon Bonaparte who took over France and then spent the rest of his active life roughing up his neighbours. Bonaparte finished his days an exile on a small island in the middle of the South Atlantic. Corsica has remained loosely glued to France ever since.

Wading ashore we took out the map. Corsica is shaped

rather like a bunch of grapes, with the capital, Ajaccio, part way down the left-hand side. With the exception of a couple of river fans on the east coast, the island is entirely mountainous. Our plan was to cycle southwards and then cut inland and follow the mountainous spine of the island northwards, before heading out to the west coast and returning to Ajaccio. It looked quite straightforward; the distance was just under 600 kilometres. By adding up the spot heights on the map, we could work how much uphill cycling we would be doing. I made it 8,202 metres. I'd oiled my bike especially for the trip.

For fifteen kilometres the road south stayed close to the sea, picking a way through the prickly *maquis*. Then it turned to climb a ridge. It took us an hour to pedal up the hairpins and into the trees near the high village of Coti-Chiavari. There was a half-built house in the village, and on the ground floor of this we laid our sleeping bags. At midnight a series of massive detonations sent us shooting from our bags like startled rabbits, but it was only another thunderstorm. The D55 south from Coti-Chiavari is one of those dreamy cycling roads that you hope will last for ever. A thousand feet up, it twists corniche-fashion towards the Capes of Muru and Neru while the bottomless blue sea reveals itself now and again in vivid fragments. All too soon however, we swooped down to cross the Taravo Valley. On the road by the river we came on four men scratching their heads and looking very puzzled. The bus they had been travelling in stood beside them, its front end stuck down an enormous hole in the road. With excited gestures, they demonstrated how the road had opened before them and swallowed the bus. 'Mines!' I said to Elaine, 'but we'll be too light to set them off.'

It is on a spur of land south of the Taravo that 3,500 years ago a tribe of megalithic people could have been found laboriously chipping statues from the rough granite of Corsica's bedrock. Some of the statues stand among the olives watching with empty eyes the tourists who drop by for ten minutes before barging on in their cars. It is thought that the sculptors of Filitosa were the first in Europe to portray man as he really is rather than as a symbolic image.

Warlike seafarers called Toreens destroyed the tranquillity of Filitosa, throwing up their own buildings with fragments of broken statue.

Above Propriano, a small port whose sunny-faced houses glow with a benign decrepitude in the evening light, we followed the narrow D91 into the hills. There is very little flat land on Corsica, and the island is remarkable for the way the gradient always changes at an acute angle. Very seldom do you come across a hesitation in the steepness of the slope. We rode higher and higher up the D91, peering into the *maquis* for any hint of a tiny ledge on which to sleep. With darkness minutes away, we settled on a small gap in the *maquis* just below the road. All that stopped us sliding down the mountain to Propriano were the massive thorns of the bush immediately below the site we had chosen.

We did not so much 'wake up' as decide that the pain threshold had been crossed. It took half an hour to extricate ourselves from the *maquis*. Each thorn feels as if it has been individually sharpened, and they are grouped so that anyone who survives penetration of the outside of the bush then becomes trapped by the intersections of backward-facing barbs. Once trapped, every little movement results in stabs of pain from new and unexpected directions. We emerged onto the road looking like worn-out dartboards.

Through soothing morning air we flew down to a river called the Rizzanese. After some sidetracking we found what we were looking for: Spin 'a Cavallu. This is one of the stone bridges built by the Genoese when they settled in Corsica. In a single, graceful span it clears the Rizzanese. It was built of stone, high to protect it from the spring floodwaters, at a time when Corsica could only be traversed by foot or hoof. The bridge is only wide enough for two people to pass, or for a loaded pack animal — and its cleanly bevelled granite bed is unmarked by the scraping of iron wheels. Grass now grows between its blocks, and part of the parapet has fallen away. Where the Genoese had contained the river, the banks have now spread and the water has carried away some of the approach paving.

It was a peaceful place, and on the dry stones of the river bed we lit a small driftwood fire to boil water for coffee. Afterwards we drenched the embers in water. Corsica is prone to devastating forest fires.

Where the Rizzanese is joined by a lively little stream called the Fiumicicoli the road curls upwards again, probing into side valleys until the terracotta rooftops of Ste-Lucie-de-Tallano can be spied peeking coyly through the trees.

The village's tall houses cluster tightly together on the steep mountainside, inward-looking and protective. In the village we talked to an old man with baggy blue trousers and white stubble that shone in the sun like frosty grass. He was quick to remember fighting with the British in the Dardanelles and at Gallipoli, and he took us to a cafe where they served hot chocolate at the bar and played the Rolling Stones on the jukebox. Outside, it looked like rain.

By the side of the mountain road leading to the next village, we stopped to cook. Semolina and ripe peaches were all we had found in Ste-Lucie-de-Tallano. Just as the semolina started to splutter in the can the sky cracked and raindrops hissed into the embers. There was nowhere to shelter, so we hastily scrabbled all our belongings together, and with the billy-can of scalding semolina in one hand and the handlebars in the other, I set off down the road after Elaine. She said she remembered passing a bus shelter on the way up. The rain thickened and the road steepened. In rising panic I realised that with only one hand free to work the brakes, my bike was going faster and faster. With both feet on the road and the steaming billy-can of semolina thrust in front of me I passed the bus shelter at 55 kph. Elaine said later that I was softly wailing. The bicycle skittered on the edge of the rain-slicked tarmac. I had a fleeting glimpse of frightening drops. The walls of Ste-Lucie-de-Tallano rushed towards me. Just missing a donkey I shot into the main street.

Two schoolchildren watched a shocked foreigner fall sideways from his bicycle and perform a circus act with a cooking pot which he passed from one hand to the other as he rolled over on the ground. Not a drop spilled from the pot, but it was a long walk back up the hill.

We slept in the bus shelter. It was very small. Just before dawn a cow pushed its head through the door and, in a morning call that had us sitting bolt upright and round-eyed, the bus shelter was filled with a reverberating bellow.

The road from Ste-Lucie-de-Tallano through to Levie and Zonza carried us into the heart of the Corsican mountains. A great basin of green opened, rimmed on the far side by the fangs of the *Aiguilles de Bavella* — the highest peaks of southern Corsica. The most exciting pass in Corsica crosses at 1,218 metres, a nick in this serrated ridge of pinkish granite. Elaine waited patiently in Zonza while I rode the 9 kilometres to the Col de Bavella; 45 minutes or so of low-geared pedalling through forest heavy with the smell of resin. The high-point had me blinking with disbelief. On the far side the road unravelled like a piece of string towards the blue haze of the distant sea. I leaned the bike on a pine tree. Wind boomed up from below in unpredictable blasts. A surprise gust knocked me to my knees. I grabbed a rock. By the time I had pulled my jacket down from over my head, my bicycle had been blown from its tree and was turning end-over-end down the mountainside.

'It's a gonner' I thought. I waited till the wind quietened and slid down to the Raleigh. A water-bottle had gone for good, and the map too. Everything else seemed intact. On all fours, I dragged the bike up the slope. Each time I heard the throaty rush of an approaching gust I lay flat to the mountain till it passed over me. By the time I returned to Zonza I was shivering.

When we reached Aullene the blue skies had been dirtied with ominous-looking storm clouds. A night indoors seemed prudent. There was a room available at the Hotel de la Poste, above a bar filled with swarthy Corsicans who were drinking rough red wine that smelled of paint-stripper. The landlord cooked us an enormous meaty meal that seemed to contain the best part of a herd of cows.

Northwards through the mountains we crossed the Col de la Vaccia and then the Col de Verde — both of them comfortably clear of 1,100 metres. The clouds bubbled below us. Separating these two passes is a little village called Zicavo. There was a bridge outside the village, over which the locals heaved anything unpleasant. Pigs rooted in the rubbish for tasty bits.

Pedalling away, I kept a wary eye on a dog snoozing at the verge. As I passed, it changed suddenly from a dozy domestic pet to a rabid-looking menace. It jumped a metre off the tarmac and lunged after us howling for blood. Elaine disappeared quick as a laser beam. I would have done, but my chain slipped. The gears jammed. I tore at the levers, thrashed the pedals. Picked up speed. The dog was closing, teeth bared. Brown. Mad. I swerved and sprinted. And looked behind. It was drawing level with the back wheel, barking, red-eyed. Another spurt of energy and trees flashed by. I shot past Elaine as if she was standing still, the dog at my heels. It chased me for five kilometres. Elaine passed the dog lying on its back with its legs in the air, exhausted. Fifty metres further she came across its prey, in a similar condition. An honourable truce.

Outside Ghisoni we found a ruined shepherd's hut. In front of it was a level patch of grass just big enough for two sleeping bags. As the last faint rays of the evening sun gave up trying to pierce the forest cover, a hawk dived past, hard on the tail of a tiny bird.

Much of the following morning was devoted to the Col de Sorba — at 1,311 metres one of the highest passes in Corsica. Through an avenue reminiscent of the shaded ways of the Black Forest we climbed, cool and intoxicated by the pine-flavoured breeze while streams that shone like liquid silver bubbled through mossy banks. *Laricio* pines of these high Corsican forests have immensely tall, bare trunks that are scaffolding for a dark canopy through which the sun sparkles like diamonds. Beyond ridges that receded to the east lay a flat silver sea.

On the other side of the Col de Sorba we joined one of Corsica's two railway lines. A single set of rusted rails rounded a bend in a series of kinks, tall grass growing between the oily sleepers. We could just hear the distant strains of an overworked engine. We sat by the track waiting for it to pass. A small locomotive, two flat-bed trucks and two covered wagons clattered by. On one of the flat-beds a pair of blond-haired travellers lay against their backpacks watching the circling mountains.

The town of Corte once held the hearts of independent Corsicans. Elected 'General of the Corsican nation' in 1755, Pascal Paoli chose this mountain fastness for his capital. His statue stands in the Place Paoli, not far from today's soulless blocks of shabby flats and offices. The town is one of the main bases for the French Foreign Legion. In a cafe we drank coffee while two soldiers with necks shaved so that they bristled like pigs backs sat at the next table watching the inconsequential street. Later we walked up the stepped cobbled alleys towards the old citadel. Exfoliation had bulged, lifted and peeled flakes of plaster from the houses. Rain had trapped the silt in corners where weeds could take root. Hanging from wires stretched between upper-floor windows, washing hung lifeless in the still air. As we stood above the rooftops, the subdued everyday resonance of old Corte was broken by a concerted thudding as a troop of legionnaires ran up the steps. They came past in twos, laden beneath packs and rifles, pouring with sweat, their breath rasping and rubber-soled boots squeaking on polished stone. It is an ugly little town.

Beyond the town and part way up a little pass — the Col di San Quilico — we came to a barn and, by standing on the saddles of the bicycles, we could scramble up into a low-beamed hay-loft. It made a good shelter for the night, despite the light-footed rodents that from time to time dashed across the down of our sleeping bags.

Dawn, and the bugles from the barracks below the pass, woke us. On a road made messy by trucks we rode north for 15 kilometres then turned west up the side valley that leads to the mountain village of Asco. Like many of the best mountain roads, this one is a cul de sac. As we climbed higher the valley walls closed in until we were riding under gorge walls that leant upwards to clouds chasing across saw-toothed ridges. The Asco drains from the slopes of Monte Cinto, at 2,710 metres, Corsica's highest mountain. The village of Asco perches precariously above the gorge, a cluster of tumbling houses connected by stepped alleys. At Asco several tracks meet, and many donkeys stood hitched and patient, waiting for the afternoon cool. That night five donkeys wandered into the tiny field where we were sleeping and managed to keep us awake by masticating indiscreetly close to our heads.

A sparsely-populated valley carried us up to the Col de Columbano. At this spectacular viewpoint we left behind the dark intensity of mountain Corsica. From here we could look over much of northern Corsica. Behind stretched hazy waves of hills fringed by the stark grey mountains of Nebbio and Castagniccia, while in front a cascade of *maquis* and rock fell to the uncomplicated sea. Fourteen kilometres away, we could just pick out the white lighthouse at L'Ille Rousse. By evening we were at calling distance from the lighthouse, standing on one of the town's small islands. In the darkness, a sea-eagle rushed from the cliff, low over our heads. There was nowhere satisfactory to sleep, and we ended up on the concrete floor of a boat shed on the quayside. In the early hours of the morning I was shaken awake by a man with bad breath who asked if we were comfortable.

To ride a bicycle down Corsica's west coast is to catch the unfolding of one of Europe's most dramatic coastlines.

Beyond the fortress town of Algajola we came to Calvi, one of the coast's more ritzy resorts. Calvi's marina is solid with fibreglass and chrome. South of here, on a bumpy road that was scaling the little ridge behind Cap Cavallo, the gears on my bicycle began to slip, and, leaning the machine on a telegraph pole, I pulled a screwdriver from the tool-kit. Having tightened the gear, I hopped on the saddle to test it.

Unknown to me, while the bike had been leaning on the telegraph pole, a great many ants of the black and red wood-eating variety had crossed from the pole to my saddle. I sat on them. My first knowledge of their presence came with a violent stabbing in my backside. I leapt over the handlebars, yelping. The pain was multiplying. Ants were all over my legs and arms; going up my shorts. Absolutely frantic, I tore all my clothes off. Elaine was cycling back to see what the commotion was about when she met me running down the road stitchless, swiping at my arms and legs with one hand, and holding a screwdriver in the other. Blood was pouring from my lip. 'They've made me bleed' I yelled. When Elaine had brought herself under control, she noticed that the shape of the cut on my lip exactly matched that of a screwdriver tip.

The River Fangio announced itself by a signpost punched full of bullet-holes. Vines grew up the hillside. At a small cafe we stopped and asked if we could have our water-bottles filled. No, we were told. We should go to the stream where the water was good. I climbed down the bank. Lying at the water's edge among the old oil-cans and tyres was a cat with its side missing.

In the forest above the Fangio valley we found a ruined farmhouse, and spread the sleeping bags on the uneven flagstones of the courtyard. A man turned up at dusk and stood staring at us, refusing to talk. Sometime in the night, a cow turned up. It had a bell around its neck that clanged with the doom-laden sonority of a marker buoy in the mist. Eventually, it bedded down in the shed next to us.

The Calanche is the name given to the red granite cliffs between Porto and Piana. From Porto the road ascends steeply then crosses the near-vertical face of a mountain. Above, the rock teeters skywards. Blocks the size of houses balance improbably above your head and solitary pines cling to distant ledges like toy trees. When the sun is high or diffused through sea mists the granite gleams pale and

42

harsh. And in the evenings the rock radiates a startling glow which seems to come from the melted magma that once gave it form. In places the tarmac is held up by 15 metres of walling and all that prevents you falling over the edge is a solid wall of tourist buses.

Just after Piana the road climbs to 500 metres before twisting down to Cargese, a town built by Greeks that spills down the hillside to a tiny, crowded harbour. The last major pass between us and Ajaccio was the Col de San Bastiano. We arrived there at dusk and lit a small fire to cook some food. We were at 415 metres. The stillness of the night was broken by the unmistakable rattling of a bicycle and the muted puffing of a tired rider. A head appeared in the light of the flames.

'Bonjour!' it said. Elaine introduced us in flawless French. The rider had tousled fair hair and a face stained with exertion. 'Ou êtes-vous from?' he asked in shaky French. 'Angleterre' we replied. 'Hey! You're Anglais!' he exclaimed. 'Then we can talk English, because *I'm* American!' Bob Wind had cycled from Bastia, on Corsica's northern coast, and was heading for Bonifacio in the south, where he was going to cross to Sardinia. After cycling across Sardinia, he planned to cross Sicily too, then take a ship to north Africa, and just keep on cycling southwards. 'I'll see how far into the Sahara I can get' he said, 'then stop.'

We talked long into the night. While Bob's father had worked as an entomologist in central America, Bob had gone off exploring on his bicycle, first along the coast of Guatamala ('no roads, so I pedalled along the hard sand when the tide was out') then down Mexico's Baja peninsula. Among other languages, he spoke fluent Arabic, and had taught in a school in the Rif Mountains of Morocco, taking his weekends in the Sahara on a single-speed bicycle. In the States he worked as a bell-hop. He'd arrived in Marseilles for the start of his present adventure having walked from Geneva along the Alps — in a pair of black lace-up shoes and a mackintosh.

There was precious little flat ground on top of the Col de San Bastiano. Bob found an old gun emplacement to sleep in; Elaine and I found an old Citroen van that had been pushed over the ridge and had by chance come to rest on its wheels. We crawled into it carefully; the two offside wheels were teetering on the edge of a steep slope. We were woken in the early hours by the baying of dogs. They grew nearer and louder. There was nowhere for us to go. I wondered what Bob would be thinking in his blockhouse up on the ridge. Something was bringing the pack up through the *maquis* to the col. As the sound came closer so it divided into individual barks and howls and suddenly it wasn't so exciting to be sleeping in the great outdoors. First a single animal crashed through the brush by the van, followed shortly by the howling, shrieking pack. We lay very still, not daring to breathe and the lunatic racket faded into the night.

In the morning the three of us rode the last 20 kilometres to Ajaccio. Bob carried on southwards towards the Sahara; Elaine and I boarded the ferry for Marseilles — and fell asleep.

4

White Mountain Tea

CRETE

'Can't take 'em mate, they're not cases. What d'yer think this is, bloody Pickfords!' The coach driver turned towards his mate and called "ere Arthur come an' look at this. Bleedin' bicycles in these boxes.' Arthur walked over, looked at our packages of brown cardboard and string, and shook his head. 'Oh no, can't take 'em mate,' he said. 'No handles. Can't take stuff wiv no 'andles.'

We wheedled and cajoled. We made handles out of lengths of pink string. Minutes before the 'express coach' was due to depart a chink, then a crack, appeared in the drivers' stonewalling. At the last moment they relented and shoved the three bicycles into the hold of the coach.

For theatrics, the men unloading the coach at Dover easily matched Arthur and his mate. They moved the three packages from the coach-hold to a trolley — a distance of about one metre — muttering and puffing as if they were single-handedly carrying a haystack over the Himalayas. On the other side of the English Channel, at Zeebrugge, we had a 'discussion' with the Belgian handlers about the definition of a bicycle once it has been dismantled and wrapped in cardboard bound with pink string. We said that our packages were 'luggage', while the Belgians regarded them as 'freight'. Anything called 'luggage' they would move, but 'freight' could only be touched by a freight handler.

'Freight, mate, ain't our pigeon' they said in Belgian. Or words to that effect. Resolution was reached by the intervention of the coach courier, a young Portuguese woman called Theresa. 'The packages are luggage to be freighted' she ruled — and loaded the bikes onto a trolley herself.

We were introduced to the two continental drivers who would be controlling the welfare of the coach and its sixty or so occupants for the journey across Europe to Greece. We will call the drivers 'Christos' and 'Theodore'. Viewed from the front, Christos' substantial bulk resembled a split horsehair mattress. Jewellry hung in his tight crinigerous curls, whose prolific growth he fertilised by regular dowsings of Cologne. Small and skinny, Theodore's main function was to hand cigarettes to Christos. When Christos saw the bicycles on the trolley, he quickly concluded that they would not fit in the storage space beneath the coach. It wasn't until he had been paid a modest advance that the coach-hold miraculously expanded to accommodate the bikes.

For the next day and a half the coach bowled down the *autobahnen* and *autoput*, into Yugoslavia. Some of the passengers were holiday makers; others were Greeks returning home from working in the U.K., and a few were Australians beginning their overland trek back to the antipodes. While the same tape of Greek pop music played over and over again for 36 hours, Christos drove the coach as if he was trying to break the world land-speed record. He wouldn't stop the bus for a call of nature unless the sufferer was on the verge of bursting. Some passengers took up smoking. Others stared ahead pale with fright as long-distance trucks filled the coach windscreen at a closing speed not much short of 150 kph. Above a footwell filled with empty beer cans, the Australians dozed on the back seat.

In the middle of the second night, somewhere south of Zagreb, Christos decided that he would like to sleep across the back seat of the coach, while Theodore drove. Christos told the Australians to move from the seat. They told him to perform the anatomically impossible with his bus. Enraged, he thundered to the front of the bus, and ordered Theodore to stop. He told Theresa that he and Theodore would return in the morning, then stamped off into the night with Theodore, his faithful corporal, at his heels.

Theresa's sympathies did not lie with the drivers: 'I smash their faces' she said 'Us Portugese can do anything!' We discussed what the next move should be. The Australians favoured slashing the tyres and setting the vehicle on fire. The courier was sent to negotiate. While she was away, Christos reappeared with a squad of armed Yugoslav soldiers who stormed down the aisle towards the back seat to be met by invitations to ''ave a beer mate'. The

46

troops retired in confusion. A truce was arranged by Theresa, who with tact and politeness negotiated for a grumpy Christos to have a portion of the rear seat.

At the border crossing between Yugoslavia and Greece, customs officials discovered two crates of bananas hidden in the hold. Christos had bought them in Austria and had planned to sell them to banana-starved Athenians at hugely inflated prices. While Christos sagged against the side of the coach, Theodore hopped from one foot to the other and the customs men walked along the queue of waiting traffic handing out a free banana to every motorist. In Omonia Square we debussed. Shaking our hands, Theresa leaned forward and with a confident smile said: 'There are different drivers for your journey back to England. No problem!'

Itinerant students and backpacks seemed to fill every dark cranny of the hotel at 48 Nikis Street behind Syntagma Square. We were given roof space with a view through the television aerials to the Acropolis. On this lofty and most agreeable eyrie we re-assembled the bikes. My cousin John, who is normally a vet, regarded the slow reconstruction of the bicycle that I had brought for him, with undisguised consternation. Even before it had been pulverised by three days of trans-European bus travel, the bike had been a wreck. Now it was hard to tell which was the front and which was the back. 'Have I got to ride *that?*' he asked.

'At least its got two wheels and a frame', I replied, hurt. 'You sit on this end.' I tapped the ruptured saddle. Elaine's bike had fared a little better. Mine, I knew from past experience, was indestructible.

With the *maitre d'hotel* we made a deal concerning the safekeeping of our precious cardboard for the next fortnight, then took a rejuvenating night's sleep under the stars while Athens' traffic jostled in the street five floors down.

At the tail-end of the next evening's rush-hour, we cycled through the opened bows of the *Kydron*. Under a thick orange dusk — Athens has terrible air pollution — the ship wove a course through the vessels moored in Piraeus harbour and headed south for Crete.

Dawn found the three of us up on the dew-damp deck watching the sun creep over the Mediterranean horizon. With the light came the spreading of our maps on a life-raft cover. Crete floats roughly half way between Athens and North Africa, and is some 240 kilometres long and 32 kilometres wide. It has three main mountain areas. The most spectacular and desolate range is in the west. The Lefka Ori, or White Mountains — so called because of their shining limestone — rise to 2,440 metres and are split by the longest gorge in Europe. Books back at home had told us that in summer it is possible to climb down into the Gorge of Samaria and walk the 19 kilometres along its bed to the coast.

Being Neolithic Man on Crete would have been fun. Caves are plentiful, obsidian is available for tools and there is plenty of wood for burning. It took 3,000 years for the hunters of the Stone Age to become bored with bashing rocks and progress to more aesthetic activities. The Bronze Age saw the introduction of copper and pottery and palaces. Earthquakes and volcanic eruptions knocked the place about from time to time and in 67 BC, twelve years before they were to land in England, the Romans arrived bringing with them their new towns and villas. The Byzantines, who held sway from the 5th to 9th century AD did a fair amount of church building, but then the Saracen Arabs invaded. A hundred years later they were ejected by the Emperor Nikephoros Phokas, who fired from a catapult over the walls of Herakleon the heads of his prisoners. Subsequent rulers included the Genoese and Venetians, the Turks and Egyptians. Since 1913 Crete has been a part of Greece.

We mapped out a route that would take us into the heart of the White Mountains and then eastwards past the Idi Mountains to the ruins of Knossos.

The *Kydron* docked in a sheltered bay beneath rumpled green hills. It is just a few kilometres from the port of Souda to Chaniá — a Venetian jewel crowning the foreshore beside the peninsula of Akrotiri. We rode along that dusty road with the light-hearted expectation of a new adventure about to begin. John asked if it was normal for touring bikes to have only one gear.

The tarmac west from Chaniá is fairly level, but on this particular day it was being blasted by a notorious sea-breeze known locally as the *meltimi*. Rocking sideways in the gusts we dashed between the high bamboo windbreaks that have been built to protect the numerous orange groves along the roadside.

It was along this fairly level section of coast that the German airborne troops landed in 1941, and from where the Australian, New Zealand and British troops made their painful withdrawal over the mountains to the south coast — a debacle graphically captured in Evelyn Waugh's novel *Officers and Gentlemen*. Several days later, we met a jovial farmer who declared himself to be an eternal 'friend of the British' — an amity born of the occasion in the last war when the RAF dropped bundles of *drachmae* into his valley.

The road on our map turned from red to brown at Kastelli, and from brown to white at Plátanos. Anything white had to be exciting cycling, and there is nothing like an appalling dirt road for keeping motorists away.

Beyond Kastelli the road climbed, and at the end of a full day it was pleasant to push the bikes, chatting and watching the landscape below broaden. The light was nearly gone when we reached Plátanos, and just through the village, down a side-road, we found a grassy terrace perched high on a hillside. It was a seat in the stalls, with the Mediterranean the stage across which played the limbs of the day's principle character.

The *meltimi* was still with us when the sun returned next morning. We cycled back to Plátanos to rejoin our road. The main street was deserted, shutters tightly closed against the gritty air and dust devils dancing between the walls. Tight-lipped and slit-eyed we rode southwards out of Plátanos. It was four days before we came across another tarmac road.

Our pebbly route took us through Sfinári, Kámbos, Amygdalokefálion, Simantiriana, and so to Kepsálion, a string of little mountain villages high above Crete's truncated western coast. Wind makes this landscape a lively companion. On the open mountain flanks the wind pushed us in exuberant surges like the hand that throws you forward on the playground swing. Once or twice the bikes rushed on so fast we had to grab the brakes. The wind shaped the trees, bending trunks and branches. Even in the stillness when the wind occasionally stopped, all the trees would remain leaning and pointing southwards, frozen in their deformity. The villages were built at the heads of valleys, sheltered from the wind, and around them were stepped the terraces of olive trees, their silver-green leaves rustling and offering welcome shelter. The houses were painted a brilliant white that burnt holes in the mountain slopes of dark coniferous scrub. A long way below, dark blue and pecked with white horses like a child's painting, the sea tossed and a small waterspout pirouetted past the island.

The August sun burned us cherry-red and for a while we sheltered beneath a gnarled old tree watching a man sitting on a bank watching his wife digging in a vegetable plot. We passed a gang of workmen heaving a telegraph pole up a slope so steep that rocks knocked by their feet skipped down in puffs of dust. They were chanting with every heave on their ropes. In a *taverna* a tractor driver sang away the siesta while one of his friends picked a small guitar-like instrument. In another village we came across two French cyclists and an Englishman who had cycled all the way from Britain.

Because it looked so inaccessible, I wanted to visit the south-west tip of Crete. It is formed by a barren Cape facing the Elaphonísi islands, and is also the most south-westerly point in Greece. On an erratic dirt track we descended from the mountains to the remote monastery of Chrysoskalitisis for some water; water that was sharp, cold and sparkling like liquid diamonds. The monastery climbed high on a rock above the sea in a jumble of cream and white rectangles. Further along the track, a priest insisted we take a bag full of red tomatoes. He also scuppered my plans, insisting that if we followed the donkey tracks towards the remote Cape, we would assuredly die of thirst. 'No water' he said, shaking his head. We turned and laboured back up into the mountains. Elaine and John looked relieved.

At a place called Plokamania we came upon the skinning of a large pig. It was strung up by its hind legs from a large tree. A couple of gore-spattered men were hard at work tearing back the pelt — rather like a diver peeling off his mate's one-piece wet suit. A small crowd was watching, as is the custom in rural Greece. Grateful for any excuse to pause in our uphill labour, we flopped to the ground and watched too, chatting to one of the skinners, who had been in the Merchant Navy. Most of the tourists, he said, were Germans. The bad roads kept the numbers down.

In the next village, Elos, we stopped for beers in a cafe heavy with the hubbub of whiskered Cretans. On first sight the traditional costume of the Cretan male could be taken for fancy dress. Long black leather boots reach high up the calves, topped by black breeches of exaggerated bagginess. Above this is worn a black wool shirt, jersey and button-up jacket, also black. A flat black hat and a thick moustache that starts below the nose, travels horizontally sideways then downwards to finish somewhere beneath the chin, completes the overall effect of comic solemnity. Unaccountably, Cretan men thus dressed never appear to get hot.

Dusk found us on a grassy platform overhung by spreading chestnuts, with a view across a broad valley. Columns of woodsmoke drifted up from homes among the trees below. Goat bells clonked as a youth followed his herd back to Kampanos. A dog barked, the breeze faltered and hushed and darkness crept along the valley. We talked of the next day, knowing that it would be the best day's cycling yet. The Milky Way grew from a wan brush-stroke across the heavens into a bright swathe. A shooting star flared, curved and died. To slip towards sleep in such a bedroom sows the finest dreams.

Dawn, and while the limestone peaks were still pink and the air still cool, we set off on the ride that would take us deep into the Lefka Ori. The road gained height laboriously, keeping an even gradient by detouring far up side valleys. The sun wasn't high enough for discomfort and we pedalled gently, reaching by lunchtime the small village of Maralia.

Picnicking on a terrace in the olives, we were joined by a young man who said that he was a teacher and a farmer. 'You like White Mountain tea? I think you do. I will send you some. What is your name? Elaine! I like you. Where do you live? England! I think you might like to marry me!' He owned many olive groves, and watered them by a pipe that came 300 metres down the mountain. He had goats too. All the villagers sent their milk to a co-operatively owned cheese factory, keeping accounts of the number of litres they despatched. Every few months they would visit the factory to claim their rightful proportion of cheese. There was little work for the young. 'Many people leave to find work, but they not find. Then they come back. Stupid.'

By mid afternoon we had reached the road junction which sits astride a major ridge of the White Mountains. The view was astonishing: from this lofty meeting of the ways we could see the Mediterranean to the north and south of

Crete. Below us the ground fell away to be swallowed in a dark green haze that merged eventually with the aqua blue of the distant sea.

Our path lay east, along a tiny and very rough road strewn with stones and pitted with holes. It followed a steep mountainside, dropped to pass a stone-works, then climbed a pleasant valley beneath forested slopes before emerging at a low col marked by a church. Here we had the second scenic surprise of the day: ahead lay the flat, fertile plain of Omalos, no more than 5 kilometres across and 1,127 metres above sea-level. It was completely surrounded by mountains and there appeared to be no valley exit from this hidden sanctuary. From one of his books, John informed us that snow lies on the Plain of Omalos till March, and that the villages are completely cut off for the winter. 'Omalas is known for *C. sieberi*, a rare type of crocus. It is also said to produce the best potatoes in Crete' he concluded, snapping shut the guide. We had arrived.

From the pass, a dusty track brought us to a *taverna*, where the arrival of three foreign bicycles caused something of a sensation among the drowsy midday drinkers. A couple of small boisterous boys insisted on riding the bikes. They were too short to reach the pedals, and kept falling to the ground amid hoots of laughter from the spectators. Dignity was restored by each boy being taken on a ride along the track, sitting astride the bike's cross-bar.

On the other side of the plain of Omalos, a road climbed to a tourist hotel. Beyond its verandah a rickety handrail marks the top of the steep climb down into the Gorge of Samaria. The place was deserted. This, we found out, was because most people set off on the 19-kilometre walk down the gorge early in the morning. Most get trapped in the central part of the gorge at the hottest time of day. John's guide book — and presumably others too — described the trek as 'a major expedition which needs careful planning . . . Fatal casualties are not unknown'. The hotel staff promised to keep an eye on the bikes over the following couple of days. As the evening sun brought a rosy warmth to the rock walls, we shouldered a couple of small bags and began the 600-metre descent into the cool depths of the White Mountains.

It would be tempting to pretend that the journey along the bed of the longest gorge in Europe is ripe with danger and difficulty, but the truth is that it's a well-trodden tourist route. Two vegetarians from Buckinghamshire's Marlboro' AC cycling club once carried a tandem through the gorge. Walking the Gorge of Samaria is like climbing a mountain ridge in reverse: following steps then a precipitous path we plunged into the cool depths to a lumpy path that dropped through pines to the bed of the gorge. At the 'Iron Gates', the gorge narrows to just a few metres. It is a secretive place, only passable in the summer when the river is dry. We slept on the beach at the gorge mouth, and retraced our steps back into the White Mountains the following morning.

We rode northwards from the Plain of Omalos. Near the top of the bare, stony pass we stopped to look at a white memorial slab cemented into the rock. Beneath the heading '1,600 metres', it recorded the death on 28 February 1944 by ambush of Dudley Perkins and a Greek partisan. Perkins, a New Zealander, was also known as 'Kiwi' and 'Vasili', and became a local legend after returning secretly to fight with the Greek resistance following the withdrawal of 1942. It was in the Cretan mountains that Patrick Leigh-Fermor and Billy Moss captured the German General Kreipe and smuggled him from the island in a submarine, an adventure related in the book and film *Ill Met by Moonlight*. It was Leigh-Fermor's book *Mani* that produced the goal for my first big bike ride. By odd coincidence, I was sitting in a park in Godalming one lunch-time when a girl walked up and began chatting about the tricycle beside me. The girl was the daughter of Billy Moss.

An eagle hung overhead while we breezed down the hairpins towards Chaniá. From the White Mountains, we pedalled eastwards behind the massif of Mount Idi. John's bike was by now shedding spokes every few kilometres, the back wheel squidging like putty under the weight of his library of hard-backed ornithological books. The boulder-strewn roads hadn't helped. Our progress was slowed further by the effect a *baklava* cake was having on my digestive tracts. For two days, all I could keep down was tea. To add to the misery, it rained for 36 hours. The road to Herakleon was covered by muddy slurries and flood-waters. By the time we reached Knossos I was cross-eyed with discomfort. 'Knossos', Elaine read from Pendlebury's *Palace of Minos* was 'the most ancient centre of civilised life in Greece and with it, of our whole Continent.' I wanted to believe it. 'Where are the loos?' I asked.

Hungry, and thinner than a *bouzouki* neck, I watched Piraeus draw near. We had been told to catch the coach for London from outside a hotel in the northern part of the city. Elaine led the way. We staggered through the hotel's swing doors towing our cardboard boxes. Theresa was waiting. She looked worried. 'What's up Theresa. Aren't you pleased to see us?' I asked, unfit for trouble. 'Not you the problem. The problem is there!' She pointed.

The lumbering form of Christos was levering itself clear of two coffee cups. He came towards us, bracelets clinking. 'No bicycles. Suitcase only. Look, too big!' Christos stooped, clumsily embraced one of our boxes, and let it fall. A look of melodramatic tragedy crossed his face: 'Impossible to take these on coach. Too much weight! Too big! You remember!'

'Yes Christos, we remember . . .'

5

Points West

IRELAND AND SCOTLAND

At first, I thought he was dead. He lay beneath me, legs splayed wide. His head had fallen forward to his chest so that I could see the frayed neck of his checked shirt. He must have hit the ground awkwardly, for he leant lopsidedly against the rough stone wall, his limbs arbitrarily arranged in the manner of a dropped puppet.

I looked down from the wall, wondering what to do. The front wheel of the man's big black bicycle was still spinning, the spokes tickling the long, wet blades of grass. I coughed, lightly. If he was alive, I didn't want to surprise him. He remained inert. I glanced down the road. It was empty. I'd have to sort this one out on my own. Everything had gone quiet.

There was a loud throaty rattle. Startled, I twisted so quickly that I had to catch the top of the wall to prevent myself falling. With an awful finality, the rattle slowly tailed away. Then, like a motorist fumbling in neutral, then finding a gear, the expiration of breath reversed. There was a sound like water in a sink trying to pass a plug-hole full of potato peelings. The cycle was completed by a snore of a volume sufficient to lift the man's head and bring into view his hedgerow eyebrows.

The sweet smell of stout hung in the air. The sun pierced the cloud-edge. The man, I noticed, had chosen a south-facing wall against which to spend the afternoon. I jumped off the wall.

Looking towards Skibereen, I wondered how far behind the others I was. To the time spent over that last Guinness I now had to add the delay caused by my contemplations over the collapsed Kerryman. With as much urgency as my hollow legs could manage, I pedalled on through the succulent countryside.

Black and white cows stood on the sides of steep, bright

pastures. I tried to whistle, but found I was breathing too heavily. I tried to remember how long ago it was that we had boarded the boat in Swansea; three days, four? Or was it five? I saw the blue five-gallon bucket belonging to William first. He carried it tied to the back of his bicycle, and used it in the evenings for washing his socks. Despite my advice to fit it to the front of his bike, where it would provide all the aerodynamics of a nose-cone, Bill carried his bucket behind his rear panniers, where it scooped the wind like a drogue parachute. He was a man not easily swayed by others.

Beyond William, and occupying the empty road with the unruliness of a herd of heifers, were the rest of the 'tour': Simon Tuite, Jeanette Woodcock, Robert Lewis, Dolly Wilkinson, 'Ali' Turnbull and Elaine. Simon came from Dublin and had been voted engineer for the duration of our stay in Eire. His tool set was big enough to unbolt the Eiffel Tower. Fed on a lifetime of propaganda about Irish weather, I'd asked Simon when we met in Cork, how much he thought it would rain. 'Not so much', he said. 'Anyway, it's heavy mist you have in Ireland, not rain.'

Pointed at the fingery peninsulas of the south west, we passed the end of Roaringwater Bay, through Ballydehob and Skull and peered over the cliffs of Mizen head before returning along the north side of the peninsula. Always it was windy but the sun could be bright enough to turn the sand to silver. On the Healy Pass, whose thrilling coils of hairpins crossed the Caha Mountains at 330 metres, we stopped and looked back to a panorama of sea inlet and rugged shore. In the distance, we could see the thin, tapering tail of Sheeps Head. 'Who wants the Mediterranean with Kerry on your doorstep?' asked Jeanette. Straightening from a wheel adjustment he'd been making with a two-foot industrial wrench, Simon commented: 'You're not wrong!'

For the first time, I was carrying a tent on my bicycle; a precaution against the weather. Having grown used to sleeping beneath the stars, the idea of being 'under canvas' was a complication which took some adapting to. Whenever I tried tying the tent poles, they would work lose then jam in the spokes. Or they would bore a hole in the back of my thigh, or fall off the bike and cartwheel down the road ringing like tubular bells.

Neither was erecting a tent a simple task. I had bought the tent secondhand through the post from a man in Wales who had lost the instructions. The two poles had to be fitted together from seven lengths of aluminium tubes of differing diameters. There are 7,560 different ways of ordering 7 pieces of aluminium tubing into 2 poles. When everybody else would be tucked up in their duck down, I would be falling over in the dark trying to make poles. Sometimes the tent looked like a tepee; at others it rose no higher than a metre from the ground. Sometimes it had no entrance.

Tenting is part art, part science. The pitching requires an eye for perspective and balance, and it also requires a grounding in physical principles such as leverage and stress points. If you pitch a tent with the outer wall — the flysheet — touching the inner part of the tent, osmosis transmits water from outside through to the inside and you wake up wet. There are other basic rules: if the doorway is pitched facing the wind, the tent may be filled by a sudden gust in the night which sends it floating like a balloon into the air. If it is pitched on a slope, then you will spend the night sliding downhill. This can lead to the impression in a shared tent that your nocturnal perambulations are a reflection of amorous regard. (There are times when sloping pitches are nowhere to be found.)

Cooking in tents is a dangerous occupation. Hol had brought me up on the paraffin pressure stove, an efficient, compact, cooker that can bring a billy-can to red heat in minutes. It does however require a subtle touch to light. Wrongly handled, pressure stoves can erupt into a geyser of flame. When he was young, Hol burnt the front off his tent. There is a correct method: having ignited the methylated spirits in the little trough, and so warmed the main jet, you pump up the pressure until the vapourising paraffin ignites with a healthy roar. It is a knack I thought I had. One morning I was demonstrating to William how to increase the pressure, when the stove exploded with a dull 'whoomphh' and covered half the camp with molten metal and Scots porridge.

Between Killarney and the sea are Macgillycuddy's Reeks, a fine range of mountains hiding Ireland's highest point: Carrauntoohill. The most celebrated route through these mountains is by way of the Gap of Dunloe, a dark cleft occupied by a string of lakes beside which runs a rough track. This has been a favourite route for cyclists for over a hundred years. In *Bicycling 1874 – A Textbook for Early Riders* the editors give the Gap of Dunloe a star grading, though they do warn that half of the ascent 'must be walked'. We came to the Gap when the clouds were low, puffing up from the Gearhameen towards a dark watery slot. We rode through in silence, tyres crunching on the gravel beneath a damp sunless ceiling. On the far side we stopped at Kate Kearney's cottage for hot scones with jam and tea.

It was hard to hurry, the pace of life in rural Ireland doesn't encourage frenzied travel. To be seen riding a bicycle fast through a village is almost a discourtesy. One morning we were woken by the clop of the milk cart, collecting churns from the wooden stand beside the field we had camped in overnight. From farms we bought fresh milk and eggs. Temptations stood in the way of the miles. We were invited in for tea round kitchen tables, and 'popping into a shop' could take an hour or more — many of the country stores double-up as bars. At one end of the counter you can purchase anything from boot-black to beetroot, and at the other a beer tap provides for thirsty shoppers. We'd drag ourselves reluctantly from the shop, then pop back in for a forgotten purchase.

Near Tralee we stopped at a small bungalow to ask the way and ended up staying for the night. Behind the bungalow, and more than twice its size, was a ramshackle wooden barn. The husband pulled back the doors. Inside, like sleeping giants, rested two traction engines he had rescued from scrap yards and painstakingly rebuilt. Where cogs were worn, he had built up each rounded tooth with blobs of weld, then filed each to its original profile. He had put in hundreds of hours of craftsmanship. On special occasions, he and his wife and daughter would dress up and take the best traction engine out for a Sunday run.

Irish rain is penetrating. We rode west with Castlemaine harbour looking like wet steel to our left and the first few metres of the Slieve Mish Mountains to our right. Water dribbled down our necks. In Dingle we watched the fishing boats unloading then took the narrow road past Dunbeg and along the cliffs below Mount Eagle. The wind strengthened. The rain grew colder. In the midst of it all, I saw a man striving to keep his ploughshare cutting while his horse struggled into the gale. The romance in hard labour is visible only to those who don't have to do it.

In Dingle they told us we would know when we reached Slea Head; 'It's where the road goes over the cliff,' they said. In mist thicker than a sheep's fleece we pedalled cautiously westwards. William went in front. 'In clear weather' I shouted at Jeanette, 'you can see the Blasket Islands from here.' Her response was blown away. We stood on the pedals. A long way below, the ocean thundered on rocks. William managed to stop his bicycle a couple of wheel revolutions before plunging to oblivion. Soaked and cold, we towed the bicycles across the flattened grass and lay down. There was too much noise to hear each other. Communication was through lip-reading. I caught Jeanette mouthing 'Why on earth have we come here Nick?' A fresh gust of wind pushed our heads down. 'It's the most western point in the British Isles! Great, isn't it!' I didn't see her reply.

Propelled on compressed air, we blew back to Cork, then hitch-hiked back to London with the bikes in the back of a meat lorry. My interest in cycling to 'furthest' places was at this stage relatively undeveloped. The goals were a necessary part of the journey, providing a challenge, and an end. The more obscure the goal, the harder and better the challenge — and the more satisfactory the end. This was an obsession not shared by Elaine, who fitted into the 'better to travel than to arrive' school of thought. I've never understood how anyone can turn back from a mountain without trying to reach the top.

★　★　★

The British Isles are crammed with adventurous challenges. Anyone with a bike and a week or two to spare can be an explorer.

After the Slea Head Expedition, Elaine and I took the night train to Glasgow. It arrived at 5 am. The streets were cold. A policeman directed us along the south bank of the Clyde. The harsh cobbled streets by the river jarred our tyres. We rode past tenement blocks and huge crook-armed cranes. We rode through ship-building yards. The south of England looked nothing like this. Everywhere there were scars; land abandoned. There was a smell, of rust and oil, of bleeding machinery.

We crossed the Clyde on a ferry from Dunoon and pedalled northwards towards the Isles. It is at places where mountains meet the sea that I enjoy cycling the most. North-west Scotland has all this. The roads were clean and bold, often unfenced, following the glens or skirting narrow shelves above the sea. Sheep wandered in our way and we watched the sky. Sun and clouds sparred for space. Pine needles whispered conversationally in the wind.

On a mossy level among the pines south of Loch Torridon we put up the tent. Beyond the water, the triangular peak of Liatach glowed orange. From the tent door I could see the gully down which a group of us had slithered on ropes amid falling rocks and ice one dark January night several years before. When we reached the road at midnight, the seat had been torn out of my trousers. Hol said we learnt some useful lessons that night.

Mountains always look better from below. In the morning we cycled past Beinn Eighe then turned north along the side of Loch Maree and over to Dundonnel village — a scattering of houses at the head of Little Loch Broom. Our clothes soaked up the smur, an opaque drizzle unique to the Highlands. Elaine put up the tent in a small wood by the road while I trudged to the farm for water. I'd been here once before: after the Liatach descent Hol had taken some of the climbing group for a long walk out along the finger of hill beside the loch. After miles of muddy cliff path we had seen houses with smoke coming from the chimneys. Darkness had prevented us from going further. I'd always wanted to go back; to reach that isolated village. I left Elaine deep in a book snug in the tent while wind buffeted the pines above.

At first, the going was good, but up on the side of that haggis-coloured hill there was no shelter. The tyres slipped in mud or banged into rocks. Now and again, I noticed the knobbly indentations of motor-bike wheels. Rounding a spur, I came on the owner. His name was Lawrence. He said the village was not far, and apologised for not stopping longer. He was going to work. His motorbike grunted through the boulders while the wind whipped a skein of blue exhaust over the cliff. Where the peninsula narrowed, the footpath broadened to the width of a four-wheeled vehicle, then curved around the hill above a mild-mannered bay. With the easing of the land came a tamer air. The wind eased and the palette brightened with hard-won pastures. The track I was riding along was level and smooth; a joy. I looked about the settlement for the vehicles that must use such a fine highway, but all I could spot was a tractor.

Halfway along the track stood a small workman's hut. Beside it were three youths. 'Ferg' was the spokesman. They were on a government job creation scheme and had been appointed to upgrade Scoraig's highway. They had a foreman, but he was not available. Ferg had lived in Scoraig since he was three, having moved with his father from America. There wasn't a lot of road-mending to do. Wear and tear caused by the tractor was limited, and it was in any case 'off the road' for the moment, awaiting repairs.

Some of the houses in the village had windmills that could charge the batteries used for televisions and lighting. At the end of the village was a concrete jetty, and on the bench beside it a man was hammering, copper nails waiting in his mouth. For the price of passing the nails I gained another conversation. He was fitting new gunwhales, and planned to sail through the islands next summer. He was a dentist, from Glasgow. Scoraig wasn't the only long-cherished goal to be reached by bike that week.

Ardnamurchan is the name given to the rough knuckle of mountain and moor that reaches further west than any other part of mainland Britain. In the same way that Lowestoft loses its eastern prominence by being nothing more than a point on a curve, so Ardnamurchan's status as a peripheral extreme is confused by the convolutions of Scotland's highlands and islands. There is only one road along the peninsula, and beyond the tiny port of Kilchoan it begins to feel like the last road in the world. There is no traffic and little beyond the road-end but white sand and sea. We left the bikes at Sanna Bay, and with an hour left of the day, walked along a threadbare track, with the biggest isle behind our backs. We cycled round Mull and Skye, and took a ferry small enough to wet its decks, from Arisaig to tiny Eigg. We climbed the keel-shaped mountain that lords over every inch of the island. On a day caressed with warmth we lay on dry turf 393 metres above the water, circled by the Cuillins and the hills of Knoydart and Moidart, Ardnamurchan, Muck and Rhum. Leaving Scotland after that summer sojourn wasn't easy, though I didn't have to wait long before an opportunity arose to return.

If Cape Matapan is the most south-easterly point in Europe, then Cape Wrath is its geometric opposite: Europe's most north-westerly point. It is pleasantly inaccessible. On an off-day from one of his winter climbing trips, Hol had led us across the bogs from Kinlochbervie, 15 kilometres to the south. Serving the lighthouse from the east is an alternative, tarmac route, cut off from the rest of Scotland by the Kyle of Durness. For motor vehicles, there is no way across the Kyle. To take a bicycle along this road is deemed sufficiently meritorious by the cycling fraternity that a 'Cape Wrath Fellowship' certificate was created for those who made it to the end. My chance to ride to the Cape came from an unexpected quarter.

Late in the summer, after the midges had lifted from the lochens, I found myself with a group of Fleet Street journalists in a place called Keodale. Keodale is closer to Iceland than it is to the Isle of Wight. Organising the three-day outing was a man wearing a red tracksuit. He was from the public relations company. We were there to test-ride a new range of bicycles. Each bicycle was fitted with two enormous panniers and a handlebar bag. Before leaving the hotel at Keodale, to which we had been transported by sleeper train and bus, the man in the red tracksuit gave us our directives: 'As you know, Cape Wrath is the most remote place in the British Isles, and can only be reached by a narrow, unfenced road entirely devoid of human habitation of any kind whatsoever. Look out for sheep! The weather in the Scottish highlands can change BHAM! Just like that! Do not split up. Stay together! Hypothermia kills! In your panniers, you will find a tent, waterproof clothing, sleeping bag and emergency supplies.' Peeping in one of my panniers I quickly found the 'emergency supplies': a bottle of malt whisky. 'Any questions? No. Good luck!'

Seven tight-lipped pear-shaped journalists freewheeled from the hotel to the stubby jetty. The choppy waters of the Kyle slapped old stone. A weather-beaten boat which had once been white, rocked on the end of a rope. At the other end stood a Scotsman.

'Excuse me' said the man from the business magazine, 'but we're looking for the Kyle ferry.'

'Aye, ye've found it', replied the Scotsman, nodding at the tiny vessel.

John Muir, the boatman, loaded the bicycles across the boat's bows, with the wheels hanging over the gunwhales. There were too many to fit in the boat all at once, so John Muir hand-picked the four smallest and told them to embark. In strong, short strokes he rowed them across the Kyle. A couple of the passengers had their eyes closed. John Muir said he would wait for us at midday on the following day.

On the far side, a single-track tarmac road leads to Cape Wrath. The distance is not extreme: about 18 kilometres. In undulating waves of peat hags the hills roll to the south. It's a steep pull up from the jetty, but then the road winds Riviera style along a hillside above the Kyle, sandbanks just visible through the water below. Past a lonely house called Aciemore the road drops, seemingly to plunge over the cliffs into the north Atlantic. But at the last moment it veers left and falls to the ford at Daill.   Then the road climbs up again, to 90 metres. The group stretched and split. Someone punctured. Below, a tail-ender fell in the ford. The sea was lost to sight as the road uncurled across tussocky moorland. Daggers of sunlight glinted on small lakes, and to the left, the rounded profile of Fashven dominated the skyline. The man from the daily paper punctured again. 'How far to the boozer?' queried another, hunched and coughing. The view back across the tobacco-coloured moor resembled Napoleon's retreat from Moscow. Dropped bikes, collapsed riders and abandoned luggage lay where they fell.

What Agustin Egurrola thought of this has never been recorded. A Basque Spaniard, Agustin had ridden all the way from the English Channel, and had caught up with us only six kilometres from his goal. He had been sleeping rough. His single-speed ladies' bike had been strengthened by adding a wooden cross-bar. The bicycle had cost him nothing; a neighbour had thrown it over his fence in Sheffield. A beret was cocked jauntily across his forehead and dark stubble shadowed his hollow cheeks. He spoke with the self-contained assurance of a man used to looking after himself. Agustin liked adventures: once, with his wife and young son, he had made a journey with mules around the mountainous border of the Basque country. While Agustin silenced everybody with his tales, the man in the red tracksuit had been heating a pan of water on a gas stove. 'Do have some tea!' he said, handing to Agustin an orange plastic mug. Before he left, I asked Agustin about cycling in the Basque Country. 'Very good for bicycles! Big mountains, they are called Picos de Europa. You must go there!'

By the time the latest crop of mechanical and physiological ailments had been rectified, Agustin had passed us again, on his way back to England. We continued past another isolated house and climbed again, the road now with a grassy parting down its centre. Ahead, the red tracksuit was waving its arms. 'Where I'm standing chaps' he shouted, 'is 174 metres above sea-level. This is the highest point on the Cape Wrath road. Fantastic!' We swooped down to the Kearvaig valley. Gravel on the corner nearly sent the business-magazine man into oblivion.

A brief struggle up from the bridge brought us back to the plateau, where a mellowing in the gradient provided an opportunity to change gear. There was the sound of chains jamming, followed by cries for assistance. Fifteen minutes later, the show was on the road again. We glided round a low brown hill before whistling down to Clais Charnach. A turn to the left, and a last climb brought the lighthouse into view. I recognised some deep peat gullies we had clambered through with Hol. The editor of the woman's magazine drew level. 'Where's everybody else?' I asked. 'More blow-outs'.

We left the bikes on a rock and walked to the edge. To the east towered black cliffs, their tops masked in mist. Southwards the coastline was lower, with a long view to the broad strand of Sandwood Loch. Offshore, statuesque, stood the rocky spires of two sea stacks. There were no trees and a perpetual wind pressed the grass. Dark peat bogs stained the hills. We knocked on the door of the lighthouse. A man in slippers glanced at us as if his every waking minute was consumed by answering the door to cyclists. He warned us that a Force Seven gale was imminent. 'Better test the emergency supplies,' said the editor.

6

End-To-End

BRITAIN

George Batt sat surrounded by brown paper, string and sticky labels in the back room on the ground floor of the Cyclists' Touring Club headquarters in Godalming. George was in charge of the mail-order department. My own room, or rather the room I shared with two others, was at the far end of the hallway. In spare moments, I would sidle down the hall to George.

In one of George's corner cupboards was a pile of yellowing cycling magazines dating from the turn of the century. To turn those brittle pages was to travel back to an era when there were more bicycles than cars on the road, and when the membership of the CTC stood at a staggering 60,000. I read of lobbyists fighting for the right to ride bicycles in public parks, or of campaigns to urge councils to erect warning signs for cyclists on steep hills. It was an age of discovery and adventure; a time when there were many 'firsts' to be claimed by anyone with a bit of nerve and a bicycle. The tales of derring-do were unsettling: how could you go back to work after reading about crossing the Devil's Punchbowl on a High Ordinary in a snowstorm? But of all the heroes of that age, one stood above the rest.

George Pilkington Mills, Lieutenant-Colonel, D.S.O., is remembered in an unpublished memoir as being 'The greatest road-racing cyclist the world has ever known'. In the days when roads were rough and tyres solid rubber, 'G.P.' Mills rode on a penny-farthing from one end of the country to the other. He did it in 5 days 1 hour and 45 seconds. It was a penny-farthing record that was still standing a hundred years later. A cartoon in *Bicycling News* of July 23rd, 1886, shows Mills staring straight from the page with dark-set eyes. He looks incredibly young. Since that July in 1886 the Land's End to John o' Groats record has been attempted many times more—on three occasions by 'G.P.' himself: he returned on a tricycle, and then with a new-fangled 'Safety' (which broke new ground by having two wheels of the same size), and finally on a tandem. According to George Batt, the current record for the ride was under two days.

Another *Bicyling News* drawing portrayed Mills in his knickerbockers and cloth cap grasping the wide semi-drops of his Safety cycle. My daydreaming wandered over the granite cliffs of Cornwall, through the West Country then up the Welsh Marches, over Shap to Beattock and the Highlands. A ride from one end to the other of a long thin land like Britain would provide a unique view of the country. It would be an interesting little physical challenge too.

'Take an organised tour mate' George said. 'You'll get time off work for that' he added. As a career perk the CTC offered extra leave to staff members who conceived, organised and lead a group of CTC members on a cycle tour. I volunteered, pencilling in to the CTC's programme of tours for the coming season, a ride from Land's End to John o' Groats. To allow time for taking photographs and writing postcards, I stretched the time limit for the ride from two days to two weeks.

Accommodation was a problem. My own inclination was to sleep under hedges, but George Batt said this was not normal CTC practice: 'Youth hostels mate, 's what you need'.

Naomi, my mother, had taken me youth hostelling when I was thirteen. We had walked up Dovedale and through Derbyshire for three days. It was brilliant. We slept in dormitories (just like school), ate lots of mashed potato and in the mornings before we left, the warden allotted us a 'task'—such as cutting wood, sweeping the yard or collecting leaves. My father, who had been obliged to whitewash lumps of coal during his National Service, did not join us.

With a youth hostel handbook and stack of Ordnance Survey maps, I plotted the route. Record-breakers had for obvious reasons stuck to the most direct line between Land's End and John o' Groats. With road-straightening and the building of new bridges, the shortest road-distance between the two points had been reduced to 858 miles—all of it using 'A' roads. My 'scenic' route went to great lengths to avoid main roads and sleight of hand with the map measurer produced a total distance of exactly 1,000 miles. The tour was advertised in the CTC's magazine *Cycletouring*.

Waiting for the response, I wondered what sort of people an 'End-to-End' challenge would attract. Most of the CTC's holiday tours were leisurely affairs, where sightseeing, rest days and modest daily distances allowed a relaxing passage through summery countryside. To fit my 1,000-mile 'End-to-End' into a fortnight would mean averaging 72 miles each day with no rest-days. Since the ride would start early in the year, on April Fool's Day, the weather would be far from predictable. Anyone wanting to reach the end would have to be committed both to the goal and to their companions. I knew it would be interesting.

We met for the first time at Land's End. The 17 members of the group represented a fair cross-section of cycling enthusiasts, from those wearing racing caps and woollen jerseys printed with the names of continental professional teams to less formal outdoor attire of combat jackets and jeans. I handed everyone a detailed route sheet and we introduced ourselves. Only Len Downs and Fred Smith, from Stockton Wheelers, knew each other. To the rest of us, everyone was a stranger. There were some old hands; enthusiasts who rode to work and with the club at weekends. Mick Moreton from Derbyshire and Bob Yellen from Surrey looked young and awesomely fit. Twenty-year-old David Morris from Birmingham, and Kevin Hamilton, a keen member of Reading Cycling Club, had trouble keeping still such was their energy.

There were two Americans. The older of the two, William A. King Jnr, was on leave from the United States Airforce. He was wearing long red tartan socks, brown cord plus-fours, two-tone blue jersey and cravat. Kevin from Reading turned up in Dr Martens boots and an army jacket on a bike with a wonky back wheel having ridden from his home to Land's End in order to save the train fare and get some pre End-to-End training. He was nineteen. Discreet enquiries revealed that I was the only one who hadn't done any training for the ride. It wasn't till Len asked me if we should start, that it occurred to me that I was going to have to be a 'leader'.

The first day was purgatory. In my eagerness to keep as

far away from the hateful motor car as possible, the route zig-zagged to and fro across the hilliest country in Britain. Enormous detours were performed in order to avoid stretches of main road. The hills were so steep that the bicycle seemed to stop dead within a few feet of the bottom. At midday a small advance party rode into Truro, stepped from their bicycles and fell onto the pavement, dead from the waist down. The rest of the group was stretched out across half of Cornwall. Some of the survivors began to take a serious interest in map reading.

Night had fallen when we reached our first youth hostel, at Tintagel, 80 miles from Land's End. With the sea thrashing phosphorescently far below I led a small band of rubber-kneed cyclists along winding cliff paths towards what I thought to be the building described in the handbook as being at Dunderhole Point.

The handbook also said 'Take care approaching after dark'. This is a reference to the ease with which it is possible to step over the cliff edge. Over in the blackness stood the ruins of Arthur's castle; somewhere too lay a 150-year-old slate quarry cottage that had been converted into a small hostel. We came on it by accident, almost falling over a precipice onto its roof. Leaving the others, I turned and began searching for the stragglers. The last in was William, who, to avoid it being stolen in the night, brought his bicycle into the dormitory.

Neither did the second day offer any rest. Where Mills batted along the A30, we set off across North Devon on tiny roads that would dip and climb every mile of the way to Exmoor.

Beneath the bridge in Boscastle the quick little River Inny bubbled past stone cottages to the high-sided harbour. A big blue fishing boat rested inelegantly on a trailer partly blocking a lane, and another boat lay tilted across the stream, its red wooden hull ripped and split by a winter storm. North of the village the group divided. Those who had seen a map took the A39 straight to Bude, the rest came with me first to Crackington Haven, then over the hill to Widemouth Bay.

Beyond Bude the hills increased in size but the exertions became less remarkable. On a corkscrew route we rode through country thick with hedges and woods that would soon be filled with the bustle of nest building and the neon-green of new leaves. In a wood near Stibb Cross a lonely crow cried from the bare branches.

An hour before dusk we met the dark form of Exmoor. Riding from South Molton we climbed a rounded hill above the little meanderings of the River Mole, then higher and higher till we crossed the 1,000-foot contour and Devon spread below us. It was a still, chilly evening, the heather and grass merging into a uniform off-brown and a feather of smoke hanging motionless above the chimney of an isolated farmhouse below Withypool Common. The warden at Exford hostel greeted us like long-lost friends.

The Somerset Levels lie low and flat between the Quantock Hills and the Mendips. Once these were swampy marshes, but the wealthy abbeys dug drains from the 10th to 14th century to create fertile farmland. We rode across the Levels late in the afternoon, skirting water-filled dykes—or *rhines*—on narrow muddy roads full of right-angled bends. Willows, deformed into stumpy knuckles by decades of pruning lined the road like ugly bollards.

It had been an 'easy' day; only 52 miles, yet I was tired enough to be dreaming of pots of tea. Somerset reminded me of Norfolk. My first bicycle expedition had been in Norfolk. When I was nine Hol decided I was big enough for a first bicycle expedition. We rode from Norwich to the North Sea at Walcot. The distance was 22¾ miles; it felt like a journey to the far end of the earth. I rode the blue and white hand-painted bicycle that I had at last grown into. Initially he had screwed wooden blocks to the pedals so that my feet could reach them. The day the blocks were unscrewed was matched only in importance by the day I first wore long trousers. Hol rode his Raleigh Record Ace. My next big bicycle ride was more ambitious. With 'Dicky' Dickson, a schoolfriend, I set off to ride around the county boundary of Norfolk in three days. We agreed to phone home every night to say where we were. For all of the first day the rain and wind came in from the North Sea as if it had been gathering speed since leaving the Urals. We arrived at Kings Lynn youth hostel soaked, frozen, starved and too exhausted to eat or think. We went straight to bed without making our telephone call. At midnight we were woken by a policeman who had been instructed to locate two missing fourteen-year-olds.

Many roads cross the high whaleback of the Mendips, but

only one attempts to cut through the rock itself. The grandeur of the Cheddar Gorge is best enjoyed on foot or by bicycle. In terms of scale, Cheddar does not rank high in the world league of gorges; the Brahmaputran and Samarian gorges could swallow it many times over. But to the English it is no less of a geographical shrine than the Grand Canyon is to Americans. In fact Cheddar is more of a steep-sided valley than a true gorge.

We pedalled from Cheddar village into the mouth of this famous chasm along a road that entirely fills its floor. To some of us, Cheddar was stupendous. But to Cy Oggins, a youthful eighteen-year-old, it was cause for some baf-flement. At the head of the gorge we paused while the English in the group re-loaded cameras or turned to cycle the gorge a second time (it only takes a few minutes). Bewildered by the interest, Cy Oggins said 'Was *that* it?'

Through Chew Stoke and Chew Magna—villages half way between the Mendips and the old city-port of Bristol—I nattered with 'Jock' Mather, who had joined us at Cheddar. Unable to take time off for the complete tour he would ride with us till he reached his home in southern Scotland. I'd been unsure whether it was fair to the group to include a rider who would not be going all the way. Later, Jock was to 'save' the tour.

In a wind that seemed intent on keeping us firmly in the West Country, little groups of three and four riders huddled together for shelter until sanctuary was reached among the walls of southern Bristol. In one of the city's more salubrious grey stone suburbs we came upon the first of three well-known suspension bridges that we would use during the ride. The oldest and most elegant of the three is Brunel's bridge over the Avon at Clifton. It was built in 1864, and crosses the Avon Gorge (Britain's home-grown, rough-hewn answer to the Corinth canal) in a single confident span.

Later that day we came to the Severn Bridge, whose abstract lattice of wires and slender metal look more like a geometric doodle than a solid piece of engineering. On the cycle-track, suspended airily above the water, we pedalled in a long, doubtful line. Cy Oggins was impressed enough to take a photograph of the Bristol Channel below. I was trying to calculate whether, if a wire broke and the bridge started to sag then pull apart, I would stand a better chance of survival by clinging to the structure or by diving clear. Cy said the impact of hitting the water from such a height would cause instant death. As I rode, I started making mental notes of good hand-holds.

The northern ramp of the Severn Bridge launched us straight into Wales. Behind Chepstow rise the steep wooded hills that conceal the secret wanderings of the River Wye. For once we followed the main road, the A466, because it tries harder than any other to stick to the valley bottom. Even so, it was a stiff pull at the end of a long day over the bluff to St Arvans and then down to join the Wye. We came to the gaunt, roofless ruin of Tintern Abbey set before damp meadows with leafless misty forests rising on the hills behind. We crossed one of the Wye's few bridges and climbed at a ridiculous angle through the embankments of Offa's Dyke to the little village of St Briavels. The youth hostel is in a moated castle built by the Normans on the edge of the Forest of Dean. It was, remarked Williams, 'a pretty neat place to stay.'

Just behind the castle is an old pub. Those of the group who could still move, limped to the bar and, by a glowing fire that crackled and spat in the grate, subsided into pints of warm bitter.

Five days out from Land's End, the group had found its pace. William was last at almost everything. Partly he was hampered by his military upbringing and partly by his equipment; the two conspiring to create a sense of order which worked contrary to action. His bright red panniers were fitted with 24 zipped pockets, each containing a particular combination of items. William always carried a map folded into a clear plastic window on the top of his handlebar-bag, and he was the only one in the group who could be guaranteed to know where we were at any given time.

Len and Fred invariably finished the day's ride first, pedalling with fluid rhythm while others further down the field struggled with punctures and pannier bags that had a habit of getting jammed in the spokes of the rear wheel. Len was sixty-six. Also up at the front was big Bill Clements, well-clear of six feet and a youngster at sixty-two. On some days, the group would be separated over several miles. I would try and oscillate around the middle—a comfortable median often occupied by stalwarts such as George Mullett, whose quiet perseverence and good-humour helped several of us over hard moments; by sprucely dressed M. Bishop; Martin Barnes in his flappy cords and by Roy Palmer, whose life of cycle-touring had tuned him to the finer aspects of such matters as route-finding and youth hostel lore. Some—like William, who had fought till near midnight on the road to Tintagel—grew stronger by the day, as did Paul Sandford, a Londoner on his first ever tour.

On roads so narrow we had to squeeze near the curb to let tractors pass, we rode beside the upper Wye through border villages like Hole-in-the-Wall, How Caple and Sollers Hope until, beyond Hereford, we joined the River Lugg. Damp fields beside the road smelled of turned soil, and just the faintest wash of green in the hedgerows hinted that spring was just a week or two away.

In a pub in Ludlow we found a folk club. It was in a back room which was half-filled with an appreciative local audience tapping their toes and staring at their beer while a young man with a finger in his ear sang nasally about fair maids. The song went on forever. Unaware of the audience emotion, Mike Kosschuk, a hard-riding Yorkshireman who wore a wollen hat pulled down over his ears, provided acoustic interludes between verses by rustling his crisp packet. The singer was pausing for a rest when Mike said in a very loud voice. ''ere, anybody like any nuts and raisins?' Furious faces turned on him and the man with a finger in his ear unscrewed his eyes. Through a mouthful of chewed peanuts Mike looked up and said loudly 'Sorry!'

The next day was clearly divided into two. First we did battle with Wenlock Edge, whose acute wooded crest rides across old Shropshire like a breaking wave. From Corve Dale our little road clambered upwards then fell down the backslope into Ape Dale. I wanted to stop in the pub at Ticklerton, but there wasn't time. And our legs were stretched most of the way to Shrewsbury by the wrinkles that link the ancient landmarks of Long Mynd, Stiperstones and The Wrekin and Caer Caradoc. After a lunch in Shrewsbury, the hills eased and we glided smoothly under a warm sky northwards into Cheshire, stalking the county town by approaching on minor roads that led us up a last hill—Fuller's Moor.

We stopped to look out across the Cheshire Plain through a gap in the naked trees. A tall elm had been felled and its fresh sawdust lay in pale drifts around the severed bole. A single bright yellow daffodil nodded in the foreground. A patchwork of fields stretched west in an unbroken rustic mosaic. Outside a grocery store in Tattenhall we sat in the sun drinking milk and munching chocolate. A sign on a cast-iron post painted pale blue, read Chester $8^{1}/_{2}$ miles. A woman walked by pushing an old black bike, its saddle covered in a plastic bag to keep off the rain, while a stooped companion chatted to her, his muddy brown corduroys wedged into the tops of his wellingtons. After the country, historic Chester appeared as a modern metropolis.

Anyone wanting to ride north from the Cheshire Plain must share the air with one of the country's densest concentrations of internal combustion engines. Main roads and motorways criss-cross the area linking Liverpool with Manchester and servicing the satellite towns that promised so much in yesterday's age of industry. A solid band of buildings and tarmac stretches from the Irish Sea to the Pennines. To ride northwards through this without using A roads you have to cross to the eastern side of the Pennines. Murmurs from the 'other ranks' suggested that a 200-mile detour just to avoid cars would be an ill-received proposition. So for a day we followed the same route used by G.P. Mills, up through Warrington and Wigan, to Preston. It had taken 'G.P.' 4 hours 35 minutes to link these three towns in 1886, a time he reduced to 2 hours 55 minutes when he later rode the End-to-End on a Safety cycle. Our time lay somewhere between the two, for we stopped for lunch at a lorry-drivers' cafe. There are few enough of these left in Britain now, most of them having been displaced by chains of sanitised glass-fronted eateries whose menus look like mail-order catalogues. For the best part of a century club cyclists (and lone riders too) have relied on a network of cosy tea shops and cafes favoured for their immense portions of no-nonsense fare and proprietal indifference to sweaty bodies and peculiar clothing. The food was high calorie and energetically fried: the puddle left on an emptied plate of eggs, sausage and chips would often be enough to lubricate a couple of bicycles. Such establishments were of national importance: the CTC used to carry a listing of them in their annual handbook, and recommended cafes and teashops were entitled to mount a CTC 'recommended' shield on their wall.

North of Preston, hills rather than chimneys lined the horizon. From the suburb of Ribbleton, the B6243 skipped over the M6, and less than half-an-hour's easy pedalling brought us to Longridge. We left the traffic here, cutting behind the Longridge Fell on narrow roads that threaded their way beside infant streams that fed the Ribble. By drystone walls and over the odd humpy bridge we rode into the heart of the Forest of Bowland which is notable for its lack of trees.

The youth hostel at Slaidburn occupies a 17th-century former inn called 'The Black Bull', and our group occupied half its total of beds. It is graded a 'Simple' hostel, which means that it has been spared the degradations inflicted on many hostels 'upgraded' by installing the very cosmetic comforts you're trying to escape from. Some hostels have even built car parks.

The road north from Slaidburn climbed straight from the village to Catlow Fell. 'That's woken me up' called Fred, sitting up as the road levelled. We hurtled down to High Bentham where a corner shop was stripped of Mars Bars.

High Bentham and Ingleton sit on opposite sides of one of the bigger trans-Pennine valleys. To avoid using the A65 and A683 we climbed out of Ingleton on a road that pointed at the sky. Clean limestone walls separated us from smooth pastures. Sheep dotted the slopes up to Whernside then the road eased and the bikes rolled on their own, picking up speed and twisting like swallows through the bends before Deepdale. We rolled into lovely Dentdale laughing and weak-legged, stopping in the cobbled main street of Dent for tea and cakes.

The Howgill Fells block the way north, forcing travellers onto high bleak slopes. Not far to the west, the main A6 road struggles over a pass called Shap. It is half way from Land's End to John o' Groats. Crossing Shap opens the door to Scotland. It is the highest, and last hill an End-to-Ender climbs in England. For Mills on his penny-farthing this must have been a memorable milestone. But for the modern record-breaker whose efforts are measured in minutes, Shap is not a place to dwell upon: to know that after 20 hours of intense, all-consuming racing you are but half way, with the harder part yet to come, is a hardly digestible mental morsel. It is your mind, not the hills that kills your legs.

For a third time that day we climbed through 300 metres

then rolled from the Pennines with legs like stretched elastic into the pretty village of Dufton. Over cottage pie that evening, Len told young Cy that he would need to show his American passport when we crossed the border to Scotland the next day.

From Dufton we rode along the wrinkled hem of the Pennines. Knock, Milburn, Skirwith, Melmerby, Gambelsby, Renwick and Newbiggin, Castle Carrock, all villages of weathered stone with their backs to the sombre moors, looking west across the Eden valley. It was the first day of our second week. According to my route-sheet, we had 92 miles to cover by nightfall.

Across Hadrian's Wall there was a brief respite from hill-climbing as we crossed the farmlands of the Border country that bridge the Eden, Lyne and Liddel before starting the long climb into the Southern Uplands of Scotland. Mick Latimer, a man with a tangled beard and blue beret, told me about his 'Curly' Hetchins bicycle—a machine so named because the frame builder had cut and filed the lugs into intricate whorls, thereby totally transforming a normally functional lump of metal. Mick was a born organiser and worked as a youth hostel warden. Jock left us here for his family in Galashiels. We did not expect to see him again.

The air carried a new hint of chill and there were fewer chances to take off our jackets. Noses glowed and we all looked forward to reaching the secluded cottage that is Snoot youth hostel (more of an isolated bunkhouse than a formal residence), which is arrived at by way of a metal footbridge spanning the pebble bed and rippling grey of Borthwick Water. We were the only visitors and it didn't take too long to steam the place into a cosy fug.

It was a cold night. In the morning a bright low sun picked out the soft folds on the rounded hill behind the hostel and Cy Oggins said it was so cold he was going to wear his gloves. The air was unnaturally still; not a breath of wind disturbed the valley. To avoid the A7 I'd routed the next part of the ride far into the hills. By now the wiser ones in the group had taken a keen interest in cartography, and quickly noted the number of contour lines my route crossed. All but four opted for the main road and we agreed to meet later in the day, at Innerleithan.

Those of us who opted for the contour lines pedalled west

past the twin waters of Alemoor Lock, its still freezing waters shining a startling blue beneath the clear sky. We cut through the sharp air on a roller coaster road without cars, silent but for the sound of whispering tyres and the abrupt clatter of gears changing. At Tushielaw Inn we leant the bikes on a wall and stamped our feet to restore circulation to numb toes. Old snow lay on the verges and the bare hills shone bright and white.

A stiff climb up to 360 metres on The Wiss took us to Mountbenger and another hill road lifted us to Innerleithen. In the High Street, Mick Latimer was waiting, worry written on his face.

'There's been an accident Nick. There was snow on the road near Selkirk. A car skidded. Just mowed into us. Les and David are in hospital in Galashiels. Len's leg may be broken. Fred's stayed with them.' In one breath the rosy exhilaration of the morning's ride was blown away. In measured sensible Yorkshire tones Mike Kosschuk said 'Let's 'ave a cuppa tea.'

A car had lost control on the hard-packed snow and smashed into them. There had been a 'bang'. It was hard to ignore the images: the twisted bicycles, inert bodies and that moment of shocking silence before new sounds begin. An ambulance had collected them. Now I had to make decisions. How badly hurt were Len and David? Should the ride go on? I decided to ride back to Galashiels hospital and asked Mick Latimer to continue north with the remainder of the group.

It was a cold, lonely and unhappy ride. It took me an hour, riding fast. In Ward 9, Len lay bandaged and sad, more disappointed by the thought that he wouldn't complete his End-to-End than by the fact that he was moderately injured. He had been X-rayed; nothing was broken, but he would be in for 'at least a week'. David wasn't so badly hurt, but was too bruised to sit on a bicycle. As he lived in Galashiels, Jock Mather had been told and immediately made for the hospital bearing comfort and support. His kind presence helped lift some of the weight from my shoulders. The coincidence of the accident happening in Jock's home town gave the tour a second chance. Len was insistent that the tour go on—urging me to leave before it was too late to catch up with Mick Latimer's group. I followed Fred round to Jock's home.

Sorrow and a certain amount of guilt (if I'd persuaded them not to use the main A7 the accident wouldn't have happened) confused the correct next step. Should I try with Fred to catch up with the group and see them through to John o' Groats, or should I stay in Galashiels and provide moral support for Len and David? With Jock happy to keep an eye on Len and David, I decided to go on.

It was dark and snowing lightly by the time Fred and I left Galashiels. The police had put barriers across the road, with a sign explaining that heavy snow had made the exposed road impassable to motor vehicles. It was 35 miles over the hills to Edinburgh. If we were to catch Mick Latimer and the rest of the group, we would have to reach Perth by the following morning.

We took it in turns to ride in each other's wheel tracks: thin black lines through snow that hissed with our passing. After the drama of the afternoon, the simple physical challenge of trying to cross mountains at night in a snowstorm had a pleasant calming effect. To our left, the crooked inky line of the river divided the pale snowscape. As the road climbed, it became colder. Flakes that had melted lower down now collected thickly on Fred's shoulders and peaked cap. He looked spectral. The valley was silent. The gears on my bicycle stopped working. Looking down, I could see a fist-size nugget of ice glued to the derailleur.

At the top, we stopped to chip pieces of ice from our brakes. Water had frozen onto the metal of the spokes until each was the diameter of a pencil. Fred was good company; he never complained. He wanted to finish. The long downhill to Edinburgh was so cold that it was difficult to grip the handlebars. In the town, we asked the way to the youth hostel. At midnight, long after he was meant to open his doors to travellers, the warden of Bruntsfield Crescent hostel admitted two cyclists who could barely speak. Our clothes were stiff with ice. I nearly wept as hot shower water brought the circulation back to my hands and feet.

We rose at 6 am and rode towards Perth. I remember nothing of the countryside, but do recall that crossing the suspension bridge over the Forth made me feel more that I was leaving two companions behind than that I was entering the last leg of the End-to-End.

At Perth, Mike Kosschuk was waiting with a pot of tea. Everyone was subdued, exhausted, needing to know about

Len and David. We swapped stories. After nearly 100 miles in sub-zero temperatures over the Moorfoot Hills then the Ochils, Mick and the others had arrived at Glendevon hostel hardly able to stand. Fred was able to say 'That was a night. I don't think I've ever had a ride like that one.' A part of me expected some of the group to pull out. Nobody did.

Just 3 days and 300 miles separated us from John o' Groats. We left Perth early. Between us and Aviemore were the Grampians. It had started to snow again. After warming up on the hilly road through Strathord Forest we dropped to the Tay Valley, and through Dunkeld began the long climb to the Pass of Killiecrankie and then Glen Garry. A head-wind tried to hold us in the valley. As the road gained height so the snow-streaked mountains dwarfed our progress. Singly and in pairs we struggled towards the top of the Pass of Drumochter. I stopped at a small store and bought a 'bridie', turning to look backwards as I munched. I could see Mick Latimer and some others far down the road. Watching a cyclist in such massive places is like looking for movement in the minute hand of a clock.

The road climbed over 450 metres but, like the Brenner pass in the Alps, Drumochter is too full of steel rails and tarmac to be authentically wild. The best pass in Scotland is Bealach na Ba—the Pass of the Cattle—which reaches 626 metres in a spiral of tortuous hairpins before dropping seawards to Applecross on the west coast. A close second is the climb from Staffin to Uig on the Isle of Skye. This must be ridden from east to west for maximum effect. The road tries to scale an inland cliff called Quirang whose broken face is split into needle-like pinnacles and tabletop rocks. The labyrinthine gullies and hidden shelves were once the hiding place for stolen cattle. Drumochter has none of this. Rolling down Glen Truim the group swelled as tail-enders caught up. We bowled through Newtonmore happier and faster as the thickening forest took the wind from the road. Shoulder to shoulder with the Spey we flew past Lochs Insh and Alvie. Later, Fred said he thought we'd been 'doing evens' for much of the afternoon. Bill explained to me that 'evens' was club-language for an average speed of 20 mph. In Aviemore, the youth hostel had heating.

We were never far from the railway for most of the next day. We shared the forested slopes of the Monadhliath Mountains as we rose gradually to 406 metres before dropping and following Strathdearn to the foot of Drum-mossie Muir. It was snowing heavily. Over to the east Bonnie Prince Charlie met his final defeat in 1746 on Culloden Muir. 1,300 lives were lost. While the railway made a long loop beyond the battlefield, the road cut at right-angles through the contours, falling to Inverness in a steep tarmac sweep. We arrived in the town with the wind roaring in our ears and our eyes streaming.

Frozen by soaking-wet clothes, part of the group dived into a launderette where they stripped off and rented a drier for an hour. By the bus station, and in a cafe whose windows ran with condensation from the heat of our bodies, we drank tea and took stock. William spread his map. We were only half way through the day's riding. I could see I wasn't the only weary one. North of Inverness three big sea-inlets—the Firths of Beauly, Cromarty and Dornoch—insinuate themselves far inland, making life difficult for End-to-Enders. 'G.P.' had used local ferries to avoid the long inland detours. My route stuck firmly to dry land.

The snow, wind and cold were not a part of the plan, however. A new desperation gripped the group. We were now close to finishing, yet the weather and miles were making each day harder than the last. To cap it all, the longest day of the entire ride was the last: 96 miles from Carbisdale Castle to John o' Groats. I worried that some might not make it.

We rode from Inverness beside the glittering surface of Beauly Firth. The wind was hard against. Rain clouds sat waiting for us over by Ben Wyvis. Beyond Dingwall we turned away from the water and began a slow ascent over the hills of Easter Ross that separate the Cromarty Firth from the Dornoch Firth. On the map, this has the appearance of a logical short cut, but with every mile it became more obvious why 'G.P.' (and most subsequent record-breakers) used the longer but flat coastal route. I wasted no opportunity to point out the scenic merits of the hilly route and maintained a continual prayer that the top would soon appear. The top came just below a mountain called Struie, overlooking the gun-metal grey of Dornoch Firth. In the last half-hour of daylight we followed a valley inland to the sanctuary of Carbisdale. While the warden checked us in I read that the castle had been built in 1914, and that during the Second World War it had been the home of exiled King Haakon of Norway. The view from the windows of the rising pines and fast-running river must have been painfully reminiscent of his own country.

Jokes and sunshine brought a cheerful start to the final day. After packing the bikes outside the hostel we crossed a tract of moor and loch from Bonar Bridge, meeting the North Sea at a small port called Golspie. The hills began to get lonely. At Helmsdale the railway line struck off inland leaving the road to tackle the notorious Braes of Berriedale. For a while there is no foreshore, forcing the road-builders to climb high. Nobody who has cycled from Land's End deserves the road that leads to Berriedale. Mills must have pushed his High Ordinary over here, cursing the roughness and steepness of the road. Leaving a cafe in Helmsdale our battered but spirited group was wrenched apart by the early bends, leaving each rider to tackle the problem as he knew best.

The sun was smothered by cloud being pushed by a northerly wind. Now it was the sheltered hills that were preferable to the wind-blasted flat stretches of road.

Through Lybster, Ulbster and Thrumster we rode. The group had formed into knots of twos and threes. At five o'clock I stopped at Wick to wait for the stragglers. William and George hadn't been seen since mid-afternoon. At six o'clock the others set off on the final 17 miles to John o' Groats. I ordered another pot of tea.

Outside, the day grew dull. I kept looking at my watch. The minute hand never seemed to move. Surely, we would all make it having got this far? I argued with myself, angry that I had not stayed with the back of the group. Maybe George had got into trouble on Berriedale? Perhaps William's bike had collapsed? I must go back. I stood up to leave; to pedal back southwards. Then sat down again. 'Ten more minutes,' I said to myself. 'No more.'

William fell through the door. He said: 'The wind!' and folded onto the table. George, he said, was doing fine; an hour back down the road. George didn't want us to wait; he would finish in his own time.

Revived by the tea, William and I pushed off for a final time. An hour's struggle brought us to a long open stretch. The wind tore into our faces. Ahead, a lone figure was plodding defiantly along the centre of the road. Yard by yard, we drew level. It was Kevin. 'Puncture?' I asked.

'Knackered!' he said. Together, the three of us walked on. The hills had subsided. Low walls divided bleak sheep pastures. Solitary houses dotted the low landscape. There is one last hill before John o' Groats. It is called Warth Hill, and it is 124 metres high. On the top, we stopped for a rest. George was not in sight. We'd all been last at some stage during the ride and I didn't envy him his solitary struggle. Fifteen minutes of cycling took us to the end.

It was a euphoric group that gathered in the tiny hostel at Canisbay that night. George arrived at nine o'clock. He was still smiling. Over a celebratory supper in the John o'Groats Hotel, we toasted two absent companions. Early the next morning, in the harsh brightness of a sky with huge horizons, we pedalled together the final five minutes to John o' Groats.

Five months later, the splints removed from his legs, Len pedalled over Warth hill and completed his End-to-End.

I was beginning to understand G.P. Mills.

★ ★ ★

The following summer I found myself at John o' Groats again. I had heard that a 29-year-old professional racing cyclist from Birmingham was going to attempt the End-to-End record. The record then stood at 1 day 23 hours 46 minutes. Paul Carbutt planned to knock 26 minutes off the record. On the grounds of gathering material for a book I was editing, I managed to get a seat in the press van.

Having waited a few days in Land's End for favourable winds, Carbutt had an uneventful first day with the exception of being stopped by police in Penzance for 'speeding'. From the press van, which followed at the 50-yard minimum distance as stipulated in Section 38 (b) of the Rules of the Road Records Association, Carbutt's performance was mesmerising. At 300 miles he was still pedalling with the fluidity of a machine locked into perpetual motion.

He rode up Shap like a train, pausing on the summit for food, clean clothes and a massage then flew on hot tarmac across the borders and into the hills of southern Scotland.

Then he collapsed. He had been slowing for a few miles. Suddenly he was wobbling. A helper ran alongside. Carbutt fell sideways. He was out for 25 minutes. I thought he was dying. Then they woke him up. He was lifted back onto his bike and rode for another 20 hours, breaking the record by 23 minutes.

Outside the John o' Groats hotel, they led him to an armchair placed on the tarmac. He slumped down, face a blank. 858 miles of agony had turned him into an old man. His excited team manager, mechanic, press officer and feeding team crowded round. For the first time in two days and two nights, the expressionless mask cracked. It flowered into a comprehending grin.

7

My First Tour de France

FRANCE

It was a great idea. John, Pete and myself had always wanted to see the Tour de France. This annual race round France is widely regarded as the toughest competition known to man. It is also the world's largest spectator sporting event. What fun, the three of us speculated, to tag our own sideshow onto this great sporting circus.

Out in front was John Rodd; just behind, Pete Inglis. John had the lean, cropped look of a racing cyclist. I'd been introduced to John by cousin Dick; the two of them had recently cycled the 'Raid Pyrenean' an end-to-end ride along the Pyrenees which has to be covered in under 80 hours to qualify for the certificate. Dick and John had managed it in 79^{1}/$_{2}$ hours. John was appallingly fit. His thighs seemed to have been inflated inside his glossy skintight shorts and his jersey had pockets in the back for carrying glucose and inner tubes. John's bicycle was so light that he had to peg it down when parking in high winds.

Pete was wearing the same clothes I remembered him using in France years before. He had a mountaineering jacket big enough to accommodate himself and a couple of Sherpas while his feet were encased in climbing boots. Pete is the ideal travelling companion: ready to try anything and able to laugh at the predicaments that normally result. One of the attributes that makes him such a fine photographer is his seemingly inexhaustible patience. Tied to the back of his bike was a rucksack loaded with bike repair essentials: hammer, coil of wire, welding kit and so on. My own equipment choice bore more similarity to Pete's than to John's.

Pete dropped further and further behind. He was finding the hill hard work. This was partly because I had lent him a bicycle which had one of those dynamo lighting systems that produces electricity by the friction of a small metal wheel running on the outside of the front tyre. These systems are not known for their efficiency. The model fitted to Pete's bike had been marinated in rain-water for ten years. It was so hard to turn that the bike felt as if it was being ridden through waist-deep semolina. When you pushed the little lever which flicked the dynamo on to the front wheel, the sudden friction loading would stop the bike dead. I could only keep up with Pete when he had his lights on.

Spaces in the trees gave a view to the lights of St Michel, now far below, and moving pinpricks of white marked the laboured progress of trucks crawling over the Alps towards Turin. A road junction emerged from the dark. The only way we could read the signpost was by John holding Pete's bicycle above his head while Pete pulled the front wheel round and round. This cast a pale yellow blob onto the word 'Valloire'. We rode on, losing sight of each other in our private worlds. Daylight crept up un-noticed, and I crested the Col du Télégraphe feeling hungry, 10 kilometres of hairpins behind; 24 in front. John was sitting on a rock wolfing a breakfast of bread and salami. In my panniers I had climbing boots and a bag of bruised apples; we ate the apples.

Pete arrived. 'At last I can turn this damned dynamo off!' he muttered, dragging a brick of pâté from a pack that chinked as if it was loaded with sawn-up scaffolding.

'Don't you think it would be safer to keep the dynamo on in case there's any traffic?' I ventured.

'Yes, you're right Nick'. His back to us, he bent over the front wheel. There was one of those short high-pitched grunts you make when lifting something very heavy, followed by a metallic rending and snapping. Pete stood up. He opened his hand. In it was a *circa* 1950s Miller dynamo, separated into a number of flanges, wires and odd shaped pieces of rusty metal.

'Oh dear' he said. 'It seems to have broken. Just fell off in my hand.' I wondered how I'd keep up with him on the Galibier.

On the rock, we idly spread the map. The mountains were curiously tranquil. Curious, because this was the dawn of one of the biggest days of European sport: in a few hours' time the Tour de France was going to claw its way past this rock towards the Col du Galibier.

The Alpine tranquillity was disturbed by the laboured drone of distant, hammering engines, which amplified explosively as two black-clad gendarmes erupted over the summit of the pass. They cranked their bikes over for the bend, trailing sparks from their footrests, then disappeared into the trees. They were the vanguard. The night time calm evaporated with the dew from the rock, and before we were back on the bikes a couple more vehicles had splintered the cool air as they hurtled southwards.

From the Col du Télégraphe it was a cold, eye-watering rush downhill to the sleeping village of Valloire. The only sign of life was the cosy warm smell of baking bread. A gentle, rising gradient out of the village warmed our frozen limbs and we cycled through fresh-cut pastures, meeting a tiny stream on the bends. Here we could mentally rest before tackling the 'double arrows' that the Michelin map marked on the final approach to the Galibier. There was a short, sharp slope, another relaxing gradient, then by Plan Lachat, the road doubled back on itself. Now for the hard part.

In a small field by the road, campers were folding their tents, bikes strewn amid piles of poles and panniers. Cars began to overtake more regularly. Valoirette was waking up.

With eight kilometres to the top, John surged off ahead as if he'd released a spring that had been winding up all morning. Pete and I reached for our gear levers. Behind me, there was a rasping of steel, followed by an indignant cry:

'What's wrong with these gears!'

'Oh! I forgot to tell you ...'

The road bent, curled and corkscrewed, with increasingly precipitous drops by our wheels. Above, grey rock walls, patches of snow and spiky peaks crept into view.

Down below, at Plan Lachat, a bevy of gendarmerie vehicles had gathered. Figures stood by open doors. The vans started up the hairpins, chugging motor cycles in escort. They crawled past us towing a cloud of choking diesel exhaust. On each corner they paused long enough for a gendarme to hop out and take station.

Out of the saddle now, and warming up quickly, we heaved up the slopes past thinning trees and listless gendarmes who were waiting for the deluge of action. For the moment they were happy to make do with grins and encouraging words for a couple of struggling foreigners.

The road began to cut through two-metre walls of snow. Passing from the balmy grass banks to these icy defiles was like riding into a refrigerator. The motor traffic had risen to a steady stream, all of it travelling our way, and in a tearing hurry. It felt as if we were caught up in a car rally. At around 2,400 metres I stopped blaming my faithful Raleigh and admitted that my difficulties were due to lack of fitness. Peter had disappeared.

At 2,401 metres I was close to expiring. I looked over my shoulder to see who was holding on to the back of my bike. I was pushing on the pedals as hard as I could; pulling on the handlebars so fiercely I feared they'd come off. The bike was hardly moving. It felt as if I was towing a condominium up the Galibier. My face was so contorted that half of it was round the back of my head. A French family sitting at a folding table by their car put down their croissants and looked the other way.

Surroundings could only be blinked at through a stinging veil of perspiration. Every watt of energy was being channelled into a pair of legs for which each revolution was a marathon of endurance. I stuffed an entire packet of glucose tablets into my mouth. Then panicked: I couldn't taste anything. Had so many of my bodily functions closed down that I could no longer taste food? Had I, in my supreme exertions, eaten my tongue? No. The Dextrosols were still in their wrapper. I chewed it off and the glucose coursed into my blood-stream.

Ahead I became aware of a rippling, colourful mass of humanity. The road was all but blocked. People were cheering, shouting, running alongside. Someone asked if I wanted a push. Through a mouth glued together with Dextrosol wrapper I tried to say 'No thanks, I'd like to make it on my own', but the words came out as 'Oui, oui, merci! merci!' and the bike leapt forward. Benevolent propellants whisked me up the last hundred metres. There was just room to squeeze along the centre of the road. It was overwhelming; fantastic. I wafted beneath the summit banner, lifted on a cushion of goodwill and personal relief.

I was on the way down the other side, towards Briançon, before Pete's urgent shouting reminded me to look for the brakes.

Spectators were already standing five deep. I wobbled off to the side, coming on a stone monument. It was dedicated to Henri Desgrange, founder in 1903 of the Tour de France. He was chief editor of the French magazine *l'Auto* and he'd dreamt up the Tour de France as a publicity vehicle for the magazine. It wasn't a bad idea: 160 million people watch it on television.

Reunited with the bearers of bread and pâté, I compared details of the climb. Both John and Pete were in suspended ecstasy. We made our way through the tight crowds to a point on the mountainside where we could see hairpins uncurling from the valley. The thin grey strip of road was bordered by a continuous sparkling frill of parked cars and picnickers. It was scarcely credible: among the snow and ice and shattered peaks, here at 2,556 metres — 8,386 feet — on the top of one of the highest of all Alpine passes was a crowd big enough to fill a football stadium. The more dedicated French race followers had brought their bicycles up the Galibier too — on the roofs of their cars.

On picnic tables standing in the snow, transistor radios rattled out the race commentary live from RTL or France-Inter O.L. Such an incongruous cacophony of sound and colour high among Alpine peaks was hard to absorb. Only the gendarmes were not in festive mood. The narrow road was blocked with stationary traffic and milling people. With much whistle-blowing and arm-waving the blue uniforms waded into the melee and scolded car drivers edged towards the cafe car park. Once again the road was cleared for bicycle wheels.

Four English cycle-tourists, standing out a mile in their showerproof green jackets, ironed black shorts and black canvas saddlebags, twiddled their way into view, dignified and completely unruffled by the mayhem that infected the Galibier. Groaning under a cargo of souvenirs and shouting its wares over a loudspeaker, a Citroen van jerked to a halt, to be swamped by a lemming-like rush of people fighting to throw away five francs in return for a race programme filled with advertisements. When the van pulled away, fifty satisfied customers tried to pull on giveaway 'Bernard Hinault' hats that were far too small. I managed to grab a hat and two special-issue magazines. What better way of filling an hour before the Tour arrives? One magazine, titled *Bernard Hinault — Un Champion d' Exception* had pictures of Hinault at five years old, as a choirboy, winning his first race, Hinault talking to a pony, Hinault sawing wood,

Hinault in the red, white and blue jersey of national champion, wearing funny caps, being kissed, Hinault laughing, grimacing and coughing. It didn't seem to matter that Hinault had dropped out of the Tour de France six days earlier. Faced with tackling the Pyrenees and Alps with a wrecked knee, 'The Badger' had uncharacteristically called it a day.

At last the caravan of publicity vehicles could be seen on the lower hairpins. They crept towards us, hooting and revving, bedecked in slogans. There were jeep-sized yoghurt cartons, Michelin's bulbous Bibendum and cars advertising insect repellent by carrying on their roofs upside-down black flies of such hugeness that they wouldn't have been bothered by an anti-aircraft gun, let alone an aerosol. 'Must be a dirty country to have flies that big,' was Pete's comment. Chasing the insects came a clutch of red-suited motorcycle stunt-riders, standing on their seats and looking suitably worried, then a frenzied queue of press saloons, radio antennae waving, carrying reporters bent over pads or chattering animatedly into microphones.

After an interval came clumsy motorcycles carrying backward-facing photographers, weaving up the slope among the first team cars whose roofs sparkled with spare bike frames and wheels. Anxious mechanics and managers hung from the windows. The final vehicle is the race director's car, a big saloon with an imperious nut-brown head poking from the roof surveying the battlefield with a Napoleonic eye. Just for a moment there was a lull, as if the crowds and the mountain were drawing breath. Down below a lone cyclist was clawing his way round a distant snow-bank, diminutive and fragile compared to the weighty entourage that had just barged by.

Binoculars swivelled; eyes strained. Who was the rider? The jersey was blue and white; somebody from the Splendor team. The name 'De Muynck' whispered on the breeze. A Belgian. He rose from the saddle to pull his bike round yet another hairpin. Nuzzling his back wheel were two press motorbikes and the Splendor team car. De Muynck's head lifted for a moment. This was the fortieth anniversary of Desgrange's death and a special bonus prize of ten thousand francs was being offered to the first rider to reach the top of the Galibier. De Muynck wanted those francs. A vortex of applause sucked him towards the summit. He was safely through the banner by the time two more riders, in the blue and yellow of Ijsboerke and green, black and white of Puch, joggled past, duelling the final metres to the top. Peeters and Willman, we were told.

Another outbreak of cheering heralded the arrival of the 'bunch'. A wall of bright jerseys forged towards us. People leaned forward as far as they dared. A photographer slipped down a snow bank, lenses skittling. Portuguese climber Joaquim Agostinho spearheaded the latest arrivals, among them Raymond Martin, who was trying to capture the red polka-dotted mountain climber's jersey but who was hanging on to the tail-end of this group by the skin of his teeth. A man wearing nothing but a tiny pair of Union Jack shorts detached himself from the crowd and sprinted beside Martin, yelling encouragement.

More, smaller groups came past, and in one of them was the twisted face of Sven-Åke Nilsson, destined to lose the polka-dots by the end of the day. Joop Zoetemelk, race leader now Hinault had dropped out came by in yellow, bandaged and obviously suffering beside two Raleigh riders who were shepherding him over this Alp. A Briton, Graham Jones, passed followed by another Peugot rider who was crying 'Poussez! Poussez!' A hundred willing hands thrust forward to help him upwards. Abruptly, the melee was over.

People turned back to their cars and radios. Almost unnoticed, a couple of stragglers heaved themselves over the Galibier; one of them was Paul Sherwen, from Britain. They had another 233 kilometres to ride that day, and three more passes to conquer before reaching Morzine where they could rest for the night.

'They go downhill at 60 miles an hour' said John lifting his bike. John's head tapered aerodynamically at the top as if he had been genetically prepared for riding bicycles very fast. Through the dribbles of water leaking out from beneath the snow banks we followed the still-damp tyre marks of the Tour. It was so steep that the bikes lunged forward when the brakes were released. We leant forward and sped down, wind tearing at our hair, eyes streaming. Below the road, sheer drops fell to the forest top. I was going as fast as I dared. Pete was going faster. The hairpin bends were shaped like question marks.

On one of the bends my back tyre skipped sideways and the bike went into a forty-mile-an-hour wobble. Behind I could hear a sound like a loose spinnaker in a gale and Pete came past, eyes slitted and a maniacal grin topping a madly flapping jacket. I tucked in behind him, hiding in his slipstream, holding his speed. With a nose that could have been designed in a wind-tunnel, Pete had a definite advantage, whereas my massive chin, shaped like a front bucket on a JCB acted with all the inefficiency of an upsidedown aerofoil. I could go much faster down hills by facing backwards.

Twenty-four hours later we were comfortably ensconced in a cafe which looked across the central square of Morzine. This town-cum-ski resort had bought its way into the Tour as a host for one of the rare 'rest days'. We had hoped to spend the day spotting the stars, as most of the teams had temporary headquarters in the town's several plush hotels. But persistent Alpine rain had kept the pros from promenading.

We spent the day drinking coffee and decoding the French daily sports paper *L'Equipe*. In it we learnt that during yesterday's mountain stage Raymond Martin had overtaken Sven Ake Nilsson by seven points in the *Meilleur Grimpeur Trophée Campagnolo*, thus laying claim to the red polka-dot jersey of the best climber. Also that Graham Jones was running third in the 'white jersey' competition for best young rider, and that Christian Seznac, born in Brest, had scooped the day's prize for most elegant rider. 'No flies on him' said Pete. The stage winner had been Mariano Martinez, who'd made the 242-kilometre dash through the Alps at an average speed of 33.837 kph (21.15 mph). And in small print at the bottom of the general classification list were the words 'Abandon: Paul Sherwen'. It seemed insufficient tribute to a rider who had survived 2,848 kilometres of the world's most gruelling sporting event.

Once we'd dissected Stage 17, we turned to the following day's race. It looked cruel: 196 kilometres from Morzine to Prapoutel-les-Sept-Laux. *L'Equipe's* 'altigraph' illustrated the day's route like the teeth of a saw. Four of the biggest teeth were the Col de la Colombière, Col des Aravis, Col de Champlaurent and Col de Barioz. We chose the Colombière. The road approaching from the north was marked with a green border on the Michelin map, meaning it should be scenic. Compared to the Galibier, it was a lightweight, with only 14 kilometres of climbing.

The gradient was comfortable. Water was sluicing down the narrow road and dripping from the overhanging trees. It was quiet, with burgeoning verges and lush woodland hiding the valley from us for the early miles. Half way up we came to the tiny village of Le Reposoir, snuggling into the valley bottom and preparing itself for the biggest invasion of the year. The village elders had moved their chairs out onto the roadside, and were patiently waiting for the entertainment to begin. Children peeked from upstairs windows.

Immediately above the village a succession of 'double arrows' had me panting so hard I was sure the trees were moving in my breath. John sneaked away. Pete was swallowing insects. A couple of teenagers ran from a family picnic and pushed us around a bend. On a hillside above us, a gaggle of school-kids formed a long line and chanted us upwards. For a while we were carried by a group of immaculately-attired *cyclo-sportifs,* then the Col came into sight — a dark slot in the steep-sided mountain. Distant cars twinkled in the sun. There was just time to pull off the road and clamber above the heads before the Tour caravan was sighted in the valley below.

The first rider to reach us wore a 'Marc' jersey, and had a number 67 bolted to his bike frame. A quick look at the team list told us that this was twenty-five-year-old Ludo Loos. Another Belgian. A minute later Alberto Fernandez and Josteen Willman heaved past in hot pursuit, and before there was time to check their pedigrees in the programme, Raymond Martin, resplendent in his new red-spotted jersey, lunged past shoulder to shoulder with Zoetemelk, in yellow. A Dutchman and Frenchman, chasing a Spaniard and Norwegian, who were in turn chasing a Belgian. But Joop looked more worried by those hanging on to his back wheel than by the escapees up front. Right on his tail were Hennie Kuiper and De Muynck, who with Martin had their eyes on the yellow jersey. Loos held his lead to the summit, and later that evening we learnt that he had won the stage by over five minutes.

Too soon they were gone. There was a short vacuum while tail-enders and the Tour's 'sag-waggon' elbowed past, then we climbed on our own machines. Le Reposoir flashed by, the village already settling back into cosy obscurity. Our tyres hummed on the tarmac, drawing smooth curves down the mountain.

'Good job we don't do this seriously' shouted Pete.

'You're right!'

Exactly three weeks later, on a Wednesday evening on the Abingdon bypass, I was launched down the Course H25/13 on my first serious time trial. I wanted to be a racing cyclist too.

My entree into the select world of skin-shorts and shaved legs came through a brush with the law.

For some time a detective from the Stolen Cycles Department at Oxford police station had been keeping an eye on a house in the Grandpont district of the city. Detective Constable Alan Deadman had observed that the front room of the house contained an unnaturally large number of bicycles. Inspecting the premises, he counted over twenty machines. Upon questioning, the householder claimed that contrary to appearances, each of the bicycles belonged to him, and that each had in fact been acquired for a different, and entirely valid, reason. There was a tricycle for riding on ice, a touring tandem, a tandem for spares, a racing bike, a fast training bike, a slow training bike, a bike for dirt tracks, a bike with 40 gears and so on. It was a story which took a bit of believing, but Alan, who was also Secretary of the Oxonian Cycling Club and an avid enthusiast, could see that this was a case of truth being stranger than fiction. He signed me up with the Oxonians and then spent the next two years reducing me to a breathless wreck on training rides to the Chilterns.

Time-trial addicts will try and tell you that this is the ultimate in pure competition; a test against the clock; a 'race of truth'. In truth it is the perfect embodiment of English sporting spirit. Intense inter-rider competition is disguised behind the pursuit of 'personal bests'. Each rider's worth is measured in hundredths of seconds, over a course which (barring changes of wind) is identical for every competitor. Ten and 25-mile time trials are the most popular, though races over 50 and 100 miles are held regularly through the season. The 12-hour and 24-hour time trials are regarded with marathon-like respect. Riders are released from the start-line at one-minute intervals. It's a solitary and intensely demanding psychological sport. The practice after a time trial is to look down the results sheet for your name and time, then, in the time it takes to say 'Bad ride that, could have done better', you memorise the names and times of every competitor who went faster. That way, you know who to beat next time.

New developments — both athletic and technical — would be noted with fanatical interest at the Oxonian evening races. The era of aerodynamics had begun. Alan Deadman cut his hair shorter and trimmed his moustache to reduce wind resistance. On his handlebars he etched into the metal the words 'More pain, More gain'. Club members turned up on increasingly radical bikes: bikes with upturned cut-off handlebars: bikes with sloping tubes; bikes with small front wheels; hidden cables; bikes with so few spokes you had to go easy on corners. Glossy, skin-tight clothing looked as if it had been applied by aerosol.

Time trialling I found to be the perfect tonic for the stress caused by training. As the starter counted down, I would be struck with a rare clarity of vision: I just *knew* that I should have stayed in watching the telly. Once pushed off, I'd try and wind up to the top gear and hang on for the prescribed miles. While some rode with a grace which looked effortless, my own body thrashed lopsidedly as heart and lungs pummelled each other in what felt like boxing gloves.

Hol has used many calculator batteries examining the most efficient ways of riding bicycles. One of his many deductions was outlined in a theory he called 'The Energy Drain'. Basically, he said, the science is to attack the hills and conserve energy on the down slopes. In a tailwind, you should increase your speed, and in a headwind, allow yourself to reduce speed. I memorised the rules. Later, they came in very handy. I longed for that elusive 'float day'; that day in a lifetime when the conditions are so perfect that your bike hums through the air to the music of rock-hard tubulars on tarmac.

Everyone else seemed to have 'float days' except me. I managed to knock a few seconds off my 10-and 25-mile times but never broke the mystical 'hour' barrier. On my first 50-mile time trial I mistook a marshall scratching his ear for an indication to leave the roundabout and raced across Oxfordshire never to find the finish. I entered a 12-hour time trial and surprised myself by finishing with a total of 228 miles despite having fallen asleep and ridden into a ditch.

'Don't give up' I told myself. 'It's just a question of waiting for the right event to come along.'

8

High Adventure

NORWAY

'Not many people come here with bicycles.' Harald poured another port. Outside, a squall boomed around the low eaves of his wooden home. 'In the winter, I have to dig through two metres of snow to find the door. Now the weather is mild.' Like a handful of flung shingle, a passing flurry of rain splattered against the window. Else walked soundlessly in her thick woollen slippers across the warm pine floor towards the kitchen. I thought 'I hope she's fetching more pancakes', and said: 'The great thing about travelling by bicycle in mountains is that you're forced to rely on your own resources ...'

Preserved by their own inaccessibility and by the shade cast upon them by the tinsled peaks of the Alps and Pyrenees, there are in Europe mountain ranges whose secrets are revealed only to the most inquisitive traveller. Few people, for instance, visit Lapland's Alookidooki range where nomadic people make clothes by stitching together giant seaweed fronds dried by hot gasses seeping from volcanic fumaroles beneath the ice.

Neither do many see the fabulous spectacle of Jostedals Bre, the largest ice cap in Europe. It sits high, hidden far above the fertile fjords and farms of Norway, like a freezer compartment on a refrigerator.

'It's going to be cold up there', said Pete through gritted teeth. I nodded enthusiastically. He regarded the map, and the pancake plate on the table with quiet resolve, his strong jaw set with determination; his eyes narrow slits. There was only one pancake left.

I lifted the plate towards him. His lips moistened. He leaned forward, reaching out his hand. I lifted up the pancake and put it in my mouth. Harald continued:

'Only once or twice a year are the clouds ever lifted from the mountains of Jostedals. Nearly always there is thick mist or snow. And the wind can be terrible. It will be difficult on a bicycle.' His finger traced a line across the map from the mountains near Bergen up towards a large area of blank whiteness.

'This is where the road goes.'

An audible gulp that had nothing to do with swallowing pancakes filled the shocked silence.

Thanking Harald and Else for their hospitality we stepped into the wild black night. Five days earlier we had left British soil and set off across the North Sea. In the tumultuous days of the eighth century, Norsemen plied this often dangerous branch of the north Atlantic in search of new lands and groceries. Storms and wrecks were common. Pete and I made the crossing in sleeperettes aboard a DFDS Lines car ferry.

Samuel Laing, a prolific author and traveller of the last century, had strong views on the corruption of travel. In his *Journal of my Residence in Norway made with a view to inquire into the Moral and Political Economy of that Country and the Condition of its Inhabitants* he wrote 'July 1834. Steamboats interfere most particularly with the vocation of the traveller who sets out in quest of all sorts of adventures and perils by land and sea and hopes to edify and astonish his friends at home by narrative of them.' He had a point. All we saw of note during our voyage was a beached oil platform near Stavanger.

Bergen has the highest rainfall in Norway. It was raining when we arrived. On the quayside, we met two British cyclists. They were wearing those urine-coloured cycling capes that smell of old rubber gloves and make crackly noises when you unroll them.

'Bloody awful place. I'd get right back on that boat if I were you. Rain every day. Never seen anything like it.'

He looked at his mate, standing in his dripping yellow tent.

'There's meant to be mountains, but we never saw 'em. Clouds everywhere. Hardly got any miles in either; spent all our time stopping to cape-up.'

He paused to blow his nose: 'Good luck. You'll need it', and the two of them splashed through the puddles towards the ferry.

We pedalled from the town in the company of two Australians whose phrases describing Norwegian weather were unprintable. So low was the cloud that our immediate impression of Norway was of a country populated by dripping pine trees planted on slopes that launched steeply upwards for at least the first twenty metres. Nothing higher was visible. We put up our small tent on a soggy slope overlooking a grey and misty inlet called Sörfjorden.

The next day we followed the Bergen to Dale road northwards. This is one of several roads in Norway along which it is illegal to cycle, the reason being that the impressively-engineered tunnels burrowed through the mountains to carry the road are unlit and can be more than a kilometre long. Entering these tunnel mouths from the bright light of day, the sudden darkness is of such impenetrable blackness that bicycle lights are useless. Many of the road tunnels have bends in them. On a bicycle, you are warned of an impending bend when your head starts scraping along the curving rock walls. We ricocheted through these fearful holes in the mountain as fast as possible, bouncing from wall to wall with pained yelps. In one tunnel, we were pinned like blinded insects to a crevice in the rock by the heavy-metal *son et lumiere* of a thundering truck.

In Dale, we stocked up on food for the coming mountains. In the squeaky-clean supermarket we were confronted by a vast array of fresh dairy products, indecipherably labelled. 'Never know when we'll find another shop' I said. 'Better stock up.' Choosing by price, we bought a kilogram of cheese. Later, we stopped by a bridge for lunch. Salivating profusely we pulled out the knife, bread and our brick-sized piece of cheese. Pete cut the cheese. 'This Norwegian stuff is soft' he commented. 'Knife's going through it like butter.' He paused. 'Hang on . . .' He licked his finger. 'It *is* butter!'

Supper was more successful. In a small village we bought some silver fish — possibly grayling — and fried them in butter over a woodfire beneath some thin birch on the shore of Hamlagro Vatnet, a rock-fringed lake 600 metres up in the mountains behind Dale. It was a chilly evening, with thin veils of fine rain drifting across the grey waters and a silence that made our voices seem unnaturally loud.

In the morning we pedalled by some wooden chalets set in grassy clearings, and past a tall-spired wooden church. In fields beside the water, men in shirtsleeves gathered hay for the drying racks which marched across the pastures like partially built walls. Then, beyond the end of the lake the road twisted down through the trees to the town of Voss — a tourist resort in summer and ski-resort in winter.

North-east from Voss the road and railway follow the valley of Raundalen until it meets with a wall of mountains rising to 1,600 metres. Where the road stops, the railway burrows its way through the rock to emerge above Aurlandsfjorden, one of the branches of Sogne Fjord — the longest in Norway. We were told at the railway station that the last train would leave the small station called Upsetè, at the tunnel entrance, at 6.30 pm. Missing the train would mean a night out in wet sleeping bags. Either we could play safe and sleep in Voss, or make a dash through the mountain tunnel and try to reach Aurlandsfjorden by nightfall.

We left Voss with three hours to cover the 40 kilometres up Raundalen to the tunnel entrance. The road was steep, and climbed through gorges above a churning river. Ahead of us, snowy summits crept slowly into view. Thick pine forests gave way to stunted birch and lichen-covered rock. At 30 kilometres, we had 45 minutes in hand. At 33 kilometres, by a hamlet called Orneberget, the tarmac unexpectedly disappeared. Drizzle began to fall. Our tyres began to slip on the wet rock. We pushed the bikes up a steep track between glistening silver birches, breathless now and glancing nervously at our watches. The track crested into a high bleak valley. Along the side ran a single-track railway line and a path. The path had braided into muddy strands as various travellers had sought dry passage. Rain could be seen falling at the end of the valley, blotting from our view the mountain watershed between Raundalen and Flåmsdalen. We tried to ride faster. The wheels slithered sideways. Leaping off, we pulled the bikes through a dark mire, feet sinking deep.

'Fourteen minutes. We're just going to make it', I shouted to Pete. 'No we're not. The train's coming', he called back. I turned to look down the valley. Cold water beat against my face. The strains of a distant locomotive rose then faded. Through streams we splashed, tyres grazing tussock and rock. With less than a kilometre to go, the train crept by on its smooth shiny rails, pausing for a minute at the distant station building. Then, like a centipede crawling indoors to shelter from the weather, it slid into the dark mouth of the tunnel. 'Well, that's a shame,' commented Pete.

Crossing the railway track to Upseté station, we pushed open the wooden door, pulled off our dripping clothes and sat steaming on a luggage cart. The two-room wooden building was appointed to hotel standard, with heating, double-glazing and all mod-cons. It was spotlessly clean. While the wind and rain drummed on the windows the light faded and night came to the high valley. We were settling down to sleep on the luggage cart when there was a tentative tap on the door.

Harald Kryvi and his little daughter peeped into the room. They had seen our race against the train from their small house on the far side of the valley, and wondered if we would like to join them for a drink.

Many contented hours later, we bedded down on the cart. Norway, filtered through home-brewed port, promised much in the coming days.

While waiting for the morning train, we climbed the mountainside above the station to reach a cleft in the lip of a high corrie where a river — the Gangdöla — rushed from above with deafening ferocity. Had we continued up the valley and into the clouds, we could have crossed a 1,341-metre col to the head of Flåmsdalen. It was tempting, but it looked a bit scary to me. Luckily Pete vetoed the idea: 'No, Nick, it's too early in the morning to start dragging a bicycle across snow-fields on a compass bearing.' We turned to jog back to the station.

The train ride through the tunnel to Myrdal station took a few minutes and cost a small fortune. We were the only passengers to alight. The station stands at 867 metres. Looking over the edge of the wooden-slatted platform, the valley fell away steeply. The gentle curves of the railway line could be seen searching for a shallow route downwards round the mountain bluffs. The rails are so steep that each carriage on the Flåm train is fitted with five braking systems. The track which we followed bore little evidence of regular use. Rocky and steep, it tipped over the lip of a hanging valley then hairpinned past tenacious little stands of birch and a tall roaring waterfall that covered us in drifting spray as we freewheeled past. The hairpins crowded each other. Every few bends we stopped to rest our hands from the bumps and constant grip on the brakes. Each turn in the track brought a new view.

We came to an easing of the valley where the river ran full

and fast and where the meadows were sprinkled with yellow and blue flowers. At a place where the river crashed through a rocky cataract a wooden bridge reached through the mist of suspended water droplets. Through this shone the sun, haloed by a circular rainbow. A crowd of schoolchildren darted and laughed at the edge of the chilling spray. Their teacher, a tall fair-haired woman, was cajoling a goat from a herd chewing the verge. She carried the animal to the children and they crowded closely around, suddenly quiet. On a grassy loop of disused track we made a fire and dried our damp clothes.

Flåm resides in splendid isolation, attached to the rest of the world by slender threads of tarmac, steel and water. The railway line stops at a set of buffers backing the still waters of Aurlandsfjorden, while the road continues by the shore for eight kilometres to Aurlandsvangen before climbing the 1,306 metres to reach the next valley. On a grassy platform shortly before Aurlandsvangen, we stopped for the night. I put up the tent, while Pete, whose combustive skills are so well developed he can set fire to seaweed underwater, searched for deadwood and soon had a fire blazing beneath our blackened billy can. While the birch smoke drifted across the mirror surface of the fjord we read paperbacks and listened to the waterfall that divided by a thin white streak the great cliff on the far shore. Daylight lingered long in these northern parts, and we were still reading at eleven o'clock. Below the snowy mountain mass to our left, a cluster of lights went out as Flam tucked itself into bed. To our right we could see the massive sombre walls of Sogne Fjord.

In the morning we rode along the smooth tarmac to Aurlandsvangen, bought bread, cheese and a caviar spread — which in Norway is sold in tubes and squeezed through a star-shaped nozzle like tooth-paste. Lying on the warm planks of the jetty we picnicked while waiting for the boat. Western Norway is so crowded with mountains and fjords that water provides a more efficient medium of transport than tarmac. This is, in part, what keeps it so unspoilt.

From Aurlandsvangen, we planned to take a small ferry up the fjord then across Sogne Fjord to Leikanger. By water, this is a distance of 40 kilometres; the road has to scale three passes of over 1,000 metres and traverse 277 kilometres of wild mountains. The ferries run like clock-

99

work, bringing to the remote farming communities everything from potato spinners to video sets.

The ferry had hardly nudged the rubber tyres hanging from the jetty before a jib-crane swung the first of 15 pallets of fertiliser onto the quayside. A few passengers disembarked. Before the unconcerned eye of its owner a car was hoisted perilously across the stern of the ferry and settled onto the tiny deck. The captain called to the boy who had been catching the pallets, the warp was slipped and we swung round towards Sogne Fjord. The whole operation had taken less than ten minutes. The voyage was pure delight. We slid across placid water beneath tumbling waterfalls and forested mountainsides patched with bright green pastures. Towering rock walls rose on both sides of the fjord compressing the water and shrinking our toy-like boat. We slid through the chasm, like the *Argo*.

In the manner of a country byway joining a trunk road, Aurlandsfjorden widened and fed into the vast Sogne Fjord — 183 kilometres long and 1,245 metres at its deepest. Around the corner we pulled into the hamlet of Fresvik. The car was off-loaded and the owner bought from the quay-side shop an ice-cream for each of the boat's crew. Rather than toss the wrapper overboard, the immaculately overalled engineer carefully folded the sticky paper and placed it in a black dustbin bag. When we asked if we could have some oil for the chains on our bicycles, the engineer handed us a can wrapped in a clean white cloth, and before descending to his engine-room, he used another clean white cloth to wipe the soles of his shoes.

From Leikanger we pedalled west along Sogne Fjord, arriving the next morning at another ferry town: Hella. *Nesøy*, the local ferry, spirited us up Fjaerlandsfjorden beneath a perfect blue sky towards the silver peaks at the head of the fjord. As we burbled closer, details emerged: above the pine-green ridges hung two glaciers, shining hard, pure and white. These two ice-falls are called Böyabreen and Suphellebreen, and form the most southern fingers of the Jostedals ice cap. Somewhere, there had to be a route up to the ice. As we crept forward the boat's bows cut Vs in the cold, still waters of the fjord and ahead, glaciers grew like two giants who had suddenly decided to stand up.

Shortly before the fjord tapers into a green valley, the

wooden jetty of Fjaerland protrudes from the painted houses on the western shore. In a small store, we bought enough food to last us three days.

In a clap-board house that contained a table-top information centre we asked about climbing on the ice-cap. A sociology student on holiday from Bergen University sold us a 1:50,000 scale 'Turkart' and pointed us up the valley.

'You should cycle to Suphelledalen and go to the big red house. Ask for Anders. He is the guide for the mountain' she said.

We cycled along a grit road past meadows lush with grass and yellow petals, to a large farmhouse. A rotund jovial woman and cheeky boy set us off across the fields towards a youth driving a tractor, who in turn pointed to a distant figure pitching hay onto a trailer beneath a huge rock. Anders, a big man with a stubbly chin, shook our hands in a hearty, knuckle-grinding greeting and wiped with his shirt-sleeve the sweat from his eyes. Yes, he could take us up onto the moutain above the ice. Also he could take us onto the ice-cap itself. But that would cost more. As tactfully as possible, we explained that we could not hire him as a guide; we wanted to climb by ourselves. He looked a little dubious. It was easy to get lost, he said, and the weather can change quickly. We assured him that we had done this kind of thing before.

Then we must use the *flatbrehytta*, he said. The hut was high on the mountain. We could sleep in it and leave some money in the tin on the mantleshelf.

We left our bicycles at the farm, taking food and sleeping bags. To start with, the track was wide enough for a tractor, but it quickly thinned to a steep footpath which clambered through the contours above the stream to reach the crest of a ridge 750 metres above the valley. With the light fading we climbed on, turning a corner to find the ice of Suphelle-breen just fifteen metres in front of us. Like a frozen waterfall the ice hung blue and green over the valley. Eerie crevasses split the ice into teetering blocks and leaning towers. The chill reached us. We walked quickly on, coming to a pair of huts — *flatbrehytta* — on a headland that looked southwards across the clear mountains. One of the huts was full of skiers; in the other we found four low beds and a paraffin lamp.

The skiers left in the morning, striding out across the ice

beyond the hut. Each skier wore a harness attached to a husky dog. Each dog was saddled with little bags containing its food. Even with the dogs to pull them, the skiers had told us that it would take them two days to cross the ice-cap. I found myself a little envious. This was the 'Ice Fall in Norway' of Ranulph Twistleton-Wykeham-Fiennes. With four others he had parachuted onto the ice-cap. 'Must be great out there', I said to Pete. 'Pity we don't have the right gear.'

We satisfied ourselves with an attempt to climb a peak called Kvanneholtnipa, the highest in the area. Looking at the map, we could see that its 1,640-metre granite summit would stand high above the ice, thus providing a bird's-eye view over some of Norway's most stunning mountain scenery.

The sky was clear when we left the hut, the air calm. Conditions were perfect. Kvanneholtnipa sticks like a promontory into the ice-cap. We reached the top in under two hours: a white desert of blinding intensity disappearing over the far horizon in an indefinite upward bulge. We sat on the dry rocks, allowing it all to sink in. We could just pick out the skiers who had left the hut earlier; tiny black dots etched on a vast and brilliant canopy. They were aiming for Briksdal, on the northern edge of Jostedals, a journey of about 25 kilometres. We too would visit Briksdal, but for us to reach it by bicycle would involve a journey of 380 kilometres.

'Time to go' said Pete. 'Don't want to be caught up here by the weather.' We made our way carefully back across the sloping snows. One of my shoes had split, and snow had packed against my sock. It seemed to be getting colder. At the col on the ridge above the huts, I said 'Let's go on to that peak, then we'll get a good view south over the fjords too.' Pete didn't reply. We climbed. To reach this second peak, we had to first climb a smaller mountain: Tyskarnipa. We were on the far side of this when I felt snow land on my neck. We turned round. Without us noticing, the sky behind had transformed from being a healthy blue to a frightening grey. It had changed in just a few minutes. We had to get back. Quickly. In falling snow, we tried to follow our footsteps.

An icy gush of wind rocked us on our feet. I fiddled for the compass. My foot was going numb. This is stupid, I thought to myself. Really stupid. We ought to have known better. To *always* watch the weather is a basic rule on any mountain. Now we were playing about above an ice-cap wearing cycling clothes and shoes with holes. We didn't even have a bivouac bag, and the only food we had was a handful of raisins.

We had to keep moving. The compass said 38° East; too far to the left and we'd drop 1,000 metres into Böyadalen. I felt the acid surge in my gut. Lots of adrenalin. We didn't speak till we reached the col. Our earlier footprints led over the edge. 'Where's the snow?' I asked. It had stopped. Then the wind blew off the cloud as quickly as it had come and we were left standing in clear air, feeling a little foolish.

Climbing a little way down the western side of the mountain we came out above the ice-fall of Böyabreen. As we watched, the narrow cleft rumbled and boomed as ice-lumps detached themselves from the parent glacier and crashed downwards in puffs of white — the sounds curiously detached by our distance from the impacts. From out of the blue a snow-cloud unleashed a flurry of clumsy flakes. We turned and made our way back to the valley and the bicycles.

On a ridge of glacial moraine in the valley, we put up the tent. 'I'm going for a wash in the river!' announced Pete. It was the moment I'd been dreading. Part of the game is not to lose points. 'Good idea. I'll come too' I replied. It was more of a heaving milky rapid than a river. Pete was already in, up to his neck and clutching a rock to prevent himself being carried off in the current. He seemed to be enjoying it. Hoping he hadn't noticed my look of utter anguish, I slithered in. The cold punched me in the stomach. Only the roaring of the river prevented Pete hearing the gasps of immeasurable pain. Unable to breathe I scrabbled for the rocks and pulled myself out, blue and completely numb. When I could speak, I shouted over to Pete, still immersed, 'Great. Terrific,' and ran off into the woods, praying fervently that I wouldn't have to repeat that performance.

Following the route mapped out for us by Harald, we planned over the next three days to cycle round to the far side of the Jostedals ice-cap.

The *Nesøy* returned us to Hella, and from there we pedalled east along the shore of Sogne Fjord then up into the mountains behind Sogndal. While the road twisted and turned pedantically through the pines, a river of astonishing power plunged straight down, filling the valley with a dull roar. Where desert hues are given life by absence of water, so in Norway senses are filled by it presence. The fiercest colours: the whites of ice, snow and raging water are paradoxically the ones that tend to lighten a landscape that would otherwise be shaded in matt greens and greys. For tranquillity the traveller can look for the blues and bright biological greens of still water. No colours relax beneath a sky that is so turbulent that snow, azure blue, rain or brilliant cumulus can occupy the same gap in the trees within one hour. Living outdoors, you develop a crick in the neck.

Beyond Sogndal the sun dropped beneath the pines and we emerged onto a high plateau decorated with pale meadows and a broad lake nestling against the rounded spurs which run down from the ice-cap. The bikes took themselves through plunging bends to Gaupne. Beyond the town we found a terrace for the tent looking out across Lustrafjorden towards the outlying peaks of Jotunheimen.

The next day we cycled 114 kilometres, climbing from sea-level to 1,440 metres across Sognefjell on a road that forces a passage between the Jostedals Bre ice-cap and the enormous massif of Jotenheimen, itself liberally sprinkled with 2,000-metre peaks and glaciers. The road is the highest in Norway.

For about 30 kilometres we pedalled gently upwards, leaving the trees and traversing bleak moorland. Above 1,000 metres the Norwegians had thoughtfully erected a large blue sign marking each successive 100-metre gain in altitude, then at around 1,400 metres the tarmac crumbled into a rutted two-lane gravel track running between tall 'snow-poles'. This was the road Harald had told us about. It was cold and wet.

We came on a lone cyclist pulling a bright orange cape from his pack, and the three of us rode together to the summit. Six more cyclists came up from the east. They had ridden all the way from Denmark. All of us stood in the cold blowing mists swapping stories and sharing chocolate. One of the Danes turned out to know Ivar Tønneson, a Danish friend who, with Mai-Britt Johansson had cycled around the world between 1977 and '79.

The town of Lom is sited by a long sinuous lake in fertile

Ottadalen. Tourists stop here to see the wooden stave church. We came to Lom in the evening, having rushed down from the heights of Sognefjell. Several kilometres upstream of the town, we camped beside the River Otta, setting out early the next morning to cycle over another high pass that crosses the northern flank of Jostedals. We pedalled in warm sunshine through stands of pine, then up through a grassy valley to the snow-line at 1,000 metres. Here we turned from the main highway and followed a dirt road through Mårådalen then Videdalen. The mountains here rise right from the verge in clean white sweeps and the road snakes between a myriad of tiny shining lakes and glacial hummocks. On the far side of the pass a few people were skiing in the high summer snow. Passing between the final snow banks we came to the start of the descent to Strynsvatn, an exhilarating corkscrew of twisting bends with no traffic to baulk our flight to the warmer airs of the valley.

The clonking of cow bells in the meadows greeted our return to low-level Norway. We stopped, and I climbed a high bank above the road for a better view. Along the top of the bank ran the wires of an electric fence, which I touched by mistake. I was surprised not to get a shock.

'Watch the fence. You'll get electrocuted,' warned Pete from below.

'No I won't. It's switched off', I replied.

'Yes you will'.

'No I won't. I bet you anything in the world I won't get a shock if I hold this wire'.

'You will.'

The gauntlet was down. I reached out. Wrapping my hand round the wire I grasped it tightly, calling down to Pete: 'Look, see you're wrong!' At which point the fence conducted a surge of 750 volts into my hand. It shot up my arm and into my chest where it detonated like a small nuclear device, throwing me off the top of the bank and over Pete's head onto the road. I bounced on the tarmac, rolled twice and hopped around the road tightly wrapped in my own arms.

'Cheat!' I shouted.' You knew I'd get a shock', but Pete was too helpless with laughter to hear. It was an hour before I could use both hands to hold the handlebars.

Over a crackling drift-wood fire on the pebble shore of

Strynsvatn, we cooked fish-cakes and drank pints of tea by the light of the flames.

The final part of the ride took us past the port of Stryn and along the edge of Innvikfjord to Oldedalen, which leads southwards to Briksdal. It was a glorious day with the sun bringing a balmy haze to the fresh meadows. Our progress was dwarfed by the immensity of the mountain walls hemming in the narrow valley. Glassy Oldevatnet reflected the greys and white of granite and snow as we passed, and when the road ended we continued along a sandy track. When the track petered out, we continued on foot, clambering between fallen boulders the size of houses to reach the milky-blue pool which lies below the snout of the tumbling Briksdal ice-fall. Above it, and out of sight, was the empty and silent world of Jostedals. Miniature icebergs floated on the water waiting for the sun to melt them into water which would rush down the Olde to the fjord far below, and thence into the Atlantic. We lay on the warm rock.

I gazed at the ice-fall, trying to remember. I thought I could see the place they'd lost the sledges, and lower down, there was the ledge where they must have bivouaced. They had reached the bottom having survived an avalanche. Then Twistleton-Wykeham-Fiennes had put them in tiny rubber boats and they had shot the rapids down to the fjord. Parachuting onto ice, climbing down ice-falls and not-quite drowning in wild rivers ... the whole caper looked mad and unneccessary. But it was a great story.

"In the heat of the handlebars he grasps the summer" / *The Cyclist* by Louis

Top: It took 21 days to cross 2,260 kilometres of the Tibetan Plateau, climbing several passes of 5,000 metres. (Photo: Nick and Richard Crane).

Above: Leaving the Ganges ferry on a day in northern India when temperatures soared to 115°F. (Photo: Nick and Richard Crane).

Facing page: North of the Himalayas, lost, without food, minutes before dark with snow on the way. We spent the night huddled in a tiny cave. (Photo: Nick and Richard Crane).

Above: Pete Inglis cycling round Europe's biggest ice-cap, Jostedals Bre, the morning I was electrocuted.
Inset: Fjaerlands Fjord.

Below: The main inconveniences to cycling north of the Arctic Circle in winter are icy roads, sub-zero temperatures and Atlantic gales. Apart from that, it's fine.
Inset: Five-star lodgings in the Lofoten Islands: a boatshed on Hinnöy.

Above: One place the traffic cannot reach cyclists is Crib Goch, North Wales. (Photo: David Higgs).

Below: A small peak in mountainbike madness came on 30 June 1984 when cousin Richard and I 'rode' all 14 of Wales' 3,000-foot mountains in 12 hours 26 minutes. (Photo: Peter Inglis).

Inset: Kilimanjaro's dense equatorial jungle is rich in unusual wildlife. (Photo: Peter Inglis).

Above: The top of 19,340-foot Kilimanjaro, Africa's highest mountain, was reached on 31 December 1984 after a five-day ascent. No other cyclists were seen on the summit. (Photo: Peter Inglis).

Above: East from Corsica's Col de Bavella, seconds before my bicycle blew over the edge.

Below: Lost (again) in the bamboo forests high above Africa's Rift Valley, cousin Adrian and I were helped on our way by Simon, who was on his way to his father with a sack of potatoes. (Photo: Adrian Crane).

9

Beneath The Bridge

YUGOSLAVIA

No motor vehicles are allowed into the medieval city of Dubrovnik, which makes it, like Venice, a shrine for those sickened by the way modern transport dirties all things beautiful. Dubrovnik lies diagonally across the Adriatic from Venice. Both cities have been preserved through time by their unusual isolations. Venice has survived by virtue of its watery moat; Dubrovnik by its tenacious hold on the bedrock of a former island.

Dubrovnik's first inhabitants were Greco-Romans on the run from the Avars and Slavs who in the 7th Century had sacked Epidaurus (now Cavtat) just down the coast. On a rocky island separated from the mainland by a narrow channel, the refugees built a settlement which in time united with Slavs living on the mainland. The whole was surrounded by defensive walls stern enough to hold off attacks by the Saracens, the Macedonians and the Serbs. The island mated with the mainland. The city of Ragusa — as Dubrovnik was then known — became an Adriatic force to rival Venice.

Ravages inflicted on Ragusa erred toward the spectacular: a huge fire destroyed much of the wooden city in 1292; 11,000 lives were lost to the Black Death of 1348; an earthquake killed over 5,000 in 1667 and during a siege by Russo-Montenegrin fleets in the early 19th century, the city was pounded by 3,000 cannon balls. Like the accretions on the shell of a clam, the walls that protected early Dubrovnik thickened with time while the organism within — the streets, buildings, trade and culture — grew. Its export of intellect was modest compared to some of the great Italian cities. Dubrovnik produced among others Marin Getaldić, the man who determined the specific weights of metals; a pre-evolutionary fundament for the bicycle.

Riding eastwards along the Put Iza Grada outside the

blank walls and bastions of Dubrovnik's defences Elaine and I wondered how and where we would find a way into the city. There are only two main entrances. At the Pile Gate, we left the bikes locked to a railing and crossed the drawbridge. From the charging, smelly traffic, we passed through an archway and into a small, calm square where movement was measured by the click and scuff of leather on marble, and where urban conversation was not conducted in hoots and revs but in peaceable murmurings from the darkened doorways of cafes. The sense of order created by the surviving geometric street pattern, the freshness of the marble buildings and the solidity of the encircling walls creates a rare air of serenity, while the encircling sea offers security.

Naohiko Murakami walked up to us in a cafe on a small square, and asked if we would like to buy his bicycle. It was a customised Nishiki, with 15 speeds, pudgy overland tyres and a speedometer. As well as two bed-rolls on the back, he had five huge packs attached to the bike. Two of the panniers were hand-painted with murals depicting camels walking past palm trees. Naohiko, travel worn in singlet and baggy trousers, had cycled from Finland to Yugoslavia, having first taken a ship across the Sea of Japan, and crossed Asia on the Trans-Siberian Express. Two of his Japanese cycling friends had recently been killed; one knocked down by a truck in Turkey after having ridden 112,500 kilometres, while the other was knocked from his bike in Canada. It was, Naohiko said, time to sell his bike.

Many narrow alleys join the smooth slabs of the Plaça, Dubrovnik's main street, a clean and wide walkway lined with high stone buildings whose grand, arched ground-floor entrances serve as both door, window and shop counter. We walked between the symmetrical rectangular shadows that projected onto the foot-worn slabs. It takes ten minutes to amble along the shady side of the Plaça to the main square where the Baroque shadow of Sv. Vlaho church nearly reaches the foot of the 15th-century bell tower that looks over the pantiled roofs of the city. From the castle walls we could look down into alleys criss-crossed by a cat's cradle of phone wires, drying lines and electricity cables. On a couple of chimney stacks — capped and vented to keep out the rain and wind — television aerials poked out incongruously. Profuse bursts of red and pink blooms crowded window boxes while on the other side of the wall, children dived from the rocks into a heaving sea.

We had flown to Dubrovnik with two bikes and the vague intention of exploring the coast and mountains of Yugoslavia's southernmost province: Montenegro. From a point high on the city walls we could look inland to the mountains. It was June, the time of year when the Mediterranean blooms with expectant vitality.

Outside the town, the hillsides were dashed with yellow broom, while the meadows were filled with flowering grasses. Wild sage and the budding freshness of spring scented the air. Early, we heard a cuckoo. The road south from Dubrovnik cuts a smooth passage through the coastal foothills. It takes less than a day to cycle to Hercegnovi, a busy town sited strategically at the mouth of the Gulf of Kotor. It was founded in the late 14th century by Stjepan I Tvrtko of Bosnia as a centre for salt production and a trading post. On the way into town we passed a bland concrete modern development advertised as 'Rent a Vile'. Beneath a sign advertising 'Slasticarnica Patisserie Kafe' we ate our way through Pizzas Beograd and Neopolitana. I tested my Serbo-Croat.

'Dvar pivo molim' produced two glasses of nose-tingling lager and we sat back and soaked in a little bit of Yugoslavia. Sitting by that clear water, it was hard to believe that the morning before we had been drinking tea in Jock's Cafe by the A4 near Slough, on our way to Heathrow. In front of us now, on the far side of the road, men in faded blue trousers were busy hosing, scrubbing, sanding and painting the hulls of their small fishing boats. Before leaving, we bought some Yugoslav salami. It comes in gnarled brown extrusions and requires a little courage to chew: one bite and the succulent spicy ingredients explode on the taste buds leaving an aroma that hangs in the strongest of breezes.

That night there was an important *vaterpolo* match between the local team and a visiting team from Rijeka. Floodlights played on the thrashing water, with the stands packed to capacity and a fiercely partisan crowd shouting and whistling for all they were worth. The players wore rubber hats in their team colours and they ducked and wove through the water as if they had been born at twenty fathoms. The pool had been built by extending three stone dams out into the sea, with an open channel to allow the sea to circulate. Waterpolo pools can be found along much of the Dalmatian coast. The fixture dates of the Yugoslav water-polo league are dictated by the lunar calendar.

The Gulf of Kotor is like a high Norwegian fjord that has been pinched at its mouth and again at its waist to form two sheltered inland seas. Of its two constrictions, the innermost is the narrower. For a while a new road ran at sea level around the indented shore-line and beneath the steep green slopes that climb to heat-blurred limestone ridges 1,000 metres above the water. There was little traffic. Near a village called Zelenika we turned from the smooth tarmac to follow the hesitant line of the old road around the Gulf. Three years earlier the area had been hit by an earthquake. In places the tarmac was twisted and split, and twice it disappeared into the sea and we had to carry the bikes through back gardens. Huge houses looked gauntly across the water, roofless, with tilting, cracked walls and eyeless windows. Where the land had suddenly dropped, dead trees stood up to their waists in the sea. It was as if some giant subterranean muscle had catastrophically flexed.

We passed by an earnest little town called Bijela, where three huge ships lay at berth, and a fourth bearing the star of the USSR sat in a dry dock. The bigger a boat the less dignity it has out of the water. Just a few kilometres further and the Gulf abruptly narrows to a gap small enough to be crossed in minutes by a car ferry. It was across this gap, measured at 325 metres, that a heavy chain once used to be stretched in order to close off the inner Gulf to hostile shipping. Little motor traffic continues into the grand and secluded majesty of the inner Gulf.

The air became still and almost steamy in its confinement. The road through Risan to Perast was newly-surfaced and fast, and acted as a courteous prelude to one of the most attractive villages in the Gulf. Baroque Perast ranges along the waterfront in weathered elegance and one of its most eye-catching buildings is an imposing balconied affair built on a bend in the road just a few feet from the sea. It was built in 1694 as the Palace Bujovic. Now it is the town's museum.

Matching in grandeur the mountains behind, Perast's *Campanile* is the tallest in Montenegro and stands like a lighthouse over the roofs; weeds and other illegitimate vegetation sprouting from the crevices of its lofty tile and stone spire. It has been there since 1691. Perast has produced some of the Adriatic's most skilful seafarers — Peter the Great sent sixty young Russian noblemen to the naval school here. From the ornate balconies of the 17th-century mansions which line the waterfront, wives and children of the captains and ship-owners would have looked out past the two tiny offshore islands to the narrow straits of the Gulf through which the wood-hulled sailing ships would have come on their journey home. By the Palaca Bujović, two small fibreglass motor-boats rocked at the stubby stone jetty. Leaning the bikes against a roadside tree, we plunged into the sea.

Through Orahovac and Dobrota, we came to Kotor and slept near the water in a grove of trees. Morning revealed a town that had suffered more than most in the earthquake. New Kotor straggles unglamorously along the narrow shelf between mountain and sea; old Kotor is confined to a triangular spit of land whose sides are formed by the sea, the Skurda river and by the sheer edge of Mount Lovcen. We walked through the Venetian gateway. The worn slabs of the main square were deserted. Three and four-storey stone buildings looked blankly inwards with windows that were boarded or partly covered by crooked shutters. Cracks zig-zagged across the stonework and above the gateway a plant had rooted. One house had collapsed inwards to hide its own debris behind a surviving ground-floor wall of perfectly-hewn limestone blocks.

Into this silent arena walked a man with a bicycle.

The man, in his fifties, had a wide mouth that quickly smiled, thinning hair, neatly furled shirt-sleeves and buckled sandals. He had been born in Kotor but had recently worked in France where he had bought the bicycle. Emblazoned on the tubes of the bicycle were the words 'Katakura Special Sports Cycle With Precision'. Looking closer we noticed a gear-lever the size of a jumbo-jet joystick and a derailleur that looked as if it had been made from re-cycled locomotive parts. Mounted on the wheels were two swollen bladders misleadingly inscribed with the words 'Silk Sports High Speed Tire'. The hub brakes were hydraulically operated and the chain was protected by a striped metal guard that flared backwards in a shape symbolising rapid air-flow. All that was missing from the enormous interior-sprung saddle was a pillow.

Between his smiles, the man had a woeful tale. He had bought the machine from a Parisian importer called M. Bellouard. It was, he said, a good bike. A little heavy but, and he said this with pained pleasure, the only one of its kind in Kotor. He had bought the bike because of its lights. On the front and back of the bike were huge moulded plastic lenses in orange, red and white. There were stop lights, side-lights, flashers and two headlights. He lifted the lid of a plastic box mounted on the rear of the bike. Inside were rows of curved slots to hold the batteries. As it cruised the night-time alleys of medieval Kotor, M. Bellouard's multi-coloured winking beams must have looked like a visiting space-ship. Sadly the energy consumption of his 'Katakura Sports Special With Precision' far outstretched Kotor's supply of available batteries and now (sad head-shaking) it would be many months before new stocks reached this remote corner of Yugoslavia.

We moved through the confused network of narrow streets and small squares. Piles of uncleared rubble lay in the streets, and in places the way had been blocked by walls thrown up to prevent people walking beneath the less stable buildings. Bikes and barrows are the only wheeled vehicles that traverse these thin thoroughfares. The quiet contributed to the shocking dilapidation. Beyond the roofs, thick walls climbed the mountain above the town to congregate in an angry little fortress.

Outside the post office a boy borrowed my bicycle pump. His mother worked in Germany. He had been to Germany, but didn't like it.

Up the mountain behind Kotor climbs one of the most spectacular roads in Europe. Some call it the 'Serpentine Road'. It ascends for 22 kilometres. We left town in the approaching cool of late afternoon, pedalling gently up a steep valley filled with tarmac loops. Six kilometres above the town, where the borders of Austria (and later Venice) once met with the edge of ancient Montenegro, is a meeting of five roads. The 'Serpentine' is the one which continues steeply upwards. A road sign read 'Srecan Put, Bon Voyage, God Bay, Goute Reise'. While the view unfolded, we rode beside lush vegetation dense with bird chatter. After several bends we could see Kotor spread out like a toy town. We stopped, hanging our legs over the road edge, to eat our way through a bag of fresh blood-red cherries.

Riding on, we were soon looking down on the tops of the lower mountain ridges. By the time the trees had disappeared from the mountainside, the entire Bay of Kotor lay before us like a map. Crowded mountains spread inland. A cruise ship crossed the Gulf leaving a wake like a water-boatman, and one by one, streetlights flicked on until a twinkling necklace lay along the shore.

On a grassy platform 20 metres above the road we spread out the sleeping bags and watched the water turn to gold. In the morning the road lifted us the last few metres over the watershed. We turned our backs on the coast and followed a winding valley that spiralled upwards to a deserted col — the 1,261-metre Bukovica Pass, that is marked by lookout posts.

Of Yugoslavia's six federal republics, Montenegro is the smallest. Mostly, it is mountainous. Looking inland from the pass above Kotor, our eyes wandered across the pale karst ridges, looking for a way the road might take. Some of the ranges rise to 2,500 metres, and between them the land is chipped into dashes of white limestone. Occasionally soil collects in a bowl and here the Montenegrins harvest pockets of corn. Thread-like paths straggle across the broken landscape. It is one of those places whose fierce countenance has in the past been matched by grisly human habits. During the centuries of feuding with the nobles of Hercegnovi the Montenegrins kept a tally by exhibiting the heads of their enemies on a tower in Cetinje.

We watched Cetinje, the ancient capital of Montenegro, swing closer as our tyres sang down 600 metres of curling tarmac. The city is squashed into a small green basin whose sparser parts are busy with little fields, trees and a scattering of pale houses. For five months of the year, snow blocks the road to Cetinje. As we rode closer the tarmac became pocked and bumpy. In the main street we stopped at a shop. Inside, the rows of wooden shelves were bare but for a few balls of string, several cans of sardines, some salami, a box of biscuits and a pile of scrubbing brushes. Six of the ten shelves were completely bare. I bought a can of sardines. Outside in the sun, Elaine was being pestered by a gaggle of grubby-faced children who were occupying themselves by massaging the tyres on our bicycles, and testing their strength by pulling on the brake levers. Two of them had bicycles: one was a Unis 'Sprint' and the other a Rog 'Elite

Sport'. The 'Sprint' had a flat tyre and the 'Elite Sport' was missing a pedal and had no brakes. Our lightweight touring bikes, complete with coloured panniers, new tyres, quick-release wheels and padded saddles must have looked enviably overdressed. The boys wanted to know if we were carrying any spare parts that might fit their bikes. All I had were five double-butted stainless-steel spokes.

Self-consciously, we pedalled from them, along streets fronted by crumbling residences that had once accommodated foreign diplomats in the days when Montenegro had been on the world map. Under Prince Nikola at the beginning of the century, Cetinje had been the smallest capital in Europe. After centuries of fighting the Turks, Venetians, Austrians and Serbians, this pocket principality became in 1918, one of Yugoslavia's republics.

A very old man was standing outside the bus station. He wore a small, pill-box-shaped black cap with a red top, and had a splendid drooping grey moustache that diverted your glance from his watery eyes and deeply lined skin. His breath was rasping; bubbly. He kept dropping his stick; people walked by.

We left the town, cycling up towards the hills. Before the roofs of Cetinje disappeared, the road leaned to the left, bracketting a squalid clutch of paste-board hovels set in a dish of rubbish and beaten earth. Picturesque this wasn't. We were following the tailboard of a heavy truck. As it dragged itself round the slope its bellowing exhaust pipe spewed black diesel between the shacks and into the low doorways. Just before she was enveloped in the cloud, I saw a young, painfully beautiful girl standing with a tiny baby in her arms, watching.

The Yugoslavs have slashed a new road through the mountains to link Cetinje with Titograd. A clean black stripe cuts through the rocky hills, now scarred and blasted with dynamite. Our bicycles rolled swiftly. After a while we found a piece of track that took us back to the old road. Above this, on a narrow ledge, we slept beneath a disturbed sky. It was overcast when we woke. A long freewheel took us most of the way to Rijeka Crnojevica. On the way we passed memorials dated June 1941. When we stopped we could hear the sound of scything coming across the valley. A tributary of the great Lake Skadar joined us, and we met a tortoise embarking on a journey across the tarmac.

Rijeka Crnojevića sits astride the sinuous arm of one of Lake Skadar's two longest tributaries. The Lake is very shallow, and about fifty kilometres long. Half of it lies in neighbouring Albania. From some angles, Rijeka Crnojevića is the perfect mountain village. Set against a rugged backdrop, two slender stone bridges arch gracefully over still waters decorated with carpets of lilies. No house looked quite like its neighbour and their stone fabric felt more as if it had been honed from the very earth rather than built piece by piece by man. Against the low, marshy banks rested two high-prowed wooden fishing boats. On the mud below the bridges lay stranded cardboard boxes, plastic bottles and a car tyre. Someone had thrown a lavatory into the lilies.

Leaving the main road to Titograd, we pedalled from Rijeka Crnojevića on a small dirt road that picked its way along the foothills south of the lake. It was very peaceful. Tall reeds sighed at the water's edge and cows stood up to their ankles in the soft meadows, chewing unconcernedly. Just beyond the town, we watched a man standing in a boat throw forward his net with an energetic sweep of his arm. For a few seconds the net sank while ripples spread outwards, then the man hauled quickly, gathering the folds of mesh as he did so. A bright silver fish flipped in the sunshine as the lake water streamed from the net.

A heron flapped clumsily over our heads, beating a half-circle over the water before dropping to the grass beyond the cows. On the road, Elaine picked up a dead snake, nearly two metres long. A sharpened stick had been stabbed through its throat.

Our road was dreamy and quiet as we gently climbed and dipped through the hills, the only noise coming from our tyres crunching on loose gravel. Lake Skadar would occasionally reveal itself in tantalising glimpses. By a tap on the roadside we met Andruja Rosnoitovic. He was filling two ten-gallon water containers that were strapped to the flanks of his donkey, a docile beast called 'Mali'. Andruja was eager to tell us about the bombing of Belgrade. He had been there. He knew Mr. Churchill.

Shortly afterwards, by a tall memorial overlooking the lake, the darkening sky was lit by lightning. Clouds grumbled in the distance. The storm seemed to hang over the lake some way from us, and we took no notice.

In a sudden untidy crackle, a bolt of lightning cut through

the heavy air, and struck the tarmac twenty metres away from us with an explosive bang. A flash the colour of marigolds stung our eyes. Smoke and the smell of splintered rock hung in the air as we ran for the bikes. With the hills booming and the sky spitting lightning we rode frantically along the dirt road looking for shelter. 'These bikes are the best conductors for miles around!' I shouted as a twin fork of jagged light dived into the hillside above our heads. We found a small cave, left our bikes well clear of its mouth and huddled inside while the bombardment continued. In heavy drops, rain began to fall. We read our books, and when the storm passed we continued towards Virpazar.

The road worsened until we were trying to ride on little more than a levelled river bed. The lake was now far below us, stretching in a grey haze eastwards to the rugged outline of that isolated, mysterious country of Albania. We had much height to lose and our rough track hairpinned down the mountainside above Virpazar. For a place with such a strategic location, Virpazar seemed ridiculously small: no more than twenty buildings tightly cluster round the foot of a rocky hillock which sits isolated in the centre of a marshy pan-flat valley. The main road from the Dalmatian coast to inland Montenegro passes Virpazar (as does the rail line) and Lake Skadar is just a few minutes away. There is a small fort on the hillock, a shop, and a little bridge. A couple of sailors were washing one of the two patrol boats tethered to the short jetty. We ate bread with salami, followed by bread with honey, and sat with our legs dangling over the bridge parapet.

Now we joined the main road, whose steep, lumpy, asphalt climbed over the mountains to the coast. Instead of grassy verges, now the roadsides were oil-stained and littered with the debris of motor traffic. We found a tortoise dithering on the white line in the centre of the road while trucks from Titograd strained past on one side, and those from the coast rattled down the hill at 90 kph on the other. Elaine carried the tortoise up the hill in her handlebar bag, where it performed a full repertory of animal functions before being released in a small field of dry grass which rustled with other tortoises.

Crushed in the road one bend further was the splintered shell of a tortoise that hadn't made it, bright yellow stuff like egg yolk oozing from the fragments of broken shell.

The next morning we rode on upwards. In one place the road engineers had tried to broaden the radius of a bend by building a new loop of road on stilts, high above a precipice. But the earthquake had moved the stilts and now the new curve didn't quite match the old. We breasted the mountains at 658 metres and sped west to the sea. The road plunged down from the coastal range in stacks of hairpins. From a rock high above the coast we watched traffic crawl towards us. As one gigantic articulated vehicle pulled itself upwards, its driver sat with a newspaper spread over the wheel, looking up every few metres to check he was still on course.

The road meets the sea at Petrovac. Here, on a narrow strip of sand we ate ice-creams and splashed in the torpid sea. Nut brown old men with saggy stomachs and nothing to do huddled conspiratorially on the sea wall. Two young men with torsos built so that each muscle overlapped the next flexed themselves, oiled and preened. And a boy, a teenager, shuffled past on a stick, his crippled legs leaving a zig-zag trail in the sand like a lizard's tail in the dust.

Three days later the microscopic world of bicycle travel was exchanged for the telescopic one of jet flight. As we rose in the air Dubrovnik receded until all we could see was a dot.

10

The Three Peaks

GREAT BRITAIN

My shoulder hit the ground. There was no noise at first, just a vague sense of friction. Then I heard the bike: a harsh, scraping of metal on stone. When I stopped moving, I looked around. The bike was ten feet away, hanging over the parapet, its back wheel still turning. Stinging, I stood up. Dust and grit covered my side. I tried to brush it off. It stuck to me. As I watched, the dust darkened. I walked to the bike. One leg was stiff. With my unhurt hand, I pulled the machine upright. It didn't look broken. I leant it on a tree.

Two men were watching. Workmen. 'Agua?' I asked, pointing at the blood. They nodded; disappeared. I waited, rocking back and forward to soothe the pain. One of the men called me. I went through a gap in the wall. They played water on me from a hose, while I brushed the dirt from the grazes. One side of me was minus a lot of skin.

Elaine's head appeared. 'What's happened?' she asked.

'Fell off.' I replied.

A wonder in a crisis, Elaine took over. The men said there was a hospital in the town below. We freewheeled down the hill.

They put me in a green-painted room. A man was carried through on a stretcher, his jacket and trousers scorched. He was a fireman. One of his mates was with him. I stopped hurting so much. Forest fire, we were later told.

I was injected and wrapped in miles of crepe bandage. I was too stiff to ride a bike. 'Life is what happens while you're busy making other plans.'

Before the accident, we had been riding blissfully through the hills above Sintra. We were on our way from Lisbon to the most western point in Europe: Cabo da Roca. The sun had been shining. Apart from messing up Elaine's holiday, my accident had reduced me from being an acceptably healthy adult to an only-just-mobile invalid. 'Maybe you'll be more careful next time' was a not unfamiliar reprimand. Unfortunately, whenever I recovered from such mishaps, it was always one that I forgot.

We did reach Cabo da Roca; it was mostly downhill from Sintra. After a few days' convalescence on the coast we cycled over the Serra de Estrela on Portugal's highest road then returned to Lisbon. Back in England I continued going downhill by taking a new and frenzied interest in competition riding. This was aided and abetted by mixing with two Australians (Tim Gartside and Peter Murphy), and with cousin Richard. Tim and 'Murph' had plans to pedal across the Sahara. Tim had just returned from cycling to India, and with his wife Melanie had set up a bicycle rickshaw taxi service in London's Covent Garden. When Tim came to England he had been engaged by a health-food shop to increase their custom by whatever means he thought most productive. Dressed in bright red dancing tights, a huge yellow Chinese hat, trick spectacles from which hung veined eye-balls, and wearing a sandwich board advertising the shop, he chose to bounce on a pogo-stick beside motorists trapped in traffic-jams. Turnover of the health-food store increased dramatically. He and Murph were an inspiration.

When cousin Dick got interested in bike racing too, it heralded the start of a series of bizarre adventures. When I was younger, I'd been rather overawed by Dick. He captained his school rugby team, collected fossils and had hundreds of 'O' levels. Furthermore, he came from Cumbria, a land of mountains and hardmen. Viewed from my position near the bottom of the class in the flatlands of Norfolk, Dick was the Clark Kent of Keswick School. On the occasions that I went faster than Dick in time-trials, my immediate assumption was that the stop-watch had malfunctioned.

With the arrival on the bike-racing scene of my cousin, the need to turn in good times took on a new importance.

The quest for seconds knew no bounds. I raced assiduously every Wednesday evening and I trained as if I were seeking a place in the Olympic squad. Over 52 days in the spring of 1981 I cycled 1,052 miles and climbed a total of 8,380 metres in the mountains of Scotland, the Lake District and North Wales, as well as doing regular 8-mile runs. This was all crammed into the time left after doing a full-time editing job. No opportunity to exercise was turned down: when Tim Gartside suggested a 15-mile run before breakfast, I accepted. When Pete Inglis wanted to climb in Glencoe we knocked off 14 mountains in 3 days. When a week later Dick wanted to watch the great Paris-Roubaix bike race, he and I rode across northern France and back in a day.

One of the first time-trials that Dick and I entered together was a 10-mile event outside Reading. In an attempt to wear each other down before the event, we rode flat out for 80 miles through the Cotswolds, arriving at the start line two minutes before we were due to be pushed off.

My bicycle became lighter each week as I found more parts in which to drill holes or cut off. Alan Deadman commissioned a new bike made from Reynolds 753 tubing. It was so slim that looked at from some angles, it became invisible. Forty miles away, Dick had joined Reading Cycling Club and was trying even harder. He bought a red lightweight racing bike and spent the evenings pounding the roads round Reading. One evening an MG sports car pulled out of a side road in front of him. When the plaster came off, he trained harder than ever, and during a 50-mile time-trial, raced into the back of a milk float. Reading Dairy sent him a bill for £240.

The problem was what to do with all this fitness. Early in the year, we went north.

* * *

We camped in Glencoe on the edge of the bogs beneath Signal Rock. Many say that it is from this rock in the late winter of 1692 that the Redcoats received the signal to begin their killings. It was also from here, while the smoke of burnt homes still hung in the valley, that Murdoch Matheson composed: 'Oh, God I am filled with gloom as I see these hills.'

We arrived in the dark, at around midnight. It was April 1982. Our tent faced east. When we woke, Hol could be seen untying bicycles and organising food into little piles. Behind him the rough slopes of Meall Mor climbed into cloud. Somewhere up there, in snow-filled hollows had lain the few MacDonalds who had escaped the slaughter below.

They would have heard the shots and cries; seen the flames. Thirty-eight died by the hand of the Redcoats. They're buried on the island in the loch.

'Breakfast!' called Karen, her voice a mixture of surprise and revulsion. Karen was shortly to marry Ados, Dick's younger brother. Behind her Ados was trying to prise spaghetti out of a very bent billy-can. It lifted out in a lump that looked like a mass of worms with rigor mortis. He added some dollops of bolognese and passed a plate each to Dick and me. It was the fifteenth meal we'd had in the last 24 hours. Under direction from my sister Liz — a dietician — we were experimenting with a technique favoured by endurance athletes, called 'carbohydrate loading'. This involves eating a protein-rich diet for a while, then, just before the 'event', switching to a diet of concentrated carbohydrate. Unfortunately we had lost Liz's list of carbohydrates, and the only ones we could remember were potatoes, bread and spaghetti. Driving up from the south of England the day before, we had eaten our way through every bread and chip shop between Scotch Corner and Glasgow.

'Think I've loaded enough' said Dick thickly, holding a stomach that had swelled so much that, if he had wanted to look at his knees, he would have needed a periscope.

This was an event that had been years in the making; minutes in the planning; a challenge which would utilise our aptitudes for over-eating and sleep deprivation. We were going to have a go at the human-powered record for the 'Three Peaks' — the highest mountains in Scotland, Wales and England: Ben Nevis, Scafell Pike and Snowdon. Times had been set for climbing and linking the peaks by car, motorbike and sailing boat, but harder still would be a combination of bicycle and foot. To make it 'sea-level', we would start and finish with our fingers in the sea.

An integral part of the programming was Hol, my father. A couple of weeks earlier, he had asked Dick and me to experiment and find what average speed we thought we could maintain for forty hours. We timed ourselves over 88 miles and reckoned that we wouldn't be able to average more than 16 mph for the Three Peaks, including stops. A week before the attempt, Hol produced a schedule based on the different average speeds we could be expected to make over the various legs of the journey. He estimated that

121

riding the 454 miles and running up the three mountains would take 41 hours 26 minutes. This tied in closely with the time taken by the only other person we could find who had tackled the Three Peaks under purely human power: Fl Lt Poulton had taken 41 hours 51 minutes, riding on his own, during the previous summer. Dick and I would have the advantage of being able to ride in each other's slipstream; against us would be the weather.

Hol calculated that for every extra pound of weight we carried over the distance, we would lose just over one minute. There was nothing I could find that could be chopped from our equipment without causing either severe pain or a loss of efficiency. On a recommendation from Liz we bought a box of Mars Bars and over a hundred glucose tablets.

At 2.18 pm on that fresh April day we knelt by a rocky creek in the harbour of Fort William. Our forefingers were in the sea. Hol stood behind us, counting down the seconds.

'3...2...1...Go!'

Like springing gazelles we turned and leapt. Dick bounded across the rocks. I slipped on the seaweed and fell in the water. It took ten seconds to reach Hol. My heart was out of control, and the still-swelling carbohydrate sat in my stomach like a sack of cement. He handed us the bikes and we raced from the car-park, leaning over to tighten our toestraps as we headed through the town.

Fort William passed in a blur. We took stock of the programme. Ride the 3 miles up Glen Nevis, run up and down the 'Ben', ride 242 miles to the Lake District, run up and down Scafell Pike, ride 166 miles to North Wales, run up and down Snowdon and then pedal the last 13 miles downhill to Caernarvon. Then have a cup of tea. It all sounded very straightforward.

At the youth hostel in Glen Nevis, Ados was waiting, already strapped into a rucksack and standing beside two pairs of boots that had been set on the ground pointing along the track towards the 'Ben'. Karen fielded the two bikes and we ripped off our cycling shoes. Up the zig-zag track we strode.

'Slow down, slow down. Take it easy. Save yourselves' Ados kept calling, shepherding us towards the 1,343-metre top. Hard snow lay deep across the summit ridge, and we paused at the cairn only long enough to touch it and turn.

We slithered down the scree, cutting corners. Ados fed us cake on the run.

'3 hours 26 minutes for the mountain,' Hol told us as we tore off the boots and were handed our cycling shoes, soup and bread.

'You're 33 minutes up on schedule.'

After the hard pounding down the rocky track, it almost felt comfortable to climb back onto the bikes. In line astern, we snaked down Glen Nevis and turned onto the A82, to find a tail-wind blowing us along the shore of Lock Linnhe. We were never to pedal this fast again. Part way down the loch the road turns eastwards to face the mountains and climb through Glen Coe. Now the wind worked against us, one of the gusts snatching the hat from my head. I saw it cartwheeling across the smudgy glen.

We rode, silent now, beneath the dark shattered faces of Aonach Eagach on our left and Bidean nam Bian on our right. Guarding the head of the glen is Buachaille Etive Mor, a fine mountain with sheer cliffs and a steep corrie that can be hacked up with axes to reach a view that is one of the best in Scotland: across the bleak sweep of Rannoch Moor, to the mighty Mamores, to Ben Nevis and backwards to Bidean. It has the same promontory-like position among its peers as does Tryfan in Snowdonia. My favourite two mountains.

At 300 metres, coming over the top of Glen Coe, we ran into a few flakes of driven snow, which quickly became a horizontal storm.

'It's because we're high. It'll be dry lower down', Dick shouted. But we still stopped to drag on jackets. We pedalled urgently across Rannoch Moor, past isolated lakes and windswept tussocks of grass, then in twilight swished down the hairpins on the far side of the Moor to Loch Tulla and the sanctuary of Bridge of Orchy. It was still snowing, and I had the uneasy feeling that we were about to embark upon an 'epic' that might turn out slightly larger than had been intended.

We fixed lights to the bikes, rolled past Tyndrum and rode along the shores of Loch Lomond while the headlights from the Land Rover behind picked out the bends in the road and the jagged rock walls. Sheltered from the wind by the steep loch side we rode fast, drawn towards the dull glow of Glasgow's distant street lights. Through Dumbarton, we fiddled to pull spent batteries from our lamps. I dropped my lamp on the road.

Past Central Station we found ourselves in a maze of one-way streets. Unable to follow us along a pedestrian precinct, the Land Rover lost us, and it was not until we emerged from the far side of the city centre that we met up again.

We stopped for five minutes to gobble bread and chocolate and drink tea. It was just after 1 am and we'd cycled a hundred miles. Hol was pleased; we were now 46 minutes up on schedule.

Tanked up with tea and calories we buzzed from Glasgow, nattering.

'There's some serious hills for a while, and grotty road surface. It's about 96 to Carlisle.'

'How d'you know?'

'Did it last week, after an evening lecture' came the reply from the dark.

'You're mad!' In his inimitable style Dick had mentally recorded the lowlights of his nocturnal ride from Glasgow to Carlisle. Once clear of Glasgow's suburbs the road climbs again to 300 metres as it crosses Scotland's Southern Uplands.

We saw the A74 before we could hear it. The moving pin-pricks of light promised several hours of mental rest. The best that can be said for riding long distances on main roads is that very little concentration is needed, and that you can switch off into the comfortable world of dreams. It seemed to be getting colder. We rode up the slip road. A voice came from the night:

'Custard!' Out of the darkness came an orange plastic mug attached to a fast-moving arm and body. It was Hol, sprinting alongside us, handing up a midnight snack.

'You're doing well' he said, and was swallowed once again by the night.

I switched the custard to my right hand, lifted it to my mouth, and, with one eye on the road's white dashes and the other swivelled like a robot camera on the mug, I tilted. Nothing came out. I blinked. My eye had nearly popped out with the strain. I tipped again. Something had gone wrong with the custard. I peered into the mug. The bike wobbled and nearly collided with Dick's back wheel. The custard was still in the mug.

'Dick!' I shouted 'Have you noticed anything funny about your custard?'

'Yeah, it's stuck!'

'So's mine.'

I could hear Dick knocking and tapping. I banged my mug on the handlebars, held the lip of the mug in my teeth, and, with my free hand, banged hard on the end of the mug. Half a pint of cold solidified custard broke free from the chemical bond it had made with the plastic, and hit me full in the face. The mug clattered to the road. I was choking. The bike swerved. For seconds I fought for breath. What a way to go: asphyxiated by cold custard while riding a bicycle down the A74 at night. I swallowed what I could. Dick was making contented slurping noises. Life was fun.

As we rode south into the hills, passing through sleeping Lesmahagow, the temperature continued to drop. We lost our rhythm by stopping every few miles to pull on more clothing. By the time we crested Beattock Summit, an hour before dawn, I was wearing two pairs of socks, two pairs of trousers, a thermal top, three jerseys, two jackets and two pairs of gloves. I could hardly move. Our feet and hands were numb with cold. I found that by riding with one hand tucked into my armpit beneath my clothes, then swapping hands, I could keep just enough blood circulating to grip the bars. When Dick tried to remove the lid of his water bottle, the plastic shattered. Inside, the water was frozen solid. In the darkness and the cold, tired and disoriented, thoughts broke and re-formed like neon lettering on rippling water. When Hol shouted the time to us, the figures had no reference in our abstract void. I longed for daylight. Later we found that a nearby weather station recorded a minimum temperature of minus 14 °C for that night.

Dawn took an age to crawl over the eastern hills. We watched it grow from a first glimmering, until the sun sparkled over a brow somewhere down in the flatter valleys near Lockerbie. We had cycled 190 miles. It was curious to be in daylight again, and reassuring to see the green Land Rover chugging along behind us, picking up the layers of clothing we were throwing to the verge. Warmed by the sun and with our spirits rekindled by daylight, we picked up speed again. We had lost a crucial 56 minutes on Beattock, and were now 10 minutes behind schedule. Carlisle was home territory for Dick, and he led through the city and out onto the long haul to Bothel. While our support team changed personnel — Dick's brother Chris was taking over from Ados and Karen — the sun climbed over the Lakes. Dick was pedalling fast and strongly. I was hanging on behind him, feeling dizzy with fatigue. My slowness was costing precious minutes. We were not yet halfway through our journey.

We cycled up Borrowdale longing for the moment when we could throw down the bikes, wanting a change of locomotion. At the head of the valley we turned left onto the little road that winds between drystone walls towards Seathwaite. Even the hump-backed bridge over the Derwent required a concentrated spurt of energy. Our mountain gear was laid out on the stones beside the farm at Seathwaite. We ate. Chris led us up Scafell Pike. Hol took the bikes round to the far side of the mountain, ready for our descent. We had scampered up Ben Nevis, being urged by Ados to slow down.

Now, 17 hours later on Scafell Pike we were trudging wordlessly while Chris forced a pace out in front. Nothing around me seemed to register any more. Someone pointed out a small lake far below us. It meant nothing more than another obstacle to go around. We came down into Langdale. Dick's sister Jo, and Chris' girl-friend Freda, and Hol were there. So was a three course meal of soup, chicken supreme, sponge pudding and custard. Never had food tasted so fine. The car-park gravel felt as comfortable as a velvet seat at the Ritz. By the time we left, we were 12 minutes down.

We rode quickly from the Lake District pumping up the hills with new legs, and the next 93 miles through Lancaster and Preston to Liverpool drifted in a smooth continuum of pedalling interrupted only by a snapped gear-cable. By the time we reached the Mersey we had pulled back three minutes and were looking for the willpower to carry us through a second night. Dick was having trouble pulling away from traffic lights, saying that his tendons were hurting.

Trying to wriggle into my jacket as I was cycling across a road intersection in Liverpool, I dropped the jacket onto the front wheel. The wheel jammed and threw me over the handlebars. Still attached by the toeclips I lay underneath the bike with headlights pointing at me from four directions. The faces of two middle-aged women appeared in the sky on the other side of the spokes.

'Eh luv, that looked dead good. You all right?'

'Yes thanks,' I said, feeling foolish. 'Fell off by mistake.'

'Ooohh! We thought you'd done it on purpose!'

Chris put me back on my bike. By the time we had cycled underneath the Mersey, Dick's tendon was worse. By the tunnel mouth we had stopped on the pavement, and were joined by an anxious-looking Chris and Hol.

'You go on Nick. I'll catch up in a couple of hours' suggested Dick. I thought it was a crazy idea. Dick would never have caught up again with a damaged leg. I said 'No, we'll wait.' Dick continued massaging his leg. We ate chocolate. I fretted about the time. Hol lowered the height of Dick's saddle a little. It would ease some of the 'stretch' out of his legs. We were now 24 minutes down on our schedule but we left Birkenhead confident we could pull it back.

Our route took us through the mountains of North Wales. We attacked the sharp climb over the Clwdian Hills from Mold to Ruthin. Dick seemed recovered. But then we came to hill after hill which piled behind the road's many bends, and in the dark we lost all sense of space. Out of the saddles we tugged the bikes through the Clocaenog Forest, the headlamps of the car spotlighting us like moths dancing in front of a bulb. Our slowness, and the need to share the mental effort of tackling such hills when our minds were muddled with tiredness meant that we rode beside each other. We zig-zagged in parallel up the slopes, muttering, groaning and heaving; desperate to maintain some kind of momentum until we could glide over a high point and rest as the gradient pulled us down the other side.

Out of the darkness on one of these excruciating climbs came a voice: 'Would you like a cup of coffee?' It was Chris. While we had been riding up the hill, Chris had managed to overtake us on foot, carrying two cups of coffee. His feet were hammering on the tarmac like a road-drill. The coffee made my eyes water. We had arranged that caffeine — in the form of Coca Cola and coffee — would be administered in increasing strengths after we reached the half-way point of the ride. This would help keep us awake. To increase its effect, neither of us had drunk any caffeine for five weeks before the ride.

We pounded along the A5. It felt as if we were nearly home. The remaining miles of cycling and the 800-metre climb up Snowdon were little more than a finishing sprint. Our tyres hissed on damp tarmac.

Through Betws Y Coed we sped, wheels inches apart, looking for the straightest line along the shiny black road. Through Capel Curig, Chris handed us coffee. It was so thick that it moved like a mud slide and stung with its acrid sweetness. But it acted like rocket fuel. We turned left, following the valley of the Gwryd, then turned right by the Pen-y-Gwryd Hotel. There's a bar in there with the signatures of Tilman, Hunt, Hilary, Odell and Bonington scrawled in black across the nicotine ceiling. No time to stop now.

As if to remind us that we were now back in the land of real mountaineers, the wind began to carry snowflakes down from Glyder Fawr. Quickly the beams of our lights filled with flying whiteness. In the gaps between the sheltering bluffs on that steep road to Pen-y-Pass the sudden gusts tried to push us from the mountain. While the wild night blew around our ears snow began to settle on our arms and thighs. Dick led to the car park at the top of the pass. Hol and Chris were waiting with chocolate, coffee and climbing gear.

For a final time we dragged off our cycling shoes and soaked and freezing, pulled on boots, waterproof trousers and jackets. We grabbed some chocolate and coffee and began up the Miners' Track towards Snowdon. Hol shouted a hoarse 'Good Luck'.

Glancing backwards through the drifting snow, I saw him standing by the car surrounded by bikes, bits of sodden clothing and lumps of food. He had been awake for 45 hours, driving and feeding us continuously. It was 3 am again.

Chris walked in front. Dick and I stumbled behind. I was being driven mad by my cycling shorts. They were so heavy with water they they kept sliding down inside my waterproof trousers. I couldn't see through my spectacles because they kept getting plastered in snow. And my worn-out treadless boots kept skating on the slippery rock. Tied at the knees by dropping shorts and half-blind, I fell along at the rear in an exhausted rage. For several agonising minutes we stopped while Chris helped Dick struggle into the only spare jersey, while I stood half-dead with the cold. As usual, I said nothing. At least by boiling over inside, I was keeping my guts warm. Dick seemed wide awake and was chatting to Chris as if they were walking by Bassenthwaite on a Sunday afternoon.

Cowering against the flying spindrift we reached Glaslyn. By a feat of navigation which I don't to this day understand, Chris located in darkness and white-out conditions the precise spot from which we had to leave the Miner's Track and start the steep scramble up Clogwyn y Garnedd. Behind him, Dick and I were on all fours, pulling ourselves upwards through the steep rocks; sometimes slipping back down in the thigh-deep drifts. To stop and rest now would not just mean losing precious minutes. No longer did I know where we were or how we would get down off the mountain. I'd been on this mountain before, on sunny June days when it had been warm enough to swim in Glaslyn. But now the cwm was wild and dangerous. Our survival depended on Chris finding the correct route through the crags. In the lee of a big rock Chris shouted at us that if we weren't on the summit ridge by 6 am we would turn back. It meant nothing to me. A series of savage gusts flattened us onto the snow. We lay immobilised like wounded animals. We lifted our shoulders once more. I couldn't understand how Chris could know where we were.

He shouted. There was flatter snow ahead. And a way through the crags. A rusty pole emerged before us. It tilted from the deep snow. We were getting close. Beyond the white roaring chaos, dawn was happening. We came over the north ridge of Snowdon to face the full force of the gale. Now there was nothing between us and the Irish Sea.

Chris pushed us into line: he in front, Dick holding on to one of his rucksack straps and I holding onto Dick's cagoule tail. At least it would stop either of us disappearing. We followed the railway track, tripping on the sleepers that were invisible in the soft snow. I looked down at my clothes. They were stiff and white. The rim of my balaclava was so laden with ice that it had stretched far below the level of my chin. The water that had soaked us earlier in the night had frozen to the skin of my face so that it cracked and dropped off when I opened my mouth to eat a dextrosol. Above the railway station, we crawled the last few feet to the summit cairn.

For the first time that night, I realised how far beyond normally acceptable limits we had gone. Striving for a summit can blind you to the risks you're taking to reach it. No one in their right minds would have set off up Snowdon in such a blizzard. To do so in the middle of the night, having cycled and climbed non-stop for two days and nearly two nights, was beyond rational explanation.

Instinct born from all the years of being trapped in blizzards with Hol on the mountains of north-west Scotland was all I had left. My body felt spent, yet my mind was continuing with the survival checks: I was asking my hands and feet whether they were numb yet. I heard myself telling Chris to slow down. We must not split.

Relying entirely on Chris to lead us off the mountain, we slithered back down the wall of the cwm to Glaslyn. In the confused wind behind the ridge the swirling eddies of snow made it impossible to see. We had to feel our way through the crags. It was an interminable plod back to Pen-y-Pass. When we saw the wall of the car park, we began talking. It seemed that we might still just be in with a chance of snatching the record if we could make a lightning ride down Llanberis Pass and over the low hills to Caernarvon.

Hol was waiting with our soaking cycle shoes and hot coffee. Beyond him we could see the Pass blocked with snow. A couple of cars were wedged crookedly across the road; snowed in. The idea of a hair-raising bicycle ride revived me. It did not appeal to Dick. On the mountain, it had been Dick who was going the strongest; now it was I who was raring to go. Astride my bike I slithered down Llanberis Pass with my feet on the snow. I was all adrenalin. Wide awake. Where was Dick? At the bottom I couldn't see him. I waited a moment, then turned round and began riding back up the Pass. At the first corner I saw him. I turned. 'What's up?' I yelled. Hol says we're going to miss it,' came Dick's exhausted reply.

We slipped into our rhythm as we pedalled out the final miles to Caernarvon.

In the town centre, traffic baulked us at some lights. I lost my balance and fell across the bonnet of a car. I was out of it again. Dick led the way to the water.

Leaning the bikes against some railings, we walked down a boat slipway, crouched on a couple of wet steps and ceremoniously dipped two fingers in the sea. It had taken us

42 hours 27 minutes; slower than Fl Lt Poulton by 36 minutes. We looked at each other, and managed a grin.

'That was a bit of a laugh.'

★   ★   ★

Back in the Vale of Oxford, the competition continued. Success to me meant finishing the race. I'm not aware of having deliberately won anything in my life. Coming last had its own amusements; the best view of a mountain is from below. A week after our Three Peaks ride Dick and I entered a 50-kilometre team time-trial which had a special category for 'composite' teams — that is teams where the two riders come from different clubs. After the event we were called by the officials. I have a dread of disqualification. But it turned out that we were to be awarded a prize for coming first in the 'composite team competition'. We were the only composite team to enter. We were presented with an aluminium water-bottle holder and pair of white socks each. Our next team event was rather harder.

In the early eighties America thoughtfully exported a fashionable new brand of self-torture. The 'triathlon' was designed to pull muscles other sports couldn't. Competitors have to enter a 2.4-mile swimming race, a 112-mile bike race and then run a 26.2-mile marathon — non-stop. I was hoping that Dick wouldn't hear about it.

The standard bearer among triathlons had been the classic 'Iron Man', held annually in the Pacific sun, sand and surf of Hawaii's golden coastline. In Dudley, home of the Dauntless Rubberline Cistern, the Metropolitan Borough had invented a race that went two stages beyond the 'Iron Man'. In this Black Country town west of Birmingham, was born the 'team quadrathlon'. In the 1982 event there were 33 teams. We would have to ride a 45-mile bike race with a break at three-quarters distance to run up the 407-metre Wrekin Hill, then paddle a canoe 24 miles down the River Severn, run 8½ miles across country and finish with an 18-mile race walk. There would be two people per team, and the result would be calculated by taking the average of the finishing positions of each team member. Some of the teams looked fearsome: among the multitude of sub-three-hour marathon runners and white-water canoe racers were two Royal marines (one of them Special Boat

Service), PE teachers, orienteers, an ex-paratrooper, a boxer, a marathon canoeist who had paddled for Great Britain and a friend who had run no less than three Karrimor Mountain Marathons. There didn't seem much room for ordinary civilians.

Dick took the event seriously enough to spend a couple of evenings practising in a canoe on the Thames, and he was very disappointed to find that there were compulsory 'rests' between each event. 'Much rather sprint from beginning to end' he said.

Me too!' I fibbed.

Somehow, we finished in fourth equal position.

★ ★ ★

Six months later, Ados and Dick teamed up to run the Himalayas. They had it in mind to raise money for a worthwhile cause, and had located in London a small charity called 'The Intermediate Technology Development Group'. Steve Bonnist, the fundraiser for I.T., was one of the few people who actually believed that Ados and Dick would set off on their run. Steve explained how I.T. specialised in helping the poor of the Third World acquire the tools and techniques they need to work themselves out of poverty. Working with local people, I.T. helps develop low cost tools and methods which can improve their ability to grow and store more food, build better homes, or increase their income though small, village-level industries. Examples of their work in the bicycle field include designing and developing the 'Oxtrike' — a cargo-carrying tricycle, and developing the bicycle ambulance from an original design used in Malawi. In poorer countries the bicycle, with its low running costs, go-anywhere capability and easy maintenance is a highly appropriate mode of transport.

Intermediate Technology's handbook was a book published in 1973 called *Small is Beautiful: A Study of Economics as if People Mattered*. It was written by a visionary German-born economist called Dr E.F. Schumacher. Mankind's unthinking pursuit of profit and progress, he argued, has horrendous costs; *people* have been forgotten in man's mad devotion to *products*. 'Small is Beautiful' forms the basis for I.T. thinking. It was through Steve's skills and enormous effort that the Crane adventures got the publicity that generated the public donations. After they returned from the Himalayas, £100,000 worth of donations came in to I.T.

It was a time of many diversions. There were marathons to run. Dick won the Fosters Quadrathlon, and then came the racing of 'HPVs' — human powered vehicles. Some of the prime movers in this specialist field were the London-domiciled American Richard Ballantine, designer Derek Henden and chief test-pilot Tim Gartside. These three had created the 'Nosey Ferret Racing Team' and had one of the fastest machines in the world with their aerodynamic pedal-machine called Bluebell. At an international race at Brands Hatch, Tim torpedoed Bluebell into the crash barriers, miraculously stepping from the wreckage of what now looked like a crashed dirigible. Dick, riding a late entry — the Hyper Hod — had to retire from the race after a paper-clip jammed in his chain. Both Tim and Dick went on to claim world records in later versions of Bluebell.

Keeping to more conventional aspects of bicycle sport but brimming with yellow-jerseyed dreams, I rode a series of mass-start criteriums then entered my first road race. On the first lap my right toe-clip snapped off, and after two more laps of one-legged riding the rear tyre punctured.

With the great question of what the point of competing was all about still unresolved, I found myself being sidetracked by a new brand of bike adventure. Its roots for me — as I'm sure they are for many a devotee — are traceable to childhood years of thrills and spills, though its current attraction has more to do with unpleasant congestion of modern roads. The cause for excitement was the arrival of a new type of bicycle: the mountainbike.

11

African Antics

KENYA

I opened my eyes and saw the scorpion. It was yellow and shiny; bigger than I would have expected, with an upturned tail like the beckoning crook of a witch's finger. It was about a foot from my face.

The scorpion shot forwards.

'Doug. DOUG! There's a scorpion on my ground sheet!' I shrieked, leaping to my feet and pulling my sleeping bag tight around my neck. Unless it could jump five feet in the air, I was safe.

'Doug. DOUG! Wake up! DO something!'

The scorpion stopped at my feet. Doug rolled over and looked at me blearily. 'Scorpion' I said again. In a blur of moving blue nylon Doug converted himself from being half-asleep horizontal to wide-awake vertical.

We stood on the parched, bare hillside, cocooned in our sleeping bags like a pair of menhirs wrapped for winter. The scorpion watched and waited.

'I'm not moving from my sleeping bag. Those things can kill' I said.

'Coward' Doug replied.

Neither of us moved. After several long minutes, as though bored, its fun over, the scorpion scuttled away with an evil crabby gait twitching its obscene tail.

'This is the last straw' I said as we hastily packed the bikes. 'Last night we got walked over by a herd of goats, we've been kicked by a shepherd, we've cycled 2,750 kilometres in 35 days, your back wheel's collapsed, I've got the shits, we've run out of water and NOW scorpions are climbing in my mouth when I'm asleep!'

'Don't exaggerate.'

'And all we've eaten in the last 24 hours is half a melon and some bad sardines.'

As usual, life brightened once we got on the bikes. Doug

rode in front. His back wheel was so bent that his bike cavorted from side to side like a cow running on three legs. We had used all our spare spokes, and were replacing those that broke in Doug's back wheel by removing them from his front wheel. The spokes broke about every 20 kilometres. But we hadn't done badly: it had taken $4^1/4$ weeks to cycle from Norwich to Morocco. It had been a lot of fun, but much harder than our ride from Norwich to Greece the year before.

It was the first time either of us had been to Africa, and it was very exciting. Beyond Tetuan we had ridden past camels and stopped to chat with Berber men dressed in long brown *djellabas* with huge hoods and floppy yellow slippers that slapped the dust as they walked. Everyone we passed called out 'Bonjour monsieur!' The women were more colourful, flouncing along in bundles of gay-coloured shawls and scarves. The children were more forward, shouting for cigarettes or money as we passed.

'Only another 200 Ks to go. Fes tomorrow!' said Doug through lips cracked by the dry air. He woke me from my dreams; the colourful bubbly part of Morocco was behind us now. The sun had yet to breach the hills. It was still cool. We had a clear two hours before the heat started hurting. It passed quickly. The road angled down across an empty wilderness of ochre hills. Across this abstract void unwound a melting line of hot black tarmac. In the incinerating August heat, the burning breath of the passing breeze sucked the sweat straight from our bodies. For the first time, we had run out of water.

Even the Rif Mountains had been preferable to this. At least it was cooler in the Rif. Even if they had thrown stones at us. And even if we had struggled up 2,000 metres on empty stomachs. And even if a man had pulled a knife on Doug. And even if kids had pestered us with hashish at every halt. There had, at least, been water in the Rif.

Here, in the scalding furnace of the Sebou, it was hard even to breathe. Doug's wheel twisted round in its perpetual, crazy spiral. It was driving him mad. Already he had thrown the bike on the ground and jumped on the wheel; it had straightened the metal better than putting in new spokes.

The tyres made a noise on the wet tar like sticky tape being pulled from skin. Empty water bottles rattled. I tried to keep my mouth closed, to keep it moist. My tongue felt fat and sticky; I couldn't swallow.

In front, Doug was shouting.

'Huts. Over there. Huts!'

We left the road, pulling the bikes across the hard ground to a couple of low mud houses. They seemed deserted. There was a well. By it rested a rusty can tied to a length of string. We dropped it over the edge. It splashed. When it was heavy we hauled it up. The water was the colour of pale tea, freckled with dark specks. 'Tablets?' I saw Doug thinking. Take too long. You had to wait ten minutes after dropping in a water purification tablet. We drank, filled the bottles, and walked back to the road. 136 kilometres after leaving the scorpion, we found another hillside and collapsed into our sleeping bags.

We reached Fes the next morning. There were two signs outside the town 'Nouvelle Ville' and 'Ancienne Ville'. We had made it.

Leaving the bikes at the youth hostel, we walked by the walls to the old Arabian town. Through a gateway, the light went out. We were in a maze of dark, twisting alleys, blocked in by three and four-storey houses that leant together at the top. Broken glass and bits of food littered the cobbles. The place was bursting with people. A tussle of kids ran in front and behind us, shouting and laughing. There were faces everywhere; faces in doorways and corners, faces with teeth missing, sores and scars. It was as if we had tripped into a world which as westerners we weren't meant to know about. This was the end of a journey.

* * *

Ten years after reaching Fes, a telephone call from cousin Adrian prompted me to reach for my atlas. 'Come to Africa, he said 'we can climb Mount Kenya then do something in the Rift Valley.' I tried to recall my fourth form geography.

Geography was one of the few lessons at school that could distract me from earnest mass-production of ink pellets, water bombs and miniature assegais made from empty pen cartridges and needles. At the merest mention of 'glaciers' my mind would carry me off to the Khumbu and a dawn start on the South-West Face of Everest; a lesson on sand-dune formation would transport me to the Sahara for half-an-hour's struggle through burning sands in search for The Lost Oasis. And when we were learning 'types of valleys', the Rift Valley was always a place of smoking volcanic vents and perilous river journeys. I never actually knew where the Rift Valley was, but I did know that it was very big because it came up so often in exam questions.

The East African Rift Valley, I quickly learnt, is the greatest landform of its kind in the world, stretching over 6,500 kilometres from the Gulf of Aquaba, beneath the Red Sea, through the Ethiopian Highlands, beneath Lakes Rudolf, Naivasha and Magadi, into Tanzania and so to the Indian Ocean near Mozambique. In another book, the eminent geographer G.H. Dury wrote that the Rift Valley was a 'depression caused by subsidence between parallel faults', a definition which smacked excitingly of earthquakes and gigantic cliffs. It sounded full of potential.

Three weeks later, Ados was viewing this natural spectacle from the lower branches of a pine in the garden of 'Trees', the little wooden home belonging to Bar and Rod (Ados' sister and brother-in-law respectively), that sits right on the edge of the Rift escarpment. The house is built at a height of around 2,500 metres. Bees hummed in the warm rising air, and beyond the explosion of red, orange and yellow flowers that rimmed the garden, a dust 'twister' spiralled across the floor of the Rift Valley, far, far below. Lake Naivasha, the highest of all the Rift Valley lakes, hovered serenely in the afternoon haze, smudges of green spreading from its shores towards the distant line of hills. It was the kind of view that makes you want to fly.

'Not sure about that one' he mused in response to a suggestion to run across the valley from side to side. Just a year earlier Ados had finished a run along the Himalayas with brother Dick, and since then it had been hard to interest him in jogs of less than 3,000 kilometres. The week before, we'd tried to climb the twin peaks of Mount Kenya equipped wth a borrowed rope and a tin of sardines, but turned back at 5,500 metres with altitude sickness and rumbling stomachs.

'What about riding bikes across the Rift Valley then?' A rustle of leaves followed by the thud of two feet hitting the ground indicated that the idea had been received, understood and put into motion. We'd start on the 3,000-metre summit of the western edge of the Rift Valley

— the Mau Escarpment — and drop down to cross the floor of the Valley at 1,825 metres, then climb up the steep eastern slope to finish in the Aberdare Mountains. The upper parts of the mountains are occupied by the Aberdare National Park. In Nairobi they say it is the highest game park in the world. It climbs to over 4,000 metres and is known for the *kali* (angry) reputation of its lions, elephants and rhinos. On the way back from carrying a tin of unopened sardines up and down Mount Kenya we'd driven through the Park, disembarking from Rod's Land Rover near Treetops Lodge to take a walk through the bush. This was foolhardy: you have to be myopic *in extremis* in order to miss all the warning signs that order you not to put so much as a little finger outside the safety of your vehicle. So we shouldn't have been surprised to find ourselves sprinting through the bush hotly pursued by a mob of giant forest hogs. For this reason, it was decided that the Great Rift Valley Bicycle Expedition would not enter the gates of the Aberdare National Park.

It took a couple of days in Nairobi to rustle up the kind of specialist machines we were looking for. Most of the journey would be on dirt roads, and we expected to cycle about 160 kilometres. Ados managed to locate a three-speed ladies' shopping bike with a bent frame, which the kind owner, the wife of a gardener, was only too pleased to lend for a few days and a nominal number of Kenyan shillings. Ados was elected expedition mechanic, and equipped himself with a large adjustable wrench. He once built a car out of scrap bits and pieces, and among other quiet accomplishments has motorcycled from Saudi Arabia to Britain. Ados is a past-master of the emergency repair or 'bodge'.

My bicycle was born of Westlands Market, where Mr. Maina of Mucatha Cycle Repair agreed to build for me, from bits lying round his workshop, a 'Rift Valley Special' bicycle. I went to collect it full of expectation. 'This is a good bike; not many punctures!' he said as he pushed it towards me with a grin '15 shillings each day.' On the front of the frame was a small badge embossed with a sleepy-faced lion and the words 'Philips — Renowned the World Over — Birmingham'. The bike had two wheels, spoked 36 and 35 respectively, and was fitted with a single-speed freewheel. The huge red plastic saddle was fringed with decorative tassles and was prevented from tilting backwards by the addition of a length of string running from its nose to the bicycle frame. It was the perfect bicycle for the job. I arranged to return it in four days, and rode off to show Ados the new machine. Half way up Spring Valley Gardens the pedal and crank fell off.

The express for Lake Victoria leaves Nairobi at six o'clock each evening. On the station platform we bought a three-day-old *Sunday Times* and checked our bikes in to the freight department. Leaning over a long list, the clerk pointed to the column showing that the minimum rate for bicycles was 48 shillings. 'And for future reference' Ados pointed out, 'we'll have to pay 9 shillings per kilometre for the transport of corpses.' We rattled north and the sun sank behind the crater of Longonot. The carriage we were in was a solid piece of rolling-stock built by Metro-Cammell in 1953. Compartment 1128A was comfortably appointed with long seats that could be converted into bunks, and in the corner a varnished wood flap could be lifted to reveal a triangular porcelain wash hand basin. We were informed by the ticket inspector — uniformed, with a red paisley tie — that a three-course dinner would be served in the dining car at eight o'clock. Then, with perfect timing, the carriage attendant knocked on the door bearing a couple of bottles of 'Tusker' beer. We reviewed our itinerary: stay overnight at a small railway town called Nakuru, then up early to catch a truck or *matatu* the 65 kilometres up to Mau Narok, on the edge of the Mau Escarpment. From there we'd cycle through the hills to their highest summit, which would be the start point for the crossing of the Rift Valley.

Twelve hours later we were waiting by a Toyota pick-up to which had been bolted a green-painted metal box fitted with windows. Sixteen of us squeezed into the box, with another three on the front seat. *Matatu* crashes are largely responsible for the high mortality rates on Kenyan roads. The bikes were tied onto the roof.

At Mau Narok, which turned out to be a road junction devoid of settlement, a small boy pointed us down a dirt track, intimating that in this direction lay Melili — the place we'd guessed to be the highest point in the hills. We made good progress, covering some 200 metres before having to stop to pick up the rear mudguard of the Philips. Rain had washed runnels in the mud surface of the track and we roller-coasted up and down the dips, dodging the bigger potholes. Small patches of farmland had been hacked from the bamboo forests, from which came a constant cacophony of squawks, screams and calls as each bird and animal gave jungle voice to its own patch of territory. Added to this natural orchestra was the steadily increasing crescendo of rattles which the Philips was developing. As each nut and bolt dropped to the passing dust we consoled ourselves that the bike was getting lighter with every mile. We passed a pretty Kikuyu girl sitting on the grassy bank, knitting, and came to a saw mill, beside which stood a thatch-roofed *chai* house. In the dark, cool interior we sipped hot, sweet tea and nattered with the proprietor. He was amazed when we told him how much a camera costs; the equivalent of five months' pay for an African worker.

We twisted and turned through the forests, joining this track and leaving that one and steering by the sun when it showed through the dense overhead canopy of foliage. Presently it became apparent that we were soon to join the long list of people who have never visited the highest point of the Mau Escarpment. In fact the longer we pedalled in that jungle, the more we came to believe there *was* no high point. We debated whether we were actually 'lost' (which can be translated as being a crisis caused by incompetence), or whether we 'didn't know where we were', which can be interpreted as a more temporary condition born of unfortunate local circumstances — like the lack of signposts and absence of passers-by to give directions.

Then, at the head of a long climb on white dust that reflected the African sun as intensely as a mirror, we came upon Peter, a tall kikuyu boy, resting at a road junction by his Raleigh. This was an elegant machine with two parallel top-tubes and a long wheelbase that provided the strength and toughness of a mule. Tied to his back rack with a strip of lorry inner-tube was a hessian sack made lumpy with several kilos of potatoes which he was going to take to his father who lived in a village several kilometres south. We set off as a threesome, Peter pedalling gracefully with a tall, straight back and a blue woolly hat pulled down over his ears, while Ados and I puffed, rattled and sweated in his wake. The Philips was suffering from a new multiplicity of ailments: three more mudguard stays had fallen off, and the rattling the machine now made at speed sounded like a suit of armour falling down a spiral staircase.

The ups and downs through the forest were enchanting, with the bowing fronds of giant bamboos waving to us from the roadside. Occasionally we passed people walking along in the sun: an old man wrapped in a brown cloak patterned with squares of ochre, a long stick across his shoulders from which he hung his arms, and then a woman tied into a bright floral *kanga* with a bag on her back supported by a strap over her forehead.

Melili emerged modestly from the trees as a collection of thatched roofs. Peter pointed us at the *chai* house and went to join a group of locals digging in a potato field. The *chai* house at Melili was wallpapered with Omo soap powder packets which had been carefully prised apart, flattened and nailed to the walls using bottle-tops as washers. The bottom metre of the walls was blackened with dirt and a darker line running at a height of about two metres round the inside of the *chai* house marked where heads had lolled against the wall over the years. The floor was beaten earth and round the edges were crude wooden benches. We folded up onto one of these while tea was poured from a big, blackened, and very battered kettle that had been simmering on the smokey wood-burner by the door. A few bemused eyes watched as we sat pouring with sweat and sipping the tea. A couple of cold chapatis (limp and clammy like a flannel, but delicious) rounded off our lunch. In the corner of the room a huddle of men were playing draughts using bottle tops (facing up for one team; down for the other) as counters, on a board made from a sheet of beaten steel with the darker squares marked out by hundreds of tiny dents. Just a few words of Swahili would have broken the ice, and not for the first time I found myself wishing I was a fluent multi-linguist. What were these people's names, where were their homes, did they have children, had they been to school, what did they think of the government? So many questions to ask, yet not the means to ask them.

The next village we had to reach was called Sakutiek, and after much enthusiastic discussion, the *chai* house concensus pointed us along a track headed south. This was a little confusing, because the Rift Valley runs roughly north to south, and therefore to cross it from side to side, we would have to travel in an easterly direction. After a few kilometres we glimpsed through a gap in the bamboo the landmark we'd been looking for all morning: the lake. Lake Naivasha sits like a puddle on the floor of the Rift Valley. It sparkled blue and inviting, 1,220 metres below us. 'All we have to do now is take the first track on the left and it'll take us down to the lake' Ados kept saying. On this optimistic note, the left pedal of the Philips dropped into the dust.

African bikes, I was thinking, only come with two pedals so you've one for a spare. At last we came to a left turn, and the road dropped away steeply over the lip of the Rift Valley. With the wind whistling by our ears, and dust spewing from the tyres, we clattered and bumped downwards. The road fell down over a series of shelves past fields of maize, patches of forest and clumps of thatched houses. A gaggle of school children clad in vivid violet dresses parted before us in a ripple of colour like wind blowing through a field of flowers. The bikes gathered a momentum of their own; gravity and mechanical purity harmoniously winging us down into the world's biggest valley. At around 65 kph the Philips and its rider reached terminal velocity.

Through wind-blasted eyes that were streaming with tears I could see Ados pulling away in front, dabbing his back brake to produce puffs of dust from his back wheel. I crouched lower to reduce the wind-resistance, and with the handlebars trying to tear themselves free, the Philips edged level with Ados. The staccato rattles on each bicycle had now increased to such a pitch and frequency that both machines whispered silently over a blur of dirt.

Eyes strained into the distance, searching for the fastest line on the road, watching for the patches of sand that could offer a little advantage. It was a duel that only one of us could win; Ados the rally driver looked sideways with the maniacal grin of a man quite at home travelling at crazy speeds over terrible road surfaces.

Thankful in defeat, I pulled hard on the brake levers. They flapped limply in my hands. I looked down. The front brake cable had shaken off its mountings. The rear brake wasn't there at all. Where was it? In the wire basket on the front of Ados' bike, where I'd put it when it had fallen off near Melili. The road took another dive down a steeper section of the Rift Valley and the Philips went faster still. In a moment of great intellectual clarity I realised that the rising graph line of speed was about to converge with the declining graph line of control, and that the only way of averting this confluence was to throw the bike into a sideways slide and use the combination of tyre friction on dirt and ballet-like balance to slew the machine to a halt. It was, after all, exactly what Ados would do, in his sleep.

I threw the handlebars round. They landed on the road several yards away. The remaining parts of the Philips described a series of somersaults down the road towards Lake Naivasha, closely followed by its rider.

Compared to crashing a car it was an unimpressive sight, and Ados was suitably unmoved. With the mole-wrench, the Philips was reconstituted enought to continue its downward journey. The remainder of the descent was a little more sedate.

We'd left behind the dense bamboo forests that clothe the 3,000-metre summits of the Mau hills, and were now crossing contours at around 2,000 metres. Here there were big open fields and tall isolated trees spread across the more level shelves of the valley sides. Sakutiek passed by on the right, a few lines of single-storey concrete housing blocks divided into claustrophobic dwellings. Three or four Land Rovers were parked outside. People walked up the road from the valley, a tired after-work walk, up a long dry hill. A nibbled sheep's carcass lay in the dust.

Below us and much closer now lay Lake Naivasha, gleaming in the early evening sun. Around it, pimpling the floor of the Rift Valley are the cones of volcanoes looking like the trace of a giant mole that's burrowed its way beneath the Valley. The shattered crater rim of Longonot, the grandest volcano of them all, turned grey in the twilight. The lower we freewheeled, the dryer and dustier the land became, till the bikes were rolling through an inch of fine dust that billowed out behind us like a smokescreen. Finally the gradient gave up. We rolled gently to a halt and prepared the bikes for pedalling. In Ados' case this meant jamming a small piece of tapered wood into the gear mechanism which pulled the gear rod out a click and thus offered him a lower gear. The Philips was now in a sorry state and could only be pedalled with one foot. Thus propelled, we made progress across the floor of Africa's Great Rift Valley, passing between the pyramidal bulk of two volcanoes as darkness quickly came.

In the dark the ruts became deeper and the dust more choking. Over some sections we pushed the bicycles, and a couple of times we crashed into the scrub beyond the road edge. By some big iron gates at the entrance to an estate we asked an *askari* (watchman) if he knew of any accommodation we could use. At that moment, a clean white Range Rover crunched down the drive. I stood in its path and Ados stuck his dusty brown head through its front window. He hadn't got half way through a polite enquiry about local accommodation when the clutch plates began to bite and four 750 x 16 tyres squirted gravel in all directions. The disappearing tail-lights gave us a focus for some well-deserved abuse, as well as providing a bearing along which to ride in the dark. Then the Philips got a puncture. We did have a puncture repair outfit, but it was on a windowsill in Nairobi 130 kilometres away.

It was a pleasant change to walk instead of ride, though a pity that the pitch dark meant there was nothing to look at. It was also a pity that the tyre fitted to the Philips turned out to be one size too big, so that when deflated it kept falling off the rim and jamming the back wheel so that it wouldn't revolve. This meant that the Philips had to be carried.

We whiled away a couple of miles with those stories that start with 'D'you remember the time when . . .'. Each story recalled a worse predicament from the past until we really did believe things were going swimmingly well on that warm African night.

There was a house, set back on the left, and with some trepidation we followed a hedge to the corner of the darkened building, where we stood softly calling 'Jambo' and 'Hallo, anyone at home', until an enormous man with shiny teeth and an even shinier *panga* erupted from the darkness carrying a swaying hurricane lantern. He was overtaken by a large, growling dog. Miming for his life, Ados did a speeded-up Marcel Marceau impression to get our message across before man, *panga* and dog saw us off the premises. Recognising a plight when he saw one, the man smiled good-naturedly. Yes, we could have a drink of water; we knelt on the grass while he jetted a hosepipe into our mouths. No, we couldn't stay in his home. Not even for money; but yes he did know a place where we could stay. He took us from his humble home along the road to another of those grand gateways, gave a shy wave and disappeared into the night.

We waited a moment expecting an *askari* or another white

Range Rover to burst from the shadows. But there was none. We trod gingerly up the crunchy drive and across a spongy grass lawn towards the lights of the house. We leant the two bicycles against a tree. From a french window came the clink of glasses and a ripple of polite laughter.

Fay Carnelley hadn't been expecting more visitors. She was returning to the drawing room to join her guests, and upon entering the room found all three twisted in their seats looking towards the north window. Framed against the night stood two dusty men holding floppy bush hats. 'Excuse me' said one, 'but we've been riding our bicycles down from the Mau hills and one of them has a puncture, and we're wondering if . . .'

'Come in. Come in. Sit down. You must be parched. Benson! Fetch two beers, please.' We sank into the enveloping embrace of two armchairs and let the Whitecap do the rest. Beyond the Persian carpet, the walls were hung with watercolours cast with flickering light from a log fire. In front of each person was arranged a small circular carved table laid with silver cutlery, ready for dinner. We felt as if we'd interrupted something. 'Now' said Fay, 'tell us your story!' It took some time.

We spent the night in a *banda* (small hut) in the garden, and Mrs Carnelley filled a cardboard box with food. We pulled on our jerseys and lay on the beds, warm in the glow of hospitality. By five in the morning we were freezing.

'Ados, why was it we didn't bring sleeping bags?'

'Too heavy. Anyway there's always something to keep you warm.'

At which point, with mute accord we rose from the beds and began carefully unplucking the curtains from the windows.

In the morning Mervin Carnelley kindly gave us a 'chit' to take to a neighbour of his who had a man who it was thought could weld the Philips' pedal back onto the crank. Peter Robertson has a compact farm on the lake shore. For 37 years he had been joint partner on one of the big Kenyan tea estates, and three years ago had come to this patch of wilderness and turned it into an irrigated garden of vegetables. Here he grew alfalfa and kept a herd of best dairy cattle ('all my labour get free milk every day'). And he grew small beans, aubergines and courgettes which were taken by regular truck to Nairobi and thence by plane to the restaurant tables of London, Paris and Frankfurt. Once a week he had to spray the crops with pesticide and herbicide to kill the tiny worms that are lifted from the lake by the irrigation pumps. He said it was cold by the lake in the mornings, because of the shade from the big overhanging trees.

But Peter Robertson's welder was away in Naivasha. We started walking, carrying the Philips, towards the town, 25 kilometres away. The dust on the road was so deep that in one place a pick-up truck was stuck fast, up to its axles in white drifts. Half-an-hour's walking brought us to a tin-roofed *duka* where we bought Fantas while one of a crowd of boys ran off to look for a bicycle pump. A bucket of water appeared, and fifteen pairs of helpful hands tore the inner tube from the Philips, pumped madly and dunked it in the water. Through all the splashing someone managed to spot the tell-tale stream of bubbles, and two Fantas later the Philips was up and running — albeit with one pedal.

We made good progress for an hour, pushing the bikes through the deeper dust, and riding along a few sections of harder dirt and frayed tarmac. Finally we turned onto the main Nairobi to Naivasha road, and in a last gesture of protest, the Philips shed the innards of its freewheel in a trickle of ball-bearings, pawls and springs. While picking up the bits 'in case they'd be useful later' I noticed that the front forks had cracked, and that the only thing holding the front wheel on was a slim piece of metal. Determined not to admit defeat, Ados set his mind to problem solving. Thirty minutes later we entered Naivasha in style, Ados in front, the Philips rolling along sweetly behind him, towed by a length of rope.

The town rests at the eastern end of the lake, 1,886 metres above sea-level, spreading across a gentle slope. In the days when malaria was rife, Naivasha became known for its 'fever trees' growing along the watercourses. But it wasn't the acacia thorns, with their striking yellow bark that was bringing disease, but the rivers themselves that were acting as breeding grounds for the mosquitoes. In 1883 a twenty-five-year-old Scottish geologist, Joseph Thomson, appointed by the Royal Geographical Society to lead the first European expedition to Mount Kenya, passed through Naivasha. He'd had trouble with Kikuyu raiding parties and his 140-strong caravan had also been attacked by lions.

146

Among his local adventrues was a climb up 2,777-metre Longonot, a scramble that one hundred years on reveals Naivasha and its lake as a scenic oasis set in the flat bottom of the Rift Valley. Fireball sailboats boats and overnighters from the Safariland Club now share the waters with hippos and herons. For the biggest fish caught each month the management of the Lake Naivasha Hotel offer a bottle of Scotch.

For the Philips, Naivasha was to be the scene of a miraculous reincarnation. It happened near the bus station, in a tiny workshop littered with the tools of a bicycle repairman's trade: a big lump hammer, a wheel truing jig, spanners, wrenches and pliers, and six inches of railway line to act as an anvil. Hanging from the ceiling was a gigantic black Raleigh with 'The All Steel Bicycle' in proud gold lettering revealed through a gap in its brown paper wrapping. Its cost was 'about 3,000 shillings'. I looked at it lovingly. Beside it was a downmarket blue Phoenix from China, going for 2,000 shillings. We listed the Philips' ailments to a man who had been trying unsuccessfully to braze the handle back onto a pair of scissors: the missing brakes, new pedal . . . the crank . . . freewheel . . . the forks that needed welding back on . . . the broken saddle . . . It was the kind of list that would cause head shaking in most bike shops. Not in Naivasha. Down the road in the 'Fish and Chips Hotel' we hadn't got half way through two plates of *maharaqwe* (beans, cabbage, potato and maize) when the bike man bounded in to say the job was done.

Now that we'd descended into the Rift Valley, and crossed its broad floor, all we had to do was ride up its eastern face, a climb of over 600 metres in 15 kilometres. Wedging his wooden chock into place Ados pushed off eastwards and upwards, followed at a distance by the Philips, now revelling in new-found form. It was hot; three o'clock in the afternoon, with six hours till dark. Through the ragged fringe of Naivasha and past a shop with a huge hoarding advertising 'Philips Gripe Medicine', we came to open country. Once wheat fields, now this is a scraggy jungle of bush used for rough grazing of goats and cattle whose herders live in a shack village set back from the road.

The road was nearly too steep for the old blue Bedford truck that took ten minutes to catch us up. It came past coughing diesel and hooting triumphantly. The catches on the tailgate were at just the right height for a cyclist's hand to rest ... hitched on for a cheeky tow, there was time to look at the deepening landscape. The lake was dropping behind, serene and blue, and in the grey haze of the distance stood the outline of the Mau Escarpment where the previous day we'd started the ride. Was it only yesterday? Ados slid round the corner of the truck and pulled himself forward on the metal body till he was level with the cab, which prompted another orgy of hooting. Not one, but *two* laughing heads poked out of the driver's window. We lost the blue Bedford when the climb eased enough for it to accelerate beyond a safe 'hanging-on speed'. Past Peppercorn Farm, then Nightingdale's Farm, the road climbed higher and higher, the air growing cooler, the vegetation greener.

Finally we came to the steepest part, and even Ados' low-geared ladies' bike couldn't make any progress. We walked a bit. The game rules according to Ados were that we were not allowed to stop and wait for a truck, and that we were to make a discernible effort to ride or walk to the top. But if a truck came past, well ... For ten grim minutes we cycled to and fro in as shallow zig-zags as is possible without actually going downhill, both of us casting surreptitious glances over our shoulders, eyes and ears fine-tuned to any approaching truck. We were saved in the nick of time by a new Isuzu.

A boy leaning on a bicycle loaded with two milk churns pointed us in the direction of North Kinangop. Up here the landscape was greener and fuller, with clumps of rustling trees and fields of maize. Between smooth curving slopes of grass was set a lake that could have been designed by Capability Brown. Far off we could see the blue line of the Aberdares topped by Elephant Mountain. Feeling the altitude perhaps, the Philips developed a slow puncture in its back tyre.

Bearing in mind the roughness of the dirt roads, it's surprising how few Africans carry a bicycle pump with them when they make a journey. The Philips' tyre was softening by the mile, and every passing cyclist we quizzed about pumps shook his head sorrowfully. We'd just heaved up a short sharp slope from a wooden-slatted bridge when our saviour appeared: a smiling man on his way home from work. He insisted on doing all the work, and laboured over an asthmatic pump till beads of sweat popped from his forehead and ran down beside his eyes. Pump connectors — those short wobbly sections of tube you use to transmit the air from the pump to the tyre — are unknown in rural Kinangop. The Kenyan practice is to hold a piece of cloth over the tyre valve, then push the pump on hard, forcing a hole through the fabric and thus forming a temporarily airtight seal. After five pump-strokes you select another piece of cloth and start again. The tyre slowly and methodically inflates, and the piece of cloth (in this case one of my socks) becomes increasingly holy.

There was a *chai* house by the crossroads, and outside, a confusion of people milling around the last bus of the day. A lady with a young child held to her back by a purple shawl poured us sweet tea and brought a couple of dough-cakes. The child was so heavy that it kept sliding downwards. Every few seconds the mother would have to put her hands behind her back and make a monumental upward heave to shift the child's weight. It must have been like putting on a loaded rucksack hundreds of times each day.

North Kinangop was as far east as we went; beyond the village the looming bulk of jungled Aberdare National Park, with all its creepies and beasties, climbed upwards towards the dying sky. Ados proposed a toast to the Rift valley, the bicycles, and the lady making the tea. We had another glass for the road, and climbed onto the bikes for a last time. The Philips' tyre was very flat.

If you suspended a powerful electro-magnet above Peter Nga 'nga Kimani's shop the clanging wouldn't stop for days. The 'New Quick Garage' is absolutely full of metal odd and ends. Wheels, broken bicycle frames, lengths of railway line, springs, sprockets, rods and hubs form a scree slope against every wall. But it took Peter just a moment to put his fingers on a tube of rubber solution. He patched the puncture using a circle of rubber cut from a car inner tube. Like everyone we met, Peter asked where our homes were, and after talking for a while about his shop and family, we talked about Kenya, and of the beauty of the hills and fields, and in that moment of listlessness that tends to come as you part from someone you like, Peter matter of factly added 'I will never see your country before I die.'

Darkness came with the swiftness of a cloak thrown over the landscape. We turned from Kinangop to face the fading glow of the day's sun that picked out every tree on the skyline as if it were a cardboard cut-out, and started the bouncing downhill run back to Naivasha. It was difficult to see. A local man came past and, with a laugh, bade us tuck in behind him because he knew where every bump and runnel lay on the road.

The man rode flat out, with Ados and the Philips trailing close behind as if attached by an invisible thread. The sounds of our laughter played tunes with the leaves in the trees.

12

Mountainbike Madness

CALIFORNIA, SPAIN, BRITAIN

'Go, go, GO!'
Behind us the pick-up fired. I let go the brake. Gravity sucked the trike forward. By the first bend I was accelerating through 30 mph. The trike was on line for a corner that was already rushing towards me far too fast. The dirt road flickered by in a pale blur. Small stones rattled on the aluminium chassis. A pebble whacked the helmet shell. The front wheel crabbed for traction on the sweeping bend. 'Too much brake' I said out loud. The wheels of the other trike edged level on the inside. Another corner. I dabbed the brake, too much again, then turned the wheel hard right.

The two twelve-inch back wheels scored through the dirt. The trike slid round the bend. 'Too fast . . . TOO FAST . . .' Off the track, a hummock lifted the offside wheel. I was going over. Another hummock. The trike was in the air, nose-diving into the brown grit. A treble impact tore the wheel from my gloves. A one-handed yank brought the machine round to the left again. Too much. Over correction. I was pointing at the rock. 'Go left . . .' the rear wheels snapped sideways and I tucked into the slipstream of Chris' machine as we raced down a straight.

Stones and dust from his back tyres streamed past my head. I pulled out to overtake. A blast of warm valley air hit me and we closed neck-to-neck on the next corner. Who'd brake first? A hole flicked by. 'Touch the brake. More brake — let go, slide. Getting the hang of it now.' The track steepened. 'Hey, this is FUN!' More brake. I could hear the pick-up horn. Chris was pulling away.

More corners collided with my eyes. Then the roaring wind, flying grit and sliding tyres were gone. The bottom. We bumped onto tarmac and braked gently. My arms were trembling. Smoke oozed from the front brake drum.

I looked towards my cousin. He was sitting absolutely

still while the fallout from the wild descent settled around him. In his borrowed padded corduroy jacket, battered motorcycle helmet and flying goggles, he looked like a cross between Farmer Giles and The Red Baron. There was a surprised grin on his face. He wriggled, trying to lever himelf out of the low-slung bucket seat.

Suddenly I was boiling over, pouring with perspiration. I fell sideways out of the seat, pulling my legs out after me, and sat on the edge of the track ripping off the gauntlets, helmet and jacket. Wonoga Park, Sierra Nevada, August 1980. It was midday, the shadows hardly visible. Below, the lake and roads in the Owens Valley were imprecise in the heat haze.

The pick-up rattled to a stop and people dropped to the ground. The driving door hung open as John Orr limped towards us. Tall, in shredded denims and scuffed boots, he carried a glint in his eye that betrayed his passion for higher octane hedonism than even the crazies of California were used to. Chris laughed. We'd descended 2,000 feet of mountain in six minutes. It had been like coming down the Cresta Run in a dumper truck. I was tingling all over; ecstatic.

'What was that!' I asked the gangling American.

'We call it freewheeling,' he said, laughing.

Mountains are a natural extension of the bicyclist's habitat. In the natural world many species like to extend their sphere of operation, whether it be to obtain better food or more prestige. The cormorant, which is technically a bird, swims underwater to catch fish. Englishmen try to ski. Donald Duck drove a car. Thus it is no less logical for cyclists to gravitate towards the trails and slopes of mountain and moor.

★ ★ ★

'Coming out' as a cyclist with a leaning towards those places where the contours are closest can be a difficult time both socially and physically. It was at the age of eight that I first became aware that I had a problem. For many weeks I'd submerged the urge, until finally one afternoon after school I pushed my sister's green tricycle up the drive in front of the house. At the top, I turned the tricycle around, locked the bin on the back, and launched myself downwards. The angle of descent of the drive was 1 in 4. I hit the house with a thump that knocked a lump from the wall and brought my mother running to the door in time to see a small boy sneaking away from a bent tricycle, holding a bleeding knee and a piece of brick.

Over the intervening years the hills became higher and the brick walls harder. The first bicycle I managed to get to the top of a mountain was my beloved Raleigh. Since its marathon rides across Europe, first to Greece and then to Morocco, the bike had had a quiet life. In 1976, fresh from graduating with a geography degree, I accepted a post in the Lake District, frying bacon and washing toilets in a youth hostel. It was a rich and varied time, and I have never lost the sense of pride and fulfilment in excecuting these two primary domestic duties. It was a job with several perks: I could for instance eat as much bacon as I wanted.

More importantly, since I worked mornings and evenings, the afternoons were free for adventuring on the fells. The nooks, crannies and moods of Coniston Old Man and Wetherlam became as familiar as the dents on the hostel frying pans. I pedalled the lanes rounded by Ruskin's house, over to High Sawry, and through Hawkshead to Grizedale and Satterthwaite. And I went beating round the rough forestry trails behind Grizedale, riding through to Little Langdale and tackled the Alpine bends of Wrynose and Hardknott.

Once a week I would have a whole day free, and this provided the chance for longer excursions. One such trip took me from Coniston down to Broughton in Furness, stopping on the way to gobble sandwiches in a wood full of daffodils on the banks of the Duddon. Over Thwaite Fell I went, then down into Ulpha, and thence to Birker Fell from where I could see the Scafells and Great Gable lording over the eastern fells. At the end of a stony track to Devoke Water an old boat-house sat, its water-door flapping in the little waves.

On the way back, I came over Birker Fell again, and took the short cut down the old coffin track to Boot. The track comes out at Stanley's Force where a waterfall churns through a green and slimy gorge. Near the top of Hardknott Pass is the Roman fort looking out over what on that day was a lonely, windswept valley. It cannot have been a popular posting for soldiers more used to Mediterranean warmth. Quickly down to Wrynose Bottom, then over the pass brought me to Little Langdale and the track that winds through the trees and brooks of Tilberthwaite. In those early weeks of the year the earth seemed to be winding its own spring, waiting for the warmth of the April sun to trigger the bracken and grass and leaves.

For some time I'd eyed with interest the rough ridge that runs along the summit of Coniston Old Man. It was, I thought, just the place to ride a bike. One afternoon in April I pedalled up the stony track that leads to the Copper Mines, and from there lifted the bike onto my shoulder and scrambled up to the ridge. It was a fickle day, with wads of cotton-wool cloud blowing across the mountain. By the time I reached the top, a clammy mist had closed round slopes which were crunchy with old winter snow. The bike made me feel faintly ridiculous, and I was glad that the cloud prevented any hikers from seeing me. I rolled off down the ridge.

It was a thrilling sensation: like running really fast or standing in a thunderstorm, unnecessary, slightly silly, but *very* exhilarating. I bumped carefully through the rocks and whizzed across the frozen grass, the handlebars bucking and twisting, tyres bouncing.

Before I could avoid them four walkers materialised right in front of me. I had to stop to let them past. 'What', one of them asked, 'are you doing?' A difficult question, that. 'Riding my bike' I replied, and scuttled off into a steep gully. Riding down a mountain on a drop-handlebar bike I found nearly impossible. With the weight so far forward, I kept being thrown over the handlebars.

*   *   *

I had to wait until 1979 for a legitimate reason to take a bike to the top of another mountain. I was reviewing for a cycling year-book a small-wheeled aluminium folding bicycle called the Bickerton, which had been designed for versatile urban living. Having found out that it could fit in car-boots, trains and under the stairs, it seemed valid that the bicycle should be tested for strength and durability. Pete Inglis had, very conveniently, moved to mountainous North Wales where, on the island of Anglesey, he kept a home well stocked with Elastoplast and Guinness. With Pete's local knowledge, a mountain called Y Garn (every other mountain in Snowdonia is called 'Y Garn') was selected as being an ideal testing ground for the Bickerton.

One of the bike's many remarkable features was that it could be folded up to occupy a very small space. We tied it to a rucksack and walked up the mountain. It was a sunny and blue June day, and Y Garn has a ridge of smooth sheep-mown grass. We larked around and found the lightweight Bickerton could be ridden over rocks and bumps. With the quick-release saddle at its lowest, it could also be ridden slalom-style down the open mountainside. And when the front wheel hit a hole the rider would go over the handlebars to be buried with a compacted spine headfirst in the bog.

★ ★ ★

One summer, I had an unexpected phone call from Pete. 'Take some time off work. Get over here. The weather's great, the mountains are great, the biking's great,' His voice sounded oddly faint.

'Where are you?' I asked suspiciously.

'In a phone-box.'

'Yes, but where's the phone-box?'

'Picos de Europa!'

'Who?'

'Picos de . . . It's a load of mountains. Spain. Take a boat to Santander. I'll meet you there.'

Grabbing panniers and a bike I took the train for Plymouth. The boat journey took 30 hours. Pete was waiting on the quay. We rode west, then south into gorges rumbling with the din of fast water. The mountains revealed themselves above the treetops as sheer teeth of gleaming limestone; the Picos de Europa. From the gorges of Hermida, Pete's Spanish map showed a rough track that seemed to cross the entire range. The track was labelled 'Pista para jeep'. It looked about 35 kilometres long and climbed to around 1,500 metres. It was a wild crossing, and an appropriate advertisement for mountainbikes.

The track was bouldery and steep. Much of the first uphill section we had to push as the bike tyres would not grip the slippery rock, nor could our gears manage the incline. At first, it was very beautiful, and the lumpy track

155

curled through whispering forest below rough-hewn rock faces. Then the cloud came down. At half-way, we rested in the mountain hamlet of Sotres, shivering in a tiny bar while a kindly Basque woman brought us hot chocolate.

Near the highpoint, a storm struck. The wind and rough stones made it quicker to walk than ride. We came on a small stone shelter. I was soaked to the skin and, not having brought a jacket, was shivering uncontrollably. 'D'you want the spare jersey?' Pete asked.

'No ta. It's for emergencies.' Pete was incredulous:

'Nick, this *is* an emergency!' I put on the jersey.

Flailed by wind and rain, we crossed a bleak col and, racing the coming darkness, pedalled like furies toward the lip of a cliff that would lead us to the valley. Then my bike punctured. In the time it took to mend it, night arrived, and those precious lost minutes committed us to a hair-raising 800-metre descent in the pitch black, on a precipitous track.

Serious mountain riding was going to need more apt machinery.

★ ★ ★

A year after courting oblivion on John Orr's Rocky Mountain trikes I was tapping at the door of a small Victorian terraced house in Aylesbury, England. Taking various types of standard bicycle off-road is something that has been long-practiced in the UK by a band of stalwart Ventile-jacketted enthusiasts who travel under the title of 'The Rough Stuff Fellowship'. And lots of un-clubbable individuals have also thrown themselves and their bicycles at mountains ever since Foster and Fraser proved the versatility of the velocipede by pedalling around the world on penny-farthings. But had anyone got around to designing a bicycle purely for off-road travel? Of course they had. In America. But then the Americans have put men on the moon and invented water-filled bicycle saddles; they are *so* far ahead.

At that very moment, in Marin County, California, men (*real* men; no zips on *their* Levis) with suntans and bandanas were burning down the dirt trails of the Coast Ranges aboard knobbly-tyred broad-bar'd hybrids cobbled together from the clunkers used to cruise the beach boardwalks. They called them 'mountainbikes'.

Geoffrey Apps opened the door to his Aylesbury workshop that drizzly autumn day and took me upstairs to his studio. A Radio Three broadcast of Schubert's Trout Quintet played softly in the background. On the drawing board was the pencilled outline of an odd-looking bicycle. Geoff pointed out some angles, and chattered excitedly about stress-points on tubing.

'Come and look at this. You'll see what I mean.' We went downstairs. He pulled back a sheet to reveal a machine the likes of which could (given the extinction of the motor car and cataclysmic chemical degradation of every piece of tarmac in the country) change the course of history. In dull gunmetal and bristling with teeth, studs and levers, it looked like an exercise machine for Conan the Barbarian.

'This bike' he said through a brown moustache 'will go *anywhere*. It's got a bottom of 20.6, tungsten studs front *and* back, Wassel bars, Grab On pads, a TA triple and VXGT clanger!'

I nodded.

'And down here' — he wriggled his hand through a cage for a thermos-flask, a metal chain-guard and a kick-stand — 'is the bash-plate!' He lifted the front wheel. 'It's designed to help you ride over logs and rocks. Very handy!'

Geoff let me borrow the 'Range Rider' for a fortnight.

It was a remarkable machine. Over the next weekend the Range Rider was pedalled up Snowdon in North Wales by a relay of riders: Elaine, Pete, myself and a short man with long hair called Rat. It was very misty, it was raining, and the ground was soaking. With its ultra low gears, easy balance and superb traction, the Range Rider could be ridden up steep wet slopes that would have had any normal bike toppling over. The transmission could develop enough torque to tear the teeth from the freewheel. Which is what happened: three of them snapped off under the strain. Apart from a couple of rock-steps, the bike was ridden from Llanberis village to the summit of Snowdon. The descent promised to be the thrill of a lifetime but in the poor visibility at 840 metres Rat rode the Range Rider straight into a boulder. The rear wheel punctured when it was crushed against the alloy wheel rim. We hadn't put enough air in the tyre.

Mountainbikes in the UK were at this time strictly the preserve of designers, closet Californians and Richard

Ballantine. Richard — the world's first bicycle guru — imported in 1982 a 'Ritchie' from Marin County. So did Richard Grant, the editor of a BMX magazine. Then Tim Gartside and Peter Murphy got a pair of Ritchies. In the winter of 1982 they set off southwards across France and didn't stop till they reached Lagos in Nigeria, 5,500 kilometres later. On the way, they pedalled and pushed their mountainbikes across the Sahara Desert, a feat 'Murph' was later to describe as 'warmish and a bit tricky'.

A year later, the first mountainbikes began appearing in London shops.

Here at last was a vehicle that could be used to escape from the hideous influence of the motor car. On a mountainbike you could leave behind the puerile executive sports cars with their flip-up headlights and 0–100-in-4-secs-acceleration; leave behind the fumes and dirty verges; leave behind the ugly car colours and engine noises. Where any old bike could manage a mountain, the purpose-built mountainbike, with its wider grippier tyres, sure brakes, low gears and easy control, promised more strength and reliability when used over rough terrain.

Free time was limited to evenings and weekends. Pulling out the maps of Oxfordshire I scoured the blanker areas for mountainbike terrain.

In Britain, wildernesses are found only in cities. The country is, for the main, intensively farmed and we are constrained to footpaths and bridleways and ancient trackways preserved through history from the hands of the landowners. Only on the moors and mountains can you wander more or less at will. In England's south-east the problem is acute, which is partly why the Ridgeway stands out as being a marvellous journey, both in time and space.

With Pete Inglis I'd cycled the section near the White Horse of Uffington, and on a solo ride had explored the tracks once walked by Thomas Hardy's sad young man in *Jude the Obscure*. With a large-scale Ordnance Survey map I'd followed the steep track up behind 'Alfredston' (Wantage), through the rings of the Iron Age fort and down the back-slope to the lost village of Fawley. In the novel, Fawley is called 'Marygreen' and Jude's surname is 'Fawley'. Just north of the village is the scooped field Jude thought so ugly, and where he scared rooks with a clacker for the farmer, Mr. Troutham. The spirits of these parts are easily stirred, so close to reality are Hardy's descriptions.

The Ridgeway is a mixture of chalk and flint, deep mud and bumpy turf. The distance from Streatley on the Thames, to the prehistoric stone circles of Avebury, is 37 miles. In 1943, my grandmother Ruth Dingley had cycled this route with her teenage daughter (my aunt) Janet, in two days. They had picked mushrooms above Avebury and fried them that night in the hostel. On a mountainbike I thought it ought to be possible to ride the Ridgeway in a single day. Marsh Norris — another designer-type who shared a loft full of Rotrings and classical music — was keen. We bumbled along that pretty chalk upland track all morning, zooming down the hill to the pub at Ashbury for lunch. It was very pleasant; just right for a sunny Sunday.

Shortly after this I had an excited phone call from Tim Gartside. He was, he said 'up on the cam', having recently broken at Indianapolis the world speed record for a bicycle. Now he was into mountainbikes, full-time. 'We're going to Wales — to Hay-on-Wye. I'll bring the bikes', he said.

Where the Ridgeway offered meditation, the Black Mountains promised drama. Tim and I started on the banks of the Wye where it bubbles beneath the bridge just outside Hay.

It was a ripe blue June morning and we left the town by way of a leafy lane climbing Cusop Dingle. A short track led us splashing through a ford and then up a steep grass bank towards the rising prow of Hay Bluff. This is what Tim wanted to ride up. From the town to the top is 580 metres of steep climbing, and we crested the grassy lip onto Hay Bluff blowing like traction engines. A German backpacker tanned to the colour of his *lederhosen* asked us if we were enjoying ourselves. Through a roaring of blood in my ears I heard Tim reply 'Betcha!' then elaborate by describing the hill as a 'cracking honey'.

It was a wild, exhilarating day, taking us flying down to the Gospel Pass then up to Twmpa with hazy Wales spreading away in a rolling quilt of blue-greens. On the left, long forested valleys snaked down to Abergavenny. The sharp ridge of Y Grib led us to the Wye Valley for a weary, satisfied pedal back to Hay. A couple of months later I was back in Wales, this time for an outing of a slightly more outrageous nature.

Dick and I travelled up from London on a Friday after work, arriving at Pete's house on Anglesey at 1.30 am. After arguing through our choice of clothes for the approaching enterprise, we crawled into our sleeping bags at 3.14 and at 3.22 respectively. At 3.30 the alarm beeped. I'd just had enough time to make my clothes into a pillow. In a daze, we drove the ten or so miles to Aber.

A whole or a half Mars Bar. That was the question. Dick said a half would do, and taped his portion to the centre of his handlebars, where, he said, he could watch it all day and test himself by seeing how long he could last before eating it. This was cousin Dick at his most entertaining: he's a master of ingenious deprivation, happier relying on his wits than on pieces of equipment. For the moment, I was excused decision making; I'd only had half as much sleep as Dick. About weight, he's obsessional. I was still smirking at his little slice of chocolate bar when he turned on my two maps and demanded that all unnecessary paper be torn from the edges of our intended route. The year before, he and Adrian had spent many happy hours in Kathmandu cutting labels and buttons from their clothing before 'Running the Himalayas'. That Dick still carried ear-lobes was only due to the difficulties of managing scissors in the mirror.

Rejected gear lay strewn about, and we hurriedly discussed tyre pressures. Much of the riding would be over rock scree, so the tyres would have to be hard enough to prevent the rims from getting crunched, yet not so hard they'd lose traction on the wet steep grass. To cement our commitment to the ride we left behind the pump and puncture repair kit. We started above Aber Falls at 5.30 am. A soggy mist clung to the khaki slopes like a dewy blanket on a sleeping tramp. It took an hour and a half to ride gently up to our starting point.

As far as we could tell, this would be the first bicycle attempt at the world famous (world of long-distance fell-walkers that is) 'Fourteen Peaks', and it would also prove once and for all that, just as herrings can't fly, bicycles can't climb cliffs. The normal aim of a 'Fourteen Peaker' is to walk over all 14 of Wales' 3,000-foot mountains in under 24 hours.

At 7.10 am we started the stopwatch and began the ride by carrying the bikes over a sharp boulder field. The weather was perfect. At the top of the grass slope on Foel

Fras we began rolling, the mist boiling below us. Clean grey peaks stretched far away beneath a clear blue sky. Fuelled by adrenalin and early-morning intoxication we had sped over the first six peaks by 9.30.

Appearing out of the mists of Ogwen bearing a packet of raisins and a bottle of lemonade, Pete administered our first pit stop, before the helter-skelter descent of Penyrole-wen. For 600 metres the rock falls away at an ugly angle down to the A5 road. Pete and Michele, Dick's girl-friend, had organised a pit-stop at Ogwen Cottage. Somebody spooned tinned rice pudding into my mouth as I pumped a few more p.s.i. into the tyres. With the drama and excitement building — and a lot of people watching from the car park — we rode off towards Tryfan with indecent bravura and come-uppance imminent. Through narrowed eyes and with jaws that would have been resolutely set had they not been trying to chew jam sandwiches and breathe at the same time, we viewed the mighty bulk of Tryfan. Manfully we wrestled the bikes over rock and grass and rode into a deep, black, sucking bog. Winded as I catapulted over the handlebars the sandwich fired forward to bury itself in the ooze.

Tryfan is one of those almost vertical mountains adhered to in varying degrees by rock climbers. We set off up the rocks with the bikes hanging from our shoulders so that our hands were free to feel for handholds. To set a decent record for the day we needed to climb fast. We passed two ropes of fiddling rock gymnasts. At times the bikes were an encumbrance: they tended to jam in chimneys and threaten to topple us from narrow ledges.

Bristly Ridge followed, and here we had to hang the bikes from projecting rock-spikes before climbing up ourselves. The pain inflicted by rock-sharpened chainring-teeth excavating the flesh of neck and arms, and of handlebars that suddenly swung round to clout us full in the cornea as we performed fingery moves over 200 metres of open air, was not inconsiderable. Pete, who had kindly offered to guide us over this technical section of the route, was laughing quietly in the background. At the top, we came onto the Glyders, where a wild jumble of car-size rocks forced us to carry further. Up here, Dick — ever the experimenter — discovered a new way of carrying a bicycle: by sticking his head through the main frame-triangle and resting the weight across his shoulders. Anyone unbalanced enough to find themselves carrying a bicycle up rock climbs will find this method the least injurious.

By 1.30 am we were on Glyder Fawr. Life began to improve. For the next few miles the gradients and rocks eased enough for continuous fast riding. Y Garn and its long ridge fell in a blur of effort. Communication between the two of us narrowed to snatched glances to check that the other hadn't dropped over the edge. Round the foot-wide track which curls level and fast along the flank of whale-backed Elidir Fawr to the summit we skimmed, then touched the summit cairn and turned the front wheels over the edge to freefall past 76 contour lines in a handful of thrilling minutes.

Pete, meanwhile, raced around the bottom of the mountains to meet us with more Mars Bars and a bottle of water. With the end but two peaks away, an element of inter-cousin competition crept into the ride as we turned onto the tarmac that climbs Llanberis Pass. Without a word, we were soon tearing ourselves apart in a lung-bursting attempt to be first to the top. This grim sweat-lathered duel concluded with a sprint finish over the high point at Pen-y-Pass, which we reached dizzy with dehydration and in a state of elaborately-disguised near-collapse. Conversation was casually re-opened as if we'd just rolled down to the pub for a pint rather than pedalled demonically up several miles of melting tarmac.

Only the Snowdon massif remained. Pete recommended the Crib Goch route as being the most direct, and therefore the fastest. It also happens to be the most dangerous ridge in the country. As if warming to a coming calamity, while still on the lower slopes, Dick crashed over a rock step and hit the ground hard. He picked himself up with blood coming out of his elbow and continued with a limp any footballer would have been proud of. The east end of Crib Goch is a rock scramble that steepens as it get higher. In places we had to hoist the bikes up near-vertical slabs. By this stage both of us were reaching that depth of tiredness where the pain of forward progress is eased by expressions of vocal discontent. Whimperings and moans mixed with grunts and muttered expletives. Later, Pete and Michele said these were the funniest moment of the day.

At 850 metres we blinked out into the bright sunlight on top of the ridge. Sheer drops fell away on both sides. It was a ridiculous place to take bicycles. Mum would not have been pleased. The ridge of Crib Goch is only an inch or two wide in places, with sheer drops on either side. We picked our way along its bare dry spine, fingers hooked over the top, feet scrabbling for thin holds out of sight below . . . and bicycles dangling above the void. It took nearly an hour to reach the safety of Crib-y-ddysgl where we managed to ride again for a few feet before the final scramble up to the narrow-gauge railway. At 7.36 pm we reached the summit of the highest mountain in England and Wales.

Below us the valleys were slowly filled with shadow. With the mountainbikes' tyres slotted into the central rack of the mountain railway, and our feet splayed out sideways like outriggers, we shot down towards Llanberis hoping not to meet a train.

Later, we studied the maps and timings. From the top of Foel-fras to Snowdon it had taken us 12 hours 26 minutes. The total height gain turned out to be 2,697 metres and the overall distance 28 miles, of which 25 miles was off-road. Since it had taken us 23^1/2 hours to walk the '14 Peaks' the year before, this day's outing could be claimed as evidence of the versatility of mountainbikes over mixed terrain.

★ ★ ★

Having found how steep and how fast a mountainbike could travel, the next obvious step was to try them in the dark. Ados, now resident in California, was in London for a couple of days. He, his wife Karen and little son Jaro and Dick were at my flat for supper.

Riding mountainbikes up Everest by night would be the kind of stunt that would really turn heads. We looked into it. Unfortunately Everest was booked for the evening we had in mind. We settled on the Ridgeway, which has many features in common with the Himalayan giant, despite being 8,569 metres lower, and grassy rather than icy. A challenge such as this demanded qualities of skill, dedication and concentration. We had none of these, but we did have a head-torch each.

We synchronised watches standing on the bridge over the Thames in the sleeping village of Streatley. It was 10 pm and a freezing night at the end of November. 'Could be interesting' commented Ados. It was the first time he'd ridden a mountainbike. Tyres crunched up the long slope as we left behind the dull orange diffusion of street lights, eyes slowly becoming accustomed to the pale reflection of the moon on the chalk track. Ethereal light bathed the fields of grass and stubble. An owl drifted low across our path.

I lost the map after about ten miles, and from there on the route-finding became less certain. I recognised none of the junctions from my previous rides. One false move on Everest can send the unwary climber falling thousands of feet to the Rongbuk Glacier; a wrong turn on the Ridgeway can land you in Swindon. It was a worrying time.

Using astral navigation — and the lights of Didcot power station — we pedalled east over frozen turf till we reached the pre-arranged grid reference. Here we were to rendez-vous with our support crew. He was sitting in a Ford Escort on the A34 eating bisuits. We chattered excitedly. In a pale blue down duvet jacket called Doris, Klon shrugged off the bitter wind; he'd seen worse. There was snow in the air. We were ready to leave. 'Which way?' we asked. Wordlessly, he lifted his arm, pointing: past a road construction site, a wrecked caravan, a heap of frozen silage and out beyond, into the darkness. 'Out there, he said, 'lies the Ridgeway.'

Most of the rest of the night was spent blundering into holes, trees and each other. We passed the gaping mouth of Wayland's Smithy burial chamber, ghostly in the pale light, then the rounded bulk of Uffington Castle. It snowed and the puddles cracked like shots as we rode over them. Above Ogbourne St George, a log reduced the derailleur on my bike to a screwed-up ball of brushed alloy. With his hands, Ados bent it straight, so that one gear worked.

Dawn, and the end, came suddenly. Riding the soaring grassy crest of Smeathes Ridge we were greeted by an uninterrupted vista of grey-green rolling Wiltshire. Into Avebury, Ados led us across the cropped grass into the ancient stone circle. We'd done it; without oxygen too. A kind truck-driver, Terry McFadden from Athlone in Ireland, took us and our bikes back to Reading.

All that remained now was to see how high a mountain-bike could go.

13

Africa

KILIMANJARO

Overhead, a Colobus monkey arced aerodynamically across the thin strip of sky and landed with a gentle swish on some convenient foliage. I lay on my back gazing idly at the rustling leaves, wondering whether the jungle air-show was going to continue, or whether, in the absence of anything further to occupy my mind, I was going to have to drag myself upright and continue with the numbing purgatory of our journey.

I'd fallen down a bank. The bike was entangled in my legs and a dark trickle of blood was oozing down a muddy shin. I tried to wriggle free. The teeth of the chainwheel gouged the umpteenth hole in my leg and a particularly nasty stinging shrub sent several volts of pain into my cheek. Its spiny leaves looked terrifically poisonous.

'This', I said loudly at a large triffid-like plant, 'is beyond a joke'. Then again, at the top of my voice:

'*It's beyond a joke, d'you hear!*' Nobody answered. Not even the triffid. I felt a bit lonely, 5 metres below the path where I'd fallen, hidden from view by a canopy of squishy vegetation that had closed back over me as I'd cartwheeled down the slope. I wondered whether those stories of Japanese soldiers being lost in the jungles of the Far East for twenty five years were true. A centipede the size of a tube train crawled out of my trousers.

It took quarter of an hour of pathetic whimpering to drag bike and body back up the bank, belaying myself on tree roots and clutching slimy fronds for handholds. The path had the clear impression of a bicycle tyre trailing zig-zag fashion around the next corner. Dick must have carried on, unaware of my jungle plunge.

I lifted the back wheel and spun the pedals. The chain was off and tightly jammed in the rear gears. More mutterings as I foul-mouthed the manufacturers of the mud-covered mechanism, the weather (it had started raining again), Dick for leaving me behind, the path for being so slippery and myself ('You stupid, STUPID, git') for going over the edge. By the time I was sorted out, the path had turned into a stream.

This was Day Two of our trip. We'd been calling it an 'expedition', though since this conjures up images of prior planning, logistical support and a general awareness of what you're letting yourself in for, it wasn't an accurate tag. Dick had suggested it was more of a 'jape'. The Blashford-Snells and Boningtons of the world would have belly-laughed at our 'organisation': we'd left our entire supply of chocolate behind in Bar and Rod's refrigerator in Nairobi; our map was more useful as a tablecloth than as a route-finding aid, and with two of us trying to be leaders, decisions could only be reached after debates of epic proportion.

'We're going cycle-touring in the southern hemisphere' is what we'd said to inquirers in England, and that normally circumvented explaining just *why* two apparently sane adults should want to ride bicycles up 5,894-metre Kilimanjaro, the highest mountain in Africa, and one of the highest volcanoes in the world. 'Bicycles up Kilimanjaro' had been put together in a hurry. Just ten weeks separated the moment when Dick and I had dreamt up the idea in wintry London and when the first of us stepped out into the balmy air of Nairobi airport and the welcoming smiles of Dick's sister and brother-in-law Bar and Rod Bennett.

At the time, Dick was working in Aberdeen. His visits to London were rare, and seldom seemed to last more than a few minutes. Our planning sessions took place at the King's Cross station chip-bar, or in the early hours of the morning at 'The Dallas', an all-night cafe in Smithfield Market. Dick had acquired the ability — through Ados and 'Running the Himalayas' — to pare away the non-essentials of life. Minimalism meant action and results. I enjoyed the details.

Hol had crystallised such family challenges into the acronym 'TEDDY'. Tough, Exciting, Difficult, Dangerous, Yourself, epitomised, he said, the winter climbing trips he led and the various spin-off expeditions that grew from them. We carried a small teddy-bear dressed in a sash bearing the words 'Intermediate Technology'. This had been provided by Hol, who sent with 'Kilimanjaro Teddy' a letter containing the following explanation:

166

*. . . 30 Oct 84 was, by the way, an important date in the
history of bearkind. Not only was it the first known occasion on
which a bear has been accepted for an expedition up
Kilimanjaro on a bicycle, but also it was the sixtieth birthday of
Winnie-the-Pooh.*

*Fully equipped with one foot of nylon saftey-rope to minimise
risk of loss on mountains, Kilimanjaro Ted weighed 1.13
ounces. My calculations showed that assuming a bike-plus-
rider weight of just under 200 lb the extra effort involved in
carrying him from sea-level to the summit would amount to the
equivalent of only an extra seven feet on the height of the
mountain.*

'On site' research was carried out for us by Bar and Rod,
who lived in Nairobi. Bar had already climbed Kilimanjaro,
and was able to give us information about routes, hiring
porters, altitude problems and so on. Rod, a rally driver like
Ados, promised to help us 'sort out' our mountainbikes.

Our goal was to raise £7,000 needed to buy and erect one
of I.T.'s low-maintenance 'Kijito' windmills in a remote
desert hospital in north-east Kenya. About 200 patients
were living in brush-wood shelters and had no convenient
water for drinking or washing. Many of them could not
walk. The more mobile adults, and the children, would
make several journeys a day to carry water in enamel bowls,
mugs and bottles to the huts. A windmill at the hospital
would lift water from underground reservoirs to storage
tanks, which could be fitted with taps for convenience.
Steve Bonnist at I.T. would co-ordinate the media and
fund-raising.

The aim of the expedition was to reach the top of the
mountain and use this achievement as a fund-raising vehicle
for I.T. Only if we reached the top with the bicycles would
the climb be noted by the press, so we had no option but to
succeed. We took certain precautions, four of them to be
exact: Pete Inglis, Maggie Birkhead, Catriona Hall and
Michèle Young. Between them they covered the fields of
parachuting, zoology, mountaineering, theatre directing,
action photography, teaching, and 11th and 12th-century
Florentine and Sienese art.

The art of successful stunting is derived firstly from the
nature of the stunt and secondly from the way in which it is
presented to the media. Some of the best adventure stunts
are those that combine two nearly-incompatible elements

167

(for example swimming and the Atlantic, running and the Himalayas, bicycles and volcanoes) into a single event which is chosen to coincide with public interest in one or both of the elements. The stunt should also be nearly impossible. Bicycles up Kilimanjaro was suitably mad, and our team well qualified. Our main concern was conveying the story to the media and Steve in time for I.T. to benefit.

The publicity effort hinged largely on our ability to send back to *The Sunday Times* in London reports and photos, and then to transport ourselves with no delay back to London so that we could promote the charity on TV and radio. Pete would take the all-important photographs; Catriona, Maggie and Michèle would co-ordinate our equipment supplies on the mountain, then run down the mountain with the summit story and photos to a waiting *Sunday Times* correspondent who would drive 320 kilometres to Nairobi airport and put film and copy on a plane for London.

That we got to the mountain at all was something of a miracle. Two days before flying out of Heathrow, we still had no bicycles, and Dick's flat was thigh-deep in unsorted equipment: puncture repair kits balanced on backpacks which leant on mounds of stoves, bottles, sleeping bags and tents. Bags spewing trousers, jerseys and jackets tumbled over ice-axes and ropes on the table. Carrier-bags of instant soup and muesli spilled in the doorway.

At the airport, the man at the check-in said we could pay him £1,300 for our excess luggage. At Nairobi airport a customs official in a white gold-braided uniform invited us to pay £1,800 import duty. At the Tanzanian border they said we didn't have enough money to enter the country. And when we finally made it to the Kilimanjaro Park Entrance they told us that since we had not obtained permission in advance, we could not go on the mountain. After that lot, we told ourselves, riding the bikes up a volcano would be a piece of cake.

Late in the afternoon of that second day we came out of the jungle. It wasn't a sorry farewell. Although the tiny red flowers with their curving translucent petals and bright yellow tongues had enchanted, and although the lush spectrum of jungle greens had shone in the late afternoon sun like deep-dappled water, the hooting, booming and screeching of invisible death-dealing wildlife had — to someone who doesn't expect to meet anything more ferocious than a pheasant — been a touch nerve-wracking. When a family of baboons ambled across the path ahead of us I rode past the gap into which they'd disappeared with hunched shoulders and a prickly neck, waiting for a hundredweight of red-bottomed mammalia to hurl itself lethally at my head.

The third day began with an equipment conference. We were carrying far too much luggage to make the top, and the bikes needed padding so that we could carry them on our shoulders without being crippled by the angular metal. A backpack full of superfluous items was left in the corner of a climbing hut, while one of our sleeping mats was ceremoniously sliced up with a knife, and taped on the bike frames. Fortified by this unusually perceptive piece of forward planning, we set off.

Fifty metres from the hut the path forked, and we took the left prong. After ten minutes of fast optimistic cycling we were making comments like 'At this rate we can reach the top tomorrow' when we met a climbing party coming up who said we'd taken the wrong turn at the fork. Back at the junction we glared insinuation at each other, and pedalled off again in a somewhat more mellow fashion up a very steep and boulder-strewn track. Thirty seconds later Dick hit a boulder, went over the handlebars — and we were laughing again.

Above our right shoulders we could occasionally glimpse the serrated ridge of Mawenzi, whose granite ramparts are only accessible to seasoned rock climbers, and which faces the main peak of Kilimanjaro across a broad desert-like plateau known as 'The Saddle'.

Our way lay up. The path spent all morning scaling stony slopes split by tumbling streams. At each stream we'd have to trickle the front wheel gingerly down the banks — some of them 15 metres high — then stamp on the pedals, splash through the water and rush the following climb with demonic intent. Normally we could get about 6 metres up the slope before the gradient or a particularly enormous boulder toppled us sideways, where we'd lie panting till one of us made a move, and the other, lest he been seen to 'cop out', would have to follow.

Kilimanjaro came into view slowly, tantalizingly out of reach and sitting snowcapped and rounded like a giant cream-topped Christmas pudding. Beyond the last rocky gully we came upon a still pool whose edges dribbled silently into the surrounding peat. A broken wooden sign on which some long gone traveller had etched 'Last Water' hung crookedly. We filled our two plastic water-bottles, reckoning we were no more than a couple of hours from the final climbing hut. Rumour had it that there was ice close to the hut which could be melted for drinking. From this point on there would be no more running water.

We reached The Saddle with yelps of success. For the first time we could see virtually the whole of our remaining route. Across on the other side of the broad dusty plateau was the steep-sided cone of Kilimanjaro, and lining its rim the great ice cliffs and glaciers that lead to the highest point: Uhuru Peak.

'Cracked the knacker!' said Dick.

We bowled across The Saddle, passing between huge boulders and small volcanic cones, and stopped for lunch in the shelter of a reef of sharp rock. A chill wind hummed morosely over our heads. We were at 5,000 metres. We ate three Ryvita biscuits each, layered with peanut butter and sprinkled with cashew nuts. It made us hungrier.

Behind our backs a huge grey cloud was tobogganning down the slopes of Mawenzi towards us, its dark shadow speeding across the plateau towards Kibo. There was a sharp gust of wind, the light went and before we could zip up our jackets we were in the midst of a full-scale blizzard. We rode close together, taking it in turns to shelter behind the other.

I was deep in a daydream, thinking of steam pudding and custard, pints of tea and warm beds when through the layers of balaclava and windproof hood I heard Dick shout: 'We're lost. The path's gone!'

It took a few moments to sink in. 'Lost?' I shouted back, wondering if I'd heard him correctly. We stopped and looked around. It was a near white-out, with snow sweeping horizontally through soup-thick cloud.

'We were on the path back there, then it kind of went faint, and now it's gone altogether. Have you got the map, or have I?'

Some wretched fumbling in rucksacks produced a sodden peanut-butter stained piece of paper. It was marked with indeterminate pecked lines which could have been contours or paths. Or streams. The surveyor must have been catastrophically myopic or else he muddled Kilimanjaro up with the flower-bed plan for his own back garden. The squiggly lines bore no relation at all to the slopes that we knew existed out there somewhere in the murk.

'Let's split up. Ride parallel courses just in sight of each other and keep heading north-west. That way we must hit the path sometime.' It was an idea that Sir Ranulph Twistleton-Wykeham-Fiennes would have been proud of. And it worked.

We reached Kibo Hut an hour after dark, pedalling tentatively by the light of head-torches and a wan moon, and feeling a little weary.

The altitude was beginning to tell, and the effort of putting the tent up (you pay to sleep in the hut) gave us both headaches and inspired a further bout of competitive whingeing:

'I've got a bit of a headache . . .'

'Yes, my head's a touch sore . . .'

'In fact it's quite painful really . . .'

'Like a severe migraine . . .'

'Could haemorrhage soon . . .'

'Might even die . . .'

'I knew someone who had cerebral oedema once ...'

We spent the night camping on a rock-shelf below the Kibo Hut. The porters, led by the ever-cheerful Simon, would wait at the hut for our return from the summit. Nicas, our Tanzanian guide, agreed to come with us to the crater rim, but no further.

Next day we carried the bikes for five hours up one continuous scree slope. It was excruciatingly exerting, and the lack of oxygen forced us to stop every fifteen paces, doubling over and sucking in great draughts of thin air. Dick, who at the time was living in an office, was in his element: 'Great stuff this. Really relaxing. No telephones up here!'

Adjusting my snow-goggles for the thousandth time I wondered whether there weren't easier ways of 'getting away from it all'. Like sitting on the beach at Brighton for instance. I launched into progressive coughs till Dick turned round. It was my speciality for the trip.

'You okay?'

'Yes, just a tickle in my throat'. I gasped dramatically

through a saliva-speckled contorted face. Dick had a particularly noticeable limp that he was working on.

We reached the crater rim at 6,000 metres looking — for brave adventurers — pretty ragged. We dumped the bikes and flopped to the ground. A brief rest, and we ran down the scree to Kibo Hut in a fifth of the time it had taken to plod up that morning. At the hut there was much last-minute packing to be done. We slept for a couple of hours, then rose at half past midnight, ready for the long slog back up the scree. This time, instead of bikes, we carried packs weighted with food and survival gear. At Gilman's Point, our bikes were still there, crusted with ice.

New Year's Eve, our fifth day out. Dawn was filling the crater, 3 kilometres wide at this point, with a tangerine light. Mawenzi, once a towering mountain, was now below us looking insignificant among a bed of clouds.

The temperature was minus 15 degrees centigrade. Ahead, the icy arete of the crater rim climbed in a gentle curve up to Uhuru Peak, clearly visible from where we were standing. A narrow trail through the deep snow looked just wide enough to ride the bikes. It took three hours to pedal that final 240 metres of ascent.

From the deepest, cleanest blue sky a burning sun cast our slow-moving shadows on the snow. The crater, 300 metres deep and floored in white, looked like a giant's swimming pool closed for winter. Very small, very lonesome, we met with Uhuru.

Reaching the top of a mountain is something of an emotional cocktail: there's the sweetness of success, the tang of tiredness, and when you've drunk the moment to its last drop, the emptiness that comes with the realisation that it's all over; that now there's nothing but downwards; that the adventure (or at least the difficult part) is now over, and that the obsession that's been ruling your life for weeks is now no more.

When you turn your back on a mountain top, you leave behind not an adversary, but your latest and most passionate acquaintance.

We stayed there an hour, riding to and fro, on the snow, at 5,895 metres, not wanting to leave. Gentle rolling clouds broke like surf against the volcanic cliffs below us, the highest people in Africa. Far away to the north-east, the other side of all that fluffy stuff and desert haze was Wajir, where every day 250 TB patients in a grass-hut hospital have no running water.

Slowing and beginning to hurt from the lack of oxygen, we tried to ride back to Gilman's Point. It was very difficult. My head felt as if it would explode. Breathing came in tortured gasps. We carried and dragged the bikes down steep ice and round the rock pinnacles of the crater rim. At Gilman's Point the six of us gathered. We pulled out tent, food, sleeping bags; Pete sorted his film, Michèle made a brew. Catriona and Maggie dropped over the edge of the volcano and disappeared from view. They would ready themselves at the hut 1,055 metres lower down.

With ice-axes, we hacked out a platform in the hard snow above Gilman's Point and put up the tent. We were at 5,640 metres. Night came like the slamming of a freezer door. Jammed together, swaddled in down, the four of us kept each other warm.

We woke in high spirits to watch the dawn of 1985. It was New Year's Day. The tent filled with light and the ice that had formed on the inside cracked and slipped down the nylon. Movement was difficult; an enormous effort in the thin air. We wrote the summit story for the *Sunday Times* and packaged the film. Stowing it safely in her pack, Michèle crept out and made her way to the top of the scree-slope down the outside of the crater. She ran down to Kibo Hut where she handed the film and copy to Catriona and Maggie. They made it to the bottom of the mountain in less than 24 hours.

Back in the tent, a crippling torpor set in. We'd ridden mountainbikes to the top of the highest mountain in Africa; we'd done what we said we would. But there was a second, much harder goal that we'd not mentioned. We wanted to descend with the mountainbikes into the crater, and ride them round the inverted cone deep in the heart of the volcano. To do this would mean abseiling down the cliffs behind Gilman's Point with the bikes, tent and enough food and fuel for three days. It was a spectacle that would make riding bicycles *up* mountains look sensible. But inside the tent, the altitude was playing us out. The headaches got worse. Just turning over in a sleeping bag required an effort of such phenomenal will-power and physical exertion that it left us speechless and gasping for minutes afterwards. We melted ice, and laboriously turned it into luke-warm soup.

173

We were dehydrating faster than we could make water. None of us could manage solid food. We lay there for hours. Nobody wanted to be the first to call off the crater attempt.

If any of us were injured inside the crater, or crippled with oedema, we could only save ourselves by climbing *upwards*, for 300 metres back to the crater rim; a bizarre reversal of the norm on mountains. The tent wracked with coughing. Conversation came in disjointed, muddled sentences, often unfinished. Although calling off the descent inside the crater went against every instinct, the facts of our situation were indisputable: we couldn't manage to eat food, we were weak, and we were having trouble breathing while lying in a tent. What would happen if we tried climbing in these conditions! It was a scary option.

When it became too late in the day to make a move into the crater, and when the lethargy made fetching new ice from outside the door a marathon effort, we agreed that the only option was to descend — down the *outside* of the mountain. Later, I felt we had failed, by not even trying. Certainly my nerve had failed, in that I was unwilling to motivate an excursion into the crater. Or was it just that we'd been visited by a rare dose of common-sense?

It was another two years before the next opportunity to cross that fearful line presented itself.

Coming down, we let gravity do all the work, stones spitting from spinning tyres and brakes jammed on knuckle-tight. With every 100 metres of descent we felt stronger and stronger. The air started to taste wholesome, our appetites came back and headaches disappeared. For three days we ricocheted down the mountain, bouncing off rocks and careering down the dusty way. It was the ultimate bike ride: 5,000 metres of continuous downhill slalom.

Back in the jungle, we met a Frenchman. When he saw us coming he began to laugh, and by the time we reached him he had doubled over and was guffawing hysterically:

'Why', he spluttered 'are you riding bicycles on Kilimanjaro? You must be English. Now I know what I must do next year: carry a refrigerator to the top!'

Two days later we were back in London, standing by our bicycles on a breakfast TV show.

The bicycles became celebrities. One of them was flown to New York to be displayed in an international exhibition. To keep the Kilimanjaro publicity alive as long as possible,

we grasped any opportunity to compete or 'achieve' in our
I.T. T-shirts.

★   ★   ★

People believed, mistakenly, that we were now mountainbike specialists. Tim Gartside organised a mountainbike
race in Wales. I entered. The other competitors were skinny
athletes on ultra-light mountainbikes. The Kilimanjaro
bikes were very strong, but weighty. To make mine lighter I
removed the saddle. A quarter of the way into the race I was
lapped; at half way I crashed and the front tyre exploded,
and I finished on a borrowed ladies' bicycle only a few feet
in front of a fifteen year old. To publicise the *Bicycles up
Kilimanjaro* book, Dick and I thought we should attempt to
ride all the 3,000-foot peaks in England non-stop. There are
four of them, all in the Lake District. Having done the
Welsh 3,000-footers already, this would be a tidy next step.
Scotland could come later.

In keeping with all record attempts, this would be a
highly-organised affair, complete with back-up team. Hol
volunteered, and brought his 1952 side-valve Morris Minor
called, appropriately, 'Bumble', as support vehicle. On the
way up the M1, with two mountainbikes on the roof, three
12-13 stone men inside and a hundredweight of food and
spares in the boot, Hol explained our schedules. The aim
was to knock off the four peaks — Skiddaw, Scafell Pike,
Sca Fell and Helvellyn — in as short a time as possible. We
would start and finish at Keswick's Moot Hall, riding the
road sections, and as much of the mountains as was possible.
We were looking for a time of about 12 hours. The Morris
Minor continued north, flat-out at 37^1/$_2$ mph. 'Shouldn't
the bikes be back-up for Bumble?' I asked. I ought to have
known better.

The chosen day was blowy, wet and cold; it was October.
We were started from the Moot Hall in Keswick before
dawn, by Hol and his brother Charles. 'Should be back for
lunch!' we said, optimistically.

On the way out of Keswick, we rode a circuit of the town's
BMX track in the dark, then set off up Latrigg. At the top of
this pimply hill we were greeted by derisive yells from Pete
Inglis and his girl-friend Lindsey McAlister, Hol, Charles,
a newspaper photographer and a TV crew. Watchers saw us

disappear into the mist of Skiddaw at 600 metres. On the way back down the summit ridge of Skiddaw, the wind was so strong that the front wheels of the bikes were snatched sideways each time we went over a bump. We flew back down the grass to the Latrigg car park, displaying for the TV crew our skill at handling mountainbikes. Unfortunately I hit a molehill and flew over the handlebars. Hol said our descent had taken 18 minutes.

The weather worsened. We pelted down the B5289 to Borrowdale then Seathwaite, and began the long plod up Scafell Pike.

On the top, clouds blew clear the sky and an angel of mercy appeared — a mysterious climber who generously poured us mugs of steaming tea from a thermos. From here we had a delicate scramble up Lord's Rake, a very steep, loose funnel of stones. The bikes kept catching on the sheer walls of the gully. At a rock-step, we had to lift the bikes above our heads, hang them to a spike of stone, then pull ourselves upwards. Each foothold was dynamic — we could only rest on it on the way to the next. Stones whistled downwards. Neither of us wanted to be the second in line.

Lord's Rake opened to Sca Fell's summit. From here we had a horrible slither over grassy boulders as we tried to lose height towards the village of Boot. We reached the hummocky grass with a pant of relief, and hurled the bikes down the slope.

Dick's bike punctured. 'Go on . . . I'll run!' he shouted. He ran so fast down Sca Fell that we reached Cockley Beck within minutes of each other. After a frenzied switching of inner tubes while Lindsey handed out jam sandwiches, and Hol told us we were behind schedule, we pressed on over Hardknott Pass and Wrynose Pass. They seemed much steeper than I remembered.

Knobbly tyres thrummed on the tarmac as we flew through Little Langdale and tackled the short climb over Red Bank. Separated on the climbs, we were both wearing down. Passing Grasmere in the dusk, we turned onto the A591 and began the long haul up Dunmail Raise towards the foot of Helvellyn. We'd been on the move for 12 hours, and were way behind schedule.

It was nearly dark. The cold wind held us on the hill. We had never dried out from the rain and mist. Suddenly there was no more energy. 'Beginnings of hypothermia?' Dick wondered later. At the top of Dunmail Raise we were straining along at walking pace. Pete was waiting. He rushed off to Grasmere to fetch fish and chips. By the time he returned, the prospect of setting off up Helvellyn in the dark was not appealing. The Kilimanjaro conquerors sat in the car, warm and cosy, eating a fry-up, and complaining about minor aches and pains. Outside, the bikes trembled in the wind.

'Look, we'll have to finish it off. Or it'll just mean coming back and doing it all over again.' The logic was inescapable. We got out of the car. With Hol for company, we stumbled up the hill, the bikes across our shoulders. At 9 pm, we reached the summit.

Passed over by the winds rushing up from below, the air on the ridge was perfectly still; a peaceful, intimate vacuum. In this curious suspension of the elements, above the cloud, with a bright moonlight raising a shine from Helvellyn's flat stones, we pedalled slowly round the summit cairn before returning along the ridge and turning down the steep path towards the distant line of black trees.

On the road again, the fuel was flowing and we raced as fast as our legs would go past Thirlmere and over the hill to Keswick. The town square was deserted. The clock on the Moot Hall read 5 minutes past 11. The Four peaks had taken 16 hours 2 minutes.

'If anyone else tries it they'll wonder what kept us' I said. But we had at least finished it, just. Hol thought that, having dropped behind our schedule, we had given up. He wrote: '. . . with no specific time target the interest had gone out of the challenge and it had become simply a matter of slogging along.'

A few months later, Dick was invited to compete in the County Garages Cumbria Quadrathlon. Entries could be teams of three, or individuals. Dick acquired a team of three: himself, brother Chris, and his cousin. He said it wouldn't be worth wearing a clean I.T. T-shirt.

The event started with a run through the town of Workington. Then we reached the river. A line of Canadian canoes lay parked on the bank. 'Which is the front?' I asked. 'Both ends look the same to me' replied Dick. All three of us jumped in, and half the Derwent poured aboard.

We dug the paddles deep. They jammed in the gravel. We

tried again, all on the same side. The canoe swung round and grounded. Other canoes were slipping away, heading into the stream. 'Go left!' we all shouted. The canoe swung right and rammed the bank. Chris climbed out and pushed us off.

Facing backwards, we splashed in a frenzy of clashing paddles down the Derwent, zig-zagging from one bank to the other, bawling orders and counter-orders at each other. Dick's and Chris' sisters Sarah and Emily shouted encouragement from the bank.

The railway bridge was rushing towards us. There were three wide gaps for us to pass through, separated by stone pillars.

'Go for the left one!'

'No, go right!'

'The left one's got faster water!'

'Yes, but the right one's better for the next bend!'

Under full power, we hit the railway bridge. The fibreglass canoe folded in the middle, then sprung open. We popped out like peas from a pod, landing in the river beneath the boat.

Drowning sounds were interrupted by more orders. Even underwater, we were shouting at each other. 'Empty the boat first!' 'Turn it round!' 'Bail it!'

Three more times the canoe capsized before we could run it up onto the beach at the harbour mouth and take to a mode of transport we could all manage: running.

The bikes were lined up outside the sports centre. Soaking wet, we pedalled madly up a disused railway track. The bike I had lent to Dick for the race was one I used for shopping in London. It punctured. In the swimming part of the quadrathlon Dick made up for lost time by aquaplaning up and down the pool in a blur of threshing limbs. Swimming with my eyes shut to prevent my contact lenses floating away, I powered head first into the end-wall of the pool. I floated to the surface like a dead carp.

The event finished with two laps of the playing field, on foot. Chasing vital seconds, Chris sprinted round the mud in bare feet and a swimming costume, throwing himself over the line to snatch a few vital seconds.

'That was a good laugh!' we agreed afterwards. And for once, it really was. We'd won.

It was the end of 'Bicycles up Kilimanjaro'. For a five-day

adventure, it had lasted well. I.T. had received public donations and royalties from the *Bicycles up Kilimanjaro* book totalling £30,000 against an initial outlay from our own pockets of £4,000 — recovered in time from lecturing, writing magazine articles and selling photos.

But *Bicycles up Kilimanjaro* was stuffed with contradictions. We had thrown an awesome amount of cash and equipment at the mountain. Bombarding a goal with money and high-technology was emphatically not a Schumacher principle. We had used a column of porters, *and* had our own specialist support team. We had scorched through 100 rolls of film. We carried 20 kilograms of spares for the bikes and enough food to feed a Sahel village for a week. All this to get two bikes to the top of a mountain. 'Small is Beautiful!'

I wasn't the only one to be confused. After I'd given a talk with slides at Shottermill Middle School, Donna Clark (10) wrote:

'What I don't understand about Africa is that it was a lot hotter at the bottom of the mountain than it was at the top but the top of the mountain was nearer the sun.'

I was stumped. Her classmate Jessica Wright added:

'Would you ever think about cycling up Mount Everest?'
I wouldn't.

Keeping still proved difficult. At the end of 1985, my grandmother Ruth Dingley — whose exotic world travels have always been a great inspiration to me — came to London and we went to an exhibition at the British Museum. It was called 'Buddhism Art and Faith'. Much of the exhibition centred on Asia. Afterwards, over tea, we talked of travel. 'Where in the world' I asked, 'would you most like to visit?'
'Tibet', she said.

I dialled Thomas Cook. 'How much would it cost to travel to Tibet from London, by train and bus?' The reply was a figure that made riding bicycles up volcanoes look cheap. I was keen. So was Granny. But the family were not. This time, I was informed, I was going too far. Did I realise Granny was ninety? What would I do if the Trans-Siberian Express broke down in the middle of an Arctic blizzard? Ruth and I talked it over, and agreed that maybe it was a little ambitious. But by now I'd gone too far down the road to Tibet to turn back.

179

A brainstorming session was held in Dick's flat. We coughed up all the crazy ways of crossing Tibet. There were plenty of them, but no media-hook on which to hang the adventure. I remembered a sentence I'd seen in the *Guinness Book of Records,* and took the book from the shelf. There it was on page 60: 'Land Remotest from the Sea . . . as yet unpinpointed spot . . . Dzoosotoyn Desert.'

We jumped up and down, clapping each other on the shoulders. 'Brilliant!' 'That's it!' 'How?' 'Which route?' 'We can call it Journey to the Centre of the Earth.' We looked at an atlas. 'Just look at the size of it!' The Tibetan Plateau looked enormous. I'd never seen a more frightening place to take a bicycle. We went away to think about it.

In California, Ados was making his own preparations. There was a mountain in South America called Chimborazo. It was 6,270 metres high; 375 metres higher than Kilimanjaro. He was going to try riding to the top on a mountainbike . . . if he made it, it would be a new world height record for a bicycle.

By March 1986, the JCE plans were well advanced. We even had a leaving date — April 27 — though no plane tickets or permission of course. Inside, I was nervous.

'Dick. I'm going to do a spot of training for this one. Going to see how racing bikes work in the snow.'

'Where?'

'Lapland.'

14

An Arctic Test

LAPLAND

A stillness in the greying day told me that dusk was on the way. The snow beside the road was cold and dead. I hadn't seen the sun. Standing on the pedals to pull the bike over a short rise, the back wheel skipped sideways, and just in time, gripped. It was getting colder by the minute. I would have to stop for the night. If I had been carrying a shovel, or ice-axe, I could have carved a cosy snow-cave from the brittle drifts piled ten-feet thick against the rocks. But the biggest tool I had was a tyre lever.

I cast about for shelter, watching the road for more ice. The beach would be the warmest place, on the tide-cleaned sand between the water's edge and the snow. The sea and me were all that weren't frozen solid. I lifted the bike over the snow bank. Trying not to scuff snow into the tops of my shoes, I trod carefully down to the sand, where I scooped a wind-hollow and spead out my jacket and overtrousers. The rib that felt broken hurt more in the cold. I put on my second pair of gloves and tied myself into my sleeping bag.

It was cold, but not dangerously so; the tide was unlikely to reach me, and although I hadn't eaten for 12 hours, I would be sure to find food tomorrow. All in all, I couldn't complain. I lay back with my head on my shoes, and waited for morning. The stars glistened like a million crystals of ice.

Ten minutes later, cold as a corpse, I shivered upright, said 'Stuff this!' and sprinted for the boat-shed where I built a platform out of wooden boards lifted from the floor of the boat. I wriggled back into my down bag muttering: 'Testing your nerve is all very well, but sleeping outdoors 200 kilometres north of the Arctic Circle in winter is going TOO far'.

This was my second week of hardening-up. It was Peter, my Swedish cousin, who had persuaded me to come to

Lapland. 'You must come skiing' he said. 'It'll be good for you. You'll learn quickly!' Out of habit, I brought a bicycle. The skiing was mildly dangerous. We scaled glaciers, skiied over high cols, crossed frozen lakes and slid up glaring white valleys. I hadn't realised till it was too late that, unlike bicycles, skis are not fitted with any braking system; while the others in the group slowed themselves by executing graceful Telemark turns, I had to rely on the friction of passing trees and rocks. Peter said he was surprised that a broken thermos and cracked rib were the only injuries I collected. Shaking their heads and commenting that I was 'crazy', they left me outside the left luggage store at Kiruna railway station. Privately, I saw cycling in the Arctic weather as a piece of cake compared to hurtling out of control down mountains on a pair of planks with 40lb of rucksack strapped to my back. Peter cheered me up by saying he'd seen the Swedish army training on bicycles loaded with shovels, skis and a machine-gun — in minus 30 degrees. 'It's fast, quiet and convenient', he said.

I fell out of the train at Narvik, buried beneath a rucksack, ski impedimentia and a large, angular blue sack. Narvik has the most northerly railway station in Europe. The cold seemed to strip my clothes away. As plump as polar bears, Norwegians waddled past the station, and every car seemed to have chains on the tyres and skis on the roof. Breath hung in the air like cotton wool.

In the seclusion of a youth hostel bedroom that night, like a spy assuming a new disguise, I kicked off the dressing of a skier. Drawing back the zips of the big blue bag, I released the restraining straps and wrapped my head round the cool smooth metal. I felt an electric surge of familiarity; a power-bond. I pulled the finely-machined tubing from the bag. It gleamed dully in the lamplight. There was a knock at the door. I froze. The door swung open. It was the man I took to be a Finn, from the room down the corridor. 'Excuse me please. It is possible you might have some toothpaste please?'

The bike was the lightest I had, an aluminium-framed racing machine from Italy, fitted with tubular tyres. It had been a good companion on past epics. It was faster than the wind. Now I had to find out how such a bike would behave in the most dire conditions bearable by its rider. When the bike was assembled, I piled in front of it some money, a map, compass, camera, spare tyre, sleeping bag, insulated mat, gloves, hat, snow-goggles and a paperback. I'd planned to carry skis with me on the bike, in case the roads had become blocked, but the combined weight of skis and boots was going to slow me down too much. Skis would in any case spoil the realism of the test. I'd dump them at the station next morning. Then I escaped from my plans by reading tourist brochures.

Narvik is the entrepôt for Sweden's iron-ore industry based around Kiruna, and it was for the shipping of the ore that the railway linking the two towns was completed in 1902. Most of Narvik was destroyed during World War II. Now the ore trade has declined and the town's 20,000 inhabitants look as much to the summer tourists and winter skiers as a source of income, as they do to the clattering trains loaded with dusty rock that snake carefully down the rails from Björnfell.

Not for the first time, I started a cycling trip on April 1st; an appropriate day to be setting off on a bicycle into the tail-end of an Arctic winter. For the time of year, it was a warmish day for Narvik: about minus 10 degrees centigrade. Mirrors of frozen water lined the road edges. I was about a metre into the journey when the bike wheels slid from beneath me and I crashed to the ice. Pain froze my ribs, and I had to pull the bike along the ground to a wall that I could lean on, before pulling my toppled machine upright.

Cautiously, I pedalled to the tourist office at Kongens Gate 66. On the counter was a district information guide urging upon visitors the qualities of Narvik as a centre for hiking, skiing, rock-climbing, hang-gliding and angling. Narvik's principal 'sights' appeared to be a Swedish locomotive dating from 1882, and the war cemeteries. I noted that among the campsite lists and directions to reach the Lutheran Church there was a list of useful addresses which included a 'Crane Breakdown Service' in Asbjørn Olsen Street. Could be useful. I asked the lady behind the counter whether she could recommend the North Cape of Norway, or the Lofoten Islands as being the most interesting destination for a five-day cycling trip. She said she hadn't personally cycled to either.

Still undecided, I made my way to the centre of town where there is a whimsical multi-boarded signpost erected to provide light relief for those tourists whose expectations of fjordland Norway have been dashed by the waterside panorama of iron ore heaps, gigantic cranes, railway sidings and dockland equipment. The signpost lists the distances from Narvik to the first 23 landmarks the town council could think of. At the top of the post is 'Nordpolen' at 2,420 kilometres, and the North Cape (Europe's most northerly point) is still 672 kilometres away. Paris (3,257 km) shares ninth equal position with Boris Gleb (1,051 km). Who *is* Boris Gleb?.

Since the North Cape and the Lofoten Islands lay along the same road out of Narvik I postponed the decision. Gingerly, I pushed myself off from a pile of ice left by the snowplough, and rode northwards. Free of the town, the elements vented their strength. Worries about the icy road were soon overshadowed by a gale-force wind that struck as I rode round the flanks of 1,220-metre Fagernesfjellet. Crouching low behind the rucksack tied to the handlebars, fingers slowly freezing up despite thermal mittens, I watched the grey water of Ofortfjorden churned into white caps by the Atlantic blast. On the far side of the fjord I could just see the thin grey line of the 'Arctic Highway' climbing a low mountain before disappearing into thin forest. Whatever it was that had happened to my rib was preventing me from pulling on the handlebars with my right arm. Salt and grit whipped against my face, pricking my eyes till they ran with tears.

If it hadn't been for the banging of her drum I wouldn't have stopped, but the sight of someone dressed in flowing orange and white robes, wearing climbing boots and a huge purple rucksack, drumming and chanting in an Arctic gale 20 kilometres from the nearest building, was just too much to ignore.

'Stockholm' she replied when I asked where she had come from.

'All the way! On foot!' I wondered incredulously.

'No, no, by hitch hike to Kiruna, then I have walked over the mountains for four days.'

'Blimey', I thought, 'I'm worn out after an hour and a half on this road, let alone four days'. We sat on a rock. She rummaged in her pack: 'Here, you must have my food, I have more than I need, I just have 20 kilometres to walk to Narvik where I have friends.' She handed me two beautifully manicured cheese sandwiches and split her orange in two. 'This here' she said as she traced her finger around the symbols painted on the side of her drum 'is my prayer for peace. They are the words of the Japanese Buddhist order Nipponzan Myohoji.' She said the people of peace-loving Sweden had been friendly to her prayer, but once she crossed the border the Norwegians had been less receptive. I told her where I was going, and she smiled.

Her drumbeats were still wafting through the wind as a convoy of British Army half-tracks thundered up the road.

Fortified in spirit and calories, the next few kilometres sped by as I made my way eastwards, back towards Sweden. Nordland is long and thin, with more islands than any other county in Norway and a ruggedly dissected coastline that causes north-south road traffic to wriggle submissively along fjord-sides until a crossing place can be found. Sometimes ferries are used; in other places bridges have been built. Part way along the shores of Rombaken I came to one of the latter-day highlights of the Arctic Highway: the Rombak Bru bridge. When it was completed in 1964 it was the largest suspension bridge in Norway with a span of 325 metres between its towers. From its highest point, a bicycle would fall 45 metres before hitting the water. With the wind shrieking in the cables above and the bike shivering and leaning with the force of the gusts I had an exhilarating few minutes making the crossing. Later that day, at Bjerkvik, I was finally obliged to decide where I was going. Here the roads split. To the left ran the road to the isles; to the right the Arctic Highway continued towards the North Cape. The North Cape road left town up a big hill. I turned to the left along the breezy shore of Herjangsfjorden. Ten kilometres later the road swung up a steep hill lined with strands of frozen pine.

Into the trees the wind was foiled and the sudden silence relieved my battered senses. I was passing occasional wooden farmhouses that dribbled smoke from their chimneys. Neatly-stacked woodpiles stood beneath the eaves. The snow, several inches deep, had hardened through the long winter into a ceramic crust. I could see for miles. The big, flat, treeless areas I guessed were lakes, frozen and snowed upon for months. Some were criss-crossed by the parallel lines of local skiers looking for a quicker route through the forest. I found the stillness eerie. Propping the bike on a snowbank, I pulled myself upwards on tree branches till I could see beyond the valley. No reindeer snuffled in the snow, nor could I spot any high wheeling eagles or solitary hares — all companions on our ski trek the previous week. The landscape was in cold storage until spring.

The first sign of life came at Skånland, a small fjord-side village 90 kilometres from Narvik. Entering the village between small detached wooden homes painted restful shades of green, yellow and rust-red I came to the elegant white-painted wooden church. Opposite the church was a small neat shack selling fast-food and hiring video tapes. In front of the shack was an ancient Volvo estate, with split windscreen, huge rounded mudguards, and a radiator grille that gave the car the expression of a grinning doughnut. Wooden struts held the bodywork together. Next to it was parked another Volvo, more modern, hand-painted orange and yellow, and thoroughly beaten-up. British rock music thudded into the evening air and in the front seat of both cars sat young Norsemen each with a girl's head on his shoulder. They were passing chips to each other through the open windows.

The man selling the chips said there was nowhere to stay in the village, so I cycled on, watching the woods for huts or caves, and the shore for boat sheds. I came to the bridge that leaps across to the first of the islands. Still I had found no shelter. It was getting colder. This was what I had come for. There were only minutes till darkness. Through the gloom I saw the pale strip of sand.

It was probably about midnight when I left the sand-hollow for the sanctuary of the boat shed. By morning, nightmares and the moaning of the wind through the gaps in the wooden walls, made sure that I regretted having chickened out of my beach bivouac.

To warm myself, I pedalled hard beneath a deliciously warm sun. After a few kilometres I climbed off the road to the sea-weathered rocks just above the waterline, and reclined into a cranny in the granite, letting the lapping of the water and sighing of the scrawny birch trees carry me away. How easy it would be to quit. Lapland was just messing around.

To survive the Tibetan Plateau, I would need an inner strength and self-sufficiency the likes of which I'd never used before. Did I have it?

Every journey is the sum of past journeys: to this one I had to add a future journey too.

The diesel gurgle of a fishing boat brought me back to the Lofoten Islands. I'd been asleep. A stone's throw from the rocks a high-sided solid vessel with a stumpy mast and sentry-box wheelhouse was butting through the choppy waves towards the open sea. With the mountains falling straight to the sea there is hardly any land available for crops, so the islanders rely on the sea. A few kilometres on from my rest the road swung suddenly right to reveal the hidden inlet of Fiskefjord.

In the calm silence of this wind-sheltered fjord, a straggle of clap-board houses stood on the rocks below the sweeping slope of the mountain. Tall drying racks made from a lattice of pine, bleached white like bones, hung with crispy paper-dry cod. Cod hung on the south-facing walls of the yellow and red houses; cod heads and cod tails lay all about. The Vikings used to carry stockfish on their longship voyages; weight for weight, stockfish has five times the nutritional value of fresh fish. The Vikings knew about survival. Poking out from a snow-drift by one of the boat sheds was the rusting carcase of a long abandoned car. No-one was in sight, but the village must have been home to twenty or thirty people at least. I pressed on to Lödingen, one of the main ports in the Lofotens, pleased that I could ride with just one arm, the other one resting across the handlebars where it couldn't pull at my rib.

A few grains of dry snow were whipping in from the sea as I leant the bike against Lödingen's only cafe. It was warm inside and smelled of coffee. I settled into a seat by the window. A tall bearded man joined me. Helge Austheim is the town's journalist, contributing to three of the Lofoten papers. He was working that day on a story concerning a local fish farm which was not paying its workers. We went for tea in his single-storey wooden home, where, by the big picture windows which watch a seascape of tiny rocky islands and heaving surf, he talked about the city life he had left and the quality of island life with his wife Anne and rampaging baby son 'Buster'. Lofoten life was changing. The fishing season revolves around the shoals of cod that make their way down from the Barents Sea to spawn in the warmer waters of the Lofotens. Every year the fishing fleets sail from as far away as Møre and Finnmarken, landing their catches at the Lofoten ports. February and March have traditionally been a time of plenty in the Lofotens, with every harbour churned by the coming and going of boats and the quays slippery with fish. Because their boats are too small to sleep on board, visiting fishermen stay in *rorbus,* the small wooden sheds built on the shore, with ten or so bunks in each, a stove, and space to store tackle. King Øystein erected the first *rorbus* in about 1100 AD. Now catches are down, and many of the *rorbus* have been converted to tourist cabins.

Helge spoke of the verdant beauty of nearby Hamaröy and its abundant wildlife, and as I was leaving I said 'After my trip to Tibet, I will visit again. But this time in the summer.'

So to Svolvaer. From Lödingen, on a bouncing hydrofoil that skipped the waves south of Hinnoy, we turned the little rocky lumps of Store Molla and Lille Molla to slide into the darkening port of Svolvaer: the main centre for the Lofoten Islands. The neon lights and shop windows were lit by the time the warps were tight, and the sound of car engines reminded me that I was back in 'the city' (4,500 inhabitants). I didn't like it; didn't need it. Several boats were in the harbour, and nosing around the quays I came across a large ship loading wooden crates. She was sailing in twenty minutes, to Stamsund, two hours away, and would dock at around 11 pm.

Stamsund Youth Hostel has cult status among those 'in the know'. It's an old fishing house built of wood on a crooked wooden jetty perched on piles above the water of the harbour. If you hold your breath you can hear the water muttering beneath your bunk. Roar Justad, the warden, is a small man with a big heart. He runs the place as if it's an extension of his own home — which it is. At the long wooden table it's never quite clear what food belongs to whom, and no-one seems to mind. Clothing hangs from the walls, big rubber boots lean on a well-worn couch and a sturdy matt black wood-burning stove hisses quietly in the corner. Masts sway gently the other side of the window. People arrive here and find it impossible to leave. A group of three from Germany and Holland had been at Stamsund for five weeks. Roar does little to encourage the itchy-footed to move on. Next morning, as I was stuffing the sleeping bag into the pack, he came down from the roof he was mending and suggested I spend the day in his boat pottering about the harbour. How could I explain to him that beautiful, idyllic Stamsund couldn't be more than a port of call?

Outside the shelter of Stamsund the wind was blowing fit to bust again, scouring the snowy verges and flinging salty spindrift in from the sea. For two hours I thought no further than the next turn of the pedals. I reached the ferry quay beyond Leknes, warm, weak and pleased. Of all the ferry crossings this was the most exciting. As the boat punched through the swell the mountains of Moskenesoy grew bigger and steeper until at the tiny harbour of Napp they seemed to hang right over the water. This was the last major island.

Grey clouds were chasing down from the north. I could see nobody. I walked the bike up the steep pitted road towards the shop, thinking that a lump of bread and cheese would set me up nicely for the next 50 kilometres. But the woman at the till had other ideas, and I was soon seated at a table in front of a massive thermos of coffee and a packet of biscuits. When I told her where I was going, she handed me another packet of biscuits.

The road climbed sharply from Napp to cross a small col. Here I met the first little blizzard of the day, though as it was going in the same direction as me, we blew along together, driven snow whistling past my ears as I dipped down towards Vareid. Square pastel-painted wooden houses with snow banked up to their windows whizzed by. Around the other side of the fjord, the solitary spire of Flakstad church came into focus through the grey swirling weather. The church stood on the foreshore, isolated, its slender spire shaped into an onion-shaped bulge near its base.

Mountains began to dominate the horizon. Not ordinary mountains, but mountains which rose sheer from the sea for 1,000 metres. Mountains jammed so close together that there seemed little room for rivers or roads. Toothy peaks leaned over the narrow foreshore along which the road picked a route. All the time the island became slimmer and steeper; tapering into the Atlantic. Propelled by the gale, the bike whirred past the little ports of Hamnoy and Reine and by late afternoon I was rolling around the edge of a cliff high above the water.

My goal came quietly out of the dusk.

The town of Å perches precariously on the granite

foreshore haloed by circling seagulls. The wind was full of snow flurries and the sea played a constant thrashing bass to the alto screams of the wheeling gulls. Among the houses, the road just stopped, mid sentence. A single man clad in cumbersome orange oilskins was hanging cod over some drying racks by the water, but every other inhabitant of Å seemed to be snugly indoors behind the double-glazing — or out at sea. Looking around it was plain to see that the people of Å had not made the same capital out of living in the place listed in the *Guinness Book of Records* as having the shortest place name in the world, as have the Welsh village folk from possessing the longest place name in Britain.

I didn't ask in Å if there was anywhere I could stay, but turned back towards Reine. It had started to snow again. Into the wind now, I paused to peer under the bigger boulders along the way, looking for the driest and most cavernous shelter for the night. No rocky hole presented itself and I found myself drawn all the way back to Reine, arriving in the main street in the last moments of daylight. I dithered. I'd already spent one night out in the cold. Doing it twice didn't appeal. Maybe I should go indoors and remind myself what I was doing it all for. A couple wrapped in thick jackets pointed me at the fisherman's hostel, a big yellow-boarded building with the sign saying 'Fiskar-heimene' above the door. Like a lesser shoal of fish, several red-painted *rorbus* were gathered round the hostel. I was the only guest. I chose Room 203 because of its view.

Reine is the most beautiful place in the Lofotens. The town is built on a curving spit of rock that thrusts into a deep-water inlet ideal for sheltering the boats and houses from the furies of the weather. Three hundred metres above the roof-tops hang rock-walls: comforting and impenetrably black by night; savage by day. The church and school occupy the highest part of the pensinsula, surrounded by tidy weather-boarded houses. At the water's edge, propped on wooden piles, are the *rorbus*. Built on stilts and linking *terra firma* with the front doors are wonky gangways high above the rock and water. Horizontal poles roof some of the gangways, and from these hang dehydrating cod, while slurries of guts below draw in the gulls.

Eilert Aijershiem introduced himself while I was stiffly pulling off the layers of Goretex, thermal mittens, balaclava and scarf. 'I teach English and physical education' he said, 'in the school here.' Eilert had walked up from his small home, where he lived alone, in order to watch the colour TV at the Fiskarheimene. Like Helge, he had moved to the Lofotens from 'the city' — in his case Oslo. With Eilert translating and advising, a meal was devised then cooked by Brigid Anderson who runs the Fiskarheimene with saintly touch. Eilert watched me nearly faint with excitement when a vast dish of grilled cod, baked potatoes, carrots and peas arrived. We talked till late. Eilert could not understand why I had come in winter. I told him about the ride due to start in a month's time. 'Himalayas!' he said 'Colder than Lofoten! The Gobi Desert. So hot! Better I think that you stay here!' he laughed. 'Yes' I said 'You could be right.' In the night I heard the windows rattling with hail.

So much snow had fallen by morning that the doorway had to be shovelled clear. The gangways out to the *rorbu* lay carpetted in snow and the water had taken on a pallid hue. Brigid Anderson wanted me to wait for the daily bus, and despite my protestations, went to to find a timetable. Outside, vapour-trails of snow streamed from the roofs. She gave me the kind of breakfast that makes you want to stay forever. It was tempting. I hauled the bike over the drifts and started walking.

Under a fresh blanket of snow Reine looked even more enchanting, and the soaring black cliffs that form an amphitheatre around the town were now plastered in white as if a careless painter had tipped a pot of whitewash over them. Shortly I met the district snowplough, and, with the odd slip and slither was able to pedal slowly back towards the north-east; slowly, because the wind that had pushed me down to Å was now doing its best to keep me there. On the uphills the bicycle's rear wheel spun on the ice, and even on mild gradients I had to walk. Snow was blasting into my face and was quickly forming new drifts across the road. This was what I had come for. Steaming with exertion I made good headway for three hours, then, on a whim, turned right off the main road to visit a place on the map called Nusfjord. No snowploughs had been here and I had to drag the bicycle up a long hill before sliding down the other side with both feet on the snow and the wheels choked with compacted ice. Nusfjord was tiny. A little gathering of red *rorbus* sat on the rocks just above the water. A fishing boat lay by the quay; crates of fish being moved by fork-lift truck into a big shed where men with knives slit and gutted. There was a shop, but I didn't stop.

A final frenzied pedal through a landscape now even more Siberian in aspect returned me to Napp where the ferry was waiting. Twenty pages of Le Carré later the boat bumped into Vestvågöy island and for the last time I pulled on jacket, gloves and hat for a final 25-kilometre dash to Stamsund. *M/S Finnmarken*, 2,189 tonnes and built in 1956, slid with elderly dignity to the wharf where a wiry islander fielded her warp and looped it around an iron bollard. *Finnmarken* is one of a disappearing breed of ships. Wooden balustrades grace her stairways, and etched flowers pattern the glass of her swing doors. Where there would now be brushed aluminium, there is brass. The *Finnmarken* is the smallest of a fleet of eleven ships that ply the coastal route between Bergen in the south and Kirkenes six days away, far beyond the Arctic Circle. In the summer the *Finnmarken* holds 146 passengers, but on this wintry evening her saloon was host to a small group from Newcastle-upon-Tyne, a German family and a few locals going to Svolvaer and Narvik for the weekend. I thought of my grandmother, Ruth Dingley, and how much she would enjoy this boat; this journey.

The wind dropped, and as the night sky filled with stars, I watched the black outline of the Lofoten Islands slip by the rail. It was a short journey. Too short. We bumped gently into Svolvaer to be greeted by coloured electric lights and the sound of youths tearing round the streets in their hot Volvos. Saturday night in Svolvaer. I was back in 'civilisation'.

★ ★ ★

One week later, in London, final preparations were being made. The concrete floor of my shoe-box flat in the city was covered in piles of clothing and equipment. The evening was bright and sunny. I'd cleaned the salt off the bike frame since Lapland, and felt like giving the old favourite a final ride (the new JCE bikes had just arrived). I crammed a few more p.s.i. in the tyres and whispered off towards Hyde Park. In Fleet Street, a van turned in front of me with no warning and I flew over its roof, somersaulting through the air. As the bike banged along the tarmac I landed on one shoulder, slid on my back, then ran back up Fleet Street to confront the driver.

In St Bartholomew's Hospital that night the duty nurse said as she wrapped the crepe: 'You can't be that unfit if you crash a bike and walk off with a couple of scratches.'

'Mmm. Maybe I'm not' I said, quite pleased.

Bandaged and sore, I carried home the crumpled remains of my aluminium bike. It had lasted longer than most. 'Journey to the Centre of the Earth', was just a few days ahead. The doubts had gone. The next day Dick and I packed our bags for Asia; we'd get the total weight down to 18lb each. This new 'adventure' was a little more serious than that first carefree trip across Europe thirteen years ago.

With just a few hours to go before flying out to Bangladesh to start our ride, a last-minute application to join the expedition arrived. It was signed by my two-year old niece, but her hand appeared to have had a little parental guidance:

DEAR UNKL NIK,
PLEESE CAN MARTIN AND I COME WITH U ON YOUR BIKE RIDE. I WIL BRING MY BIK SEET AND MARTIN WIL GO IN YOUR SADDEL BAG. I WILL EAT THE SAME FOOOD AS U BUT MARTIN ONLIE DRINK MILK SO WE WIL HAVE TOO FIND SUM COWS.
                                LUV SARAH
                                   XXX

15

Journey To The Centre Of The Earth

INDIA, NEPAL, TIBET

The ceiling fan slowly stirred the air of Room 309 of the Golden Gate Hotel in downtown Dhaka. It was 3 am. Sweat beaded on Dick's face and arms as he punched a grimy finger at the key-pad of our solar-powered calculator.

'What's the Obskaya co-ordinate again?' I smoothed Operational Navigation Chart ONCC4 (US Defense Mapping Agency) on the concrete floor squinting once more at the convolutions of the northern Russian coastline. Two cockroaches watched from the doorway. '66 degrees 14 minutes north, 72 degrees 6 minutes east.' More mutterings, then, a few minutes later:

'Wow!' There was another pause. 'Guess where it is.'

'I'd rather not.'

'In the Gobi Desert!'

Twelve hours later we were in a train rattling south through the paddy-fields, an Irish missionary telling us about the bandits operating in the Chittagong Hills. 'Sometimes they come down to the villages, but you should be all right.' The missionary wondered whether we were riding bicycles to the beach at Cox's Bazaar. No, we said, the idea was to go in the opposite direction, northwards to India, then Nepal and over the Himalayas, across the Tibetan Plateau and the Gobi Desert to the centre of the earth. 'Centre of whaaat?'

The centre of the earth, we explained, was the place in the world most remote from the open sea. This place happened to be in the north-west corner of China. We were going to pedal from the open sea to the centre of the earth. The distance was roughly 5,000 kilometres; we wanted to do it in 50 days. The missionary looked at us and said dubiously: 'Where are you from?'

'England' we said.

'Ah. I understand now.'

We started the ride at noon the next day, at a place called Patenga Point on the Bay of Bengal about twelve kilometres south of Chittagong. A crowd of kids splashed with us in the shallows.

It took us a little over an hour to get lost. In a maze of cobbled alleys lined with tumbledown homes spilling scores of children, we tried to ask directions. Laughing, shouting humanity hemmed us in. We couldn't move. The heat, noise and humidity, squeezed the oxygen from the air. A young boy helped. We rode for another hour then collapsed into a shady *chai* house dizzy with the heat. We drank. Bangladesh swam into focus. Somehow we'd already lost a pair of waterproof overtrousers. 'A good start, eh!' We both laughed.

Timing for the ride was critical. Slowness on the early section of the ride meant we'd be caught by the approaching monsoon then have to finish the ride when the Gobi Desert would be at its hottest. Yet we couldn't start earlier because the passes of the Himalayas and Tibet would still be blocked by snow. Through this tiny window in the seasons we planned to race pell-mell halfway across Asia. Speed was only possible if we travelled light. The combined weight of luggage and bicycle for each of us was 40 lb.

Raleigh, the Nottingham-based bicycle manufacturer had built for us two bicycles that were light, fast and tough. These had been created by Gerald o' Donovan, who designs the bikes used by many pro teams that race the Tour de France. He chose Reynolds '753' tubing for the frames, and we had ten gears. To save weight we had just one gear-lever: changing gears on the front was effected by a kick of the heel. We carried the bare minimum of equipment: a sleeping bag and one set of clothes, but no tent or food and just one litre-bottle of water. The strap was cut from our watch. Zips, labels and buckles removed from our clothing and pannier bags — and later on we even shortened and cut slots in our chopsticks. With our tiny knife I cut the mountains from the background of the photograph of my girlfriend Penny. The picture was still too heavy. I hesitated before making the next cut, then taped her head to the back of a credit card. The only items to escape the trimming and drilling were our contact lenses.

The monsoon struck as we raced through the afternoon of that first day, trying to make up lost time. Banks of grey and white cumulus began piling up on the low green hills to our right. Then the sky darkened and large drops of rain began to collide with the hot tarmac. Seconds later the downpour arrived. People ran for cover. We pedalled on through spraying water. Beyond the storm the sun was setting. Later came the lightning: violent instants of bright white — almost blue — light. Every few seconds it ripped the night to jagged shreds. Ahead, the road pulsed with water. Lamps had been too heavy to carry so we pedalled by the sky's flashes. As if flexing itself for the coming monsoon season, the wind began tearing at the roadside trees. Savage gusts pushed the bikes this way and that. A jagger of light exposed, like a camera flash-gun, two rickshaws locked together in urgent companionship, their riders' bodies arced and straining against the wind. It got cold. From a soothing warmness the water changed to chilly hailstones that bruised our faces.

We came to a *chai* house packed with Bangladeshis. We dived in, and squeezed on to the end of a bench. A hundred pairs of eyes turned and stared. We asked for tea. Cataracts poured from the thrumming roof and we squeezed the water from our T-shirts.

That night we spent in a rest house in the small village of Misurai, writhing beneath a mosquito net memorable for the number of mosquitoes it trapped on the inside. To beat the heat, we left early the next morning. The road ran along the edge of the Ganges delta, built high on an embankment above a sea of paddy-fields. The ripeness of the rice in each paddy was measured in greenness, the brightest green of all coming from the fields of very young shoots. Interspersed amongst the greens would be the odd patch of blue where the rice had yet to be planted and the empty water reflected the sky. Men ploughed, sploshing through muddy water behind leaning buffaloes. Cows stood munching the verges and amiable dogs wandered. On the causeways between the paddies stood small thatched huts, low enough to get swept away by the waters that periodically break the banks. Bangladesh is the second poorest country in the world, beset with environmental and political problems. Floods, plagues of rats, ferry sinkings that drown hundreds, hailstones that kill, epidemics and a refugee crisis are but a few of the human catastrophes disguised by the green virility of the Ganges.

By late afternoon we were approaching the Meghna River, watching a great anvil-shaped cloud grow in the sky; wondering whether we'd be in for another aquatic thrashing. But today's surprise wasn't water. At dusk the air suddenly filled with millions of bugs. Insects got in our mouths, blocked ears and noses and hair. Breathing became a struggle. With thermal long-johns wrapped round our faces, we made the Meghna, where, in a small dusty village called Daudkhandi we found a hotel called the Modena and paid for a room that was so small the bikes had to stand on the double bed. Even the cockroaches looked cramped for space.

That night, after chapatis, *dahl* and vegetable curry, we were marched off to the police station by an angry crowd who thought we were taking too much interest in local politics. Earlier in the day one man from the 'Rickshaw Party' had been killed in a riot in Daudkhandi, and many others had been injured. We were taken to the headquarters of Mr Nazruil Haq, Officer Commanding Daudkhandi police force. He grilled us about something he called our 'mission' (an elevation from the 'social welfare philanthropic activity' that Bangladesh TV had called our ride the week before). Tiredness pulled my eyelids closed every few seconds; Dick, wide awake and warming to a new diplomatic challenge, presented Mr Haq with the details of our innocent enterprise. It occurred to me how dependent for success Dick and I were on only one of us weakening at a time.

Mr Haq was cordial and kind. He sent a soldier to buy us Pepsi Colas. But he wasn't happy. 'Today' he announced with eloquent understatement, 'we have had a certain degree of trouble here in Daudkhandi. You see, we are having our general elections!' The Pepsis arrived. 'And you should not stay at the Modena; it is *not* sophisticated.' We agreed, but there was nowhere else to stay in Daudkhandi. Past midnight he allowed us to return to the Modena, escorted by a soldier.

Dhaka embraced us in a hooting, chaotic riptide of charging yellow buses, lopsided trucks and clanging rickshaws. The British Consulate restrained us for 24 hours while a few bombs went off and Bangladesh's political pressure cooker let off a bit more steam. We slipped out of the city before dawn on Day 5. Time was not on our side.

Election day was in two days' time, and all but one of the frontier crossings had been closed. Now we had to detour 200 kilometres to escape to India along the main road to Calcutta.

For two days we raced west, crossing the Ganges on a ferry called *Oxfam Kamini*. Approaching Faridpur, the road was blocked by a chanting crowd, brandishing banners. They were from the 'Rickshaw Party', and looked fervent. A bus came up behind us, horn blaring, driving straight at the crowd. We slithered through in its backwash. I was shouting 'Up the Rickshaws' as loud as I could; earlier, some members of the crowd had kicked out at Dick's bike. We spent the night in the 'Hotel Luxury' at Faridpur while trucks overflowing with yelling electioneers careered past and a shrieking storm tore off tin roofs. Rain thundered, lightning flashed, we poured with sweat in the humidity, and a power failure cut the lights. By the light of a candle guttering with uncertainty, Dick grumbled 'Why is life so cruddy'.

At 4.15 next morning we lifted the bikes over the sleeping forms in the corridor, and headed for India. Over the torn trees crept the sun, benign and apologetic for the previous day's climatic aberration. Birds woke and sang and herders switched the rumps of cattle ambling down the road. Outside Jessore a young boy handed me a flower with slender white petals and an intoxicating scent. 'Razanighanda', he said it was called.

India is much less poor than Bangladesh. Many Indians ride bicycles, which in Bangladesh was a sign of unusual wealth. The women dress flamboyantly. Entering the border town of Bangaon we rode beneath a hugh billboard advertising the 'Belle Non-Slip Bra' with a painting of a woman dressed in something that looked as if it had been inspired by the Forth Road Bridge. We found a place described as 'Fooding and Lodging', and spent the night sharing double bedding.

It took us five magical days to cycle across the north-east corner of India. One evening we came to Katoya. For many miles we'd been pedalling a single-track strip of frayed tarmac to cross a tabletop of flat paddies. Small groups of people were walking home in a dusty tangerine dusk. By some huts the road ended; beyond was a broad dry river bed, divided in the distance by the grey solidity of a river.

Against the skyline was the outline of many buildings. We rode down the steep river bank and onto the sandy bed which was criss-crossed with the tracks of animals, humans, carts and bicycles. At the water's edge stood two or three thatched huts, with knots of people drinking tea, talking quietly or climbing gently aboard the ferry — a broad-beamed boat about 10 metres long, low in the water, with a deck of split bamboo. The sun dripped into the trees beyond the river.

We lifted the bikes onto the boat to join twenty or so other passengers, a two-metre pile of jute, 6 bicycles, some goats and two boatmen. Not a ripple showed. The boy in the bow poled mightily into the mud and the boat swung slowly into the stream. Into the deeper water the long bamboo poles were shipped and two great oar blades snatched from their resting places at bow and stern. With one boy straining at each end, in short, choppy strokes, the heavy ferry crabbed across the current towards the evening silhouette of Katwa. The town was sited on the outside of the river's bend, and here the current was strongest, obliging both boys to row from the bow. Now their strokes became urgent enough to arch their sitting bodies until their backs curved like longbows over the bamboo deck. The boat touched with precision at the foot of a flight of stone steps leading up through a carved arch to the town. We carried the bicycles upwards, and began the search for lodgings.

In Siuri we entertained the locals by taking a hacksaw and hammer to two of the most expensive bicycles ever seen in India, in order to cut the wheel guides from the brakes, shorten the gear levers, and chisel a handful of plastic 'D' rings from the panniers. One of the many manifestations of the competition between the two of us was in the arena of weight-savings: he who travels lightest, wins. The surgery provided a modest pile of amputations weighing at least two or three grams. We rode happily into the Rajmahal Hills while long elastic shadows danced on the cooling tarmac beside us. Onto the time taken to change gear we now had to add two minutes of fumbling for the diminutive but streamlined knob of metal that had once been a gear lever.

Dick woke me one sweltering Indian dawn by singing 'Happy Birthday'. I wriggled on the sticky mattress. My cousin burst naked from the mosquito net over his bed and trod across the gritty concrete floor to the table, where, with due ceremony he arranged a single birthday card that he'd hidden since Dhaka. It was from Mum and Dad, with the edges trimmed to save weight. As a birthday gift ten years ago Ruth Dingley had given me a copy of Schumacher's book *Small is Beautiful*. In the front, she had written: 'This seems to me to be an important book'.

At Monghyr we once again met the Ganges, arriving at the river bank just before dawn on Day 10. Below the town a broad flight of stone steps led down to a lazy sweep of water the colour of *dahl*. In the young sunlight early-risers stood wringing out clothes, dipping and swimming, spouting like bleary gargoyles before going to work. The ride across the northern plains of Bihar was excruciatingly hot, on molten tarmac that stuck to the tyres. Dick measured our daily consumption of liquid at 14 litres each. We were working well together, and covered 240 kilometres in temperatures of 115°F.

Nepal happened on the morning of Day 12. We'd been woken at 5 am in the border town of Raxaul by the discordant shrieking of a brass band backed by a thumping that was either the percussionist or the sound of bricks bouncing off the backs of the trombonists' heads. 'Bonkers!' I wrote in my notebook. On the wall of the Nepalese immigration office was a map showing two routes to Kathmandu: the new highway detouring far to the west, and the old road, a serpentine climb northwards through gorges and over three high passes. The Immigration Officer recommended the new road; we chose the old.

The storm struck while we were eating rice and *dahl* in Hetauda, a flyblown dump in the foothills of the Himalayas. I was itching to get moving; Dick was down the street flattening rivets in his saddle with a borrowed hammer and punch. He seemed to take ages, and when finally we started cycling, it was 7 pm. It was a delay that saved us the inconvenience of being crushed beneath hundreds of tons of earth and rubble.

We were the first to arrive at the landslide. In light rain we rode the bikes through a hub-deep torrent of mud and water sweeping across the road, while to our left the river, ten times its normal size, was excavating the bank and claiming chunks of tarmac. Whole lumps of mountainside had been ripped down, burying the road beneath six metres of mud and rocks the size of refrigerators. We gingerly carried the bikes over the debris, ears filled with the roar of the swollen river below us. A few trucks stood stranded between rockfalls; drivers disappeared. A man in the village of Bhainse let us sleep on the wooden floor of his one-room home.

Next morning the steep green-terraced hillsides were still sat upon by weighty cloud. We rode up and down passes all day, crossing the 2,488-metre Simbhanjyang at 11.13 am, then the 2,030-metre Tistung Pass at 1.35 pm, finishing the afternoon by racing each other up the 1,000-metre Nardunga Pass. In the moments between cresting the Nardunga and being submerged beneath the heaviest monsoon outburst of the trip, we had a tantalising glimpse of far-off snowy peaks catching the last sun of the day. The Himalayas — and Tibet — were just up the road.

The spectre of that enormous, inhospitable plateau, the biggest in the world, had been growing and mutating in my mind for weeks. It was as if we were cycling through a magnetic field, with impulses polarised toward an invisible point of unimaginable force through which we somehow had to pass. The plateau, with its thin air, freezing conditions, lack of habitation and fierce storms was, we thought, the only part of the route likely to create problems. Until we crested that plateau, no drama was worth worrying about; noting mattered until we were up *there*.

The stress of coping with sordid teeming Kathmandu was relieved by a trip to the dentist, where an American motorcycle enthusiast called Dr Elliot B. Higgins removed from my mouth half a tooth while music by Eddie and the Cruisers bounced round the room. For four dispiriting days we listened to pessimistic rumour about entry to Tibet, contracted 'Kathmandu Quickstep', and tried in vain to recover a bag of spare clothes and bike parts from the airport. We argued until we couldn't bear to be near each other.

Our adventure holiday was becoming serious. We had contingency plans should the Chinese prevent us from entering Tibet with bicycles: one was to cycle the entire length of the Himalayas and cross the Karakoram Highway into China; another was to carry the bikes illegally over one of the high snowy passes by Everest. But when we came to the Chinese border, we were waved past the Immigration Office with a smile and a nod. It all seemed too easy.

Above the border the rough track climbed through forest and into cloud. It was getting colder and darker. The euphoria of the border crossing had disappeared. We were in Tibet. Now nothing stood in our way. The tension detonated into an acrimonious slanging match. Tired, cold, hungry, we stood in wet shoes beneath the pines shouting at each other about whether or not we should have stopped at a stream to fill the water bottles. By early evening it was raining.

An army barracks emerged from the mist, but a Chinese soldier waved us away. So we tried a stone building nearby. We pushed our way through a stiff wooden door. Inside were four men sitting round a single electric ring. By the front door were small wooden bird traps, and in an outhouse, tethered by string to their legs, flapped a couple of the unfortunate creatures. The men said their taste was good. While the wind and rain whistled outside and our clothes steamed by the stove, one of our hosts practised his harmonica, then a couple of them began singing duets, reading their lines from a notebook. Inside the notebook was page after page of meticulous calligraphy. One of the pages was filled with a red and blue watercolour of a beautiful bird. The artist and owner of the notebook had a shock of thick black hair and a fountain pen the size of a frankfurter. All six of us slept on the single bed jammed together nose-to-tail.

We set off to cross the Himalayas next morning, wrapped in every stitch of clothing we carried. The bumpy brown road climbed, passing between high snow banks while the mighty ice spires of Shishapangma grew cathedral-like above our heads.

A herd of yaks wallowed ruminatively down the pass, their bells clonking dolefully in the thin air.

At 5,214 metres we came to the summit of the Lalung Le. Breathing came hard at this altitude. Wind-frayed prayer flags of purples, reds, blues, yellows, greens, whites and off-whites flapped madly in a freezing gale that tore invisibly through the clear blue sky. Behind us the silver serrations of the Himalayas stood as a wall between the teeming heat of busy Asia and the buff ridges of the high barren plateau that stretched northwards before us for over a thousand kilometres. Dick, the expedition databank, later calculated that since leaving the Sun Kosi river in Nepal we'd cycled continuously uphill for 153 kilometres and 4,633 metres. It would be 22 days before we dropped off the far end of the Tibetan plateau into the warmer oxygenated air of the Gobi.

Beyond the pass we freewheeled down in chilling evening shadows and stopped at the first building we came upon. We slept on the earth floor with four Tibetan horsemen, boisterous rogues with long leathery faces, pigtails, wide-brimmed felt hats, thick coats and big, brass-handled sheath knives. They gave us handfuls of *tsampa*, the roast barley flour that is the staple diet in Tibet, washed down with salt tea. The tea is usually served up with lumps of rancid yak's butter that float in it like dissolving yellow icebergs.

For four days and 450 kilometres we pedalled on a terrible combination of sand, gravel, deep corrugations and rock. Each pass was a monumental challenge; one of them — the Jia Tsno La — rose to 5,252 metres. For two of the days the dark pyramidal north face of Mount Everest dominated the southern skyline; Gaurishankar, Menlungtse and Cho Oyu too. In the Lhaze valley we watched yaks decorated in red wool plumes ploughing the tiny fields while the men and women sang and chanted, and wind whipped plumes of dust from the plough shares.

Soon we would have to turn north, away from the populated valleys of Tibet. We spent our sixth night in Tibet as we had spent the fifth: sleeping outdoors, unable to reach shelter by nightfall. Day 17 began badly and got worse. Below the sandy stream bed which we had slept in, we had an emotional row about the relative merits of two routes to Lhasa. One followed the tarmac road over a high pass: the other cut the corner to Lhasa by taking an exciting line up the bed of the Brahmaputra gorge. Our map showed no roads or tracks through the gorge.

For half a day we followed a small track above the river, dwarfed by the gorge walls. Then the track divided. Which led to Lhasa? We went to the right. All afternoon we pedalled uphill on rocks and slippery boulders. By nightfall we were up in the clouds, cold and hungry. And lost. Our miniature compass told us that we were too far south. We pressed on, hoping for a village or hut for shelter. The rain made us even more miserable. We climbed higher. It grew colder. In the dark, with no lights to see by, the handlebars of the bikes kept trying to twist from our numbed grip. We collided with rocks and holes. With each corner in the valley we hoped for a house. Each corner revealed a new, bleaker sweep of snow-filled valley. There was an overhang in the rock. By piling rocks in front of the overhang we created a cave big enough for two — just. The floor was strewn with animal dung.

'Claustrophobic' Dick said. We waited for morning.

'It's light!' There was a rustling and grunting; cursing. An elbow jabbed my side.

'You warm?'

'More or less.'

'Let's move, it's nearly dawn.'

Inside the cave, we were jammed together. The rock was an inch above our faces. I wriggled out. The bikes were covered in new snow. Out of the sleeping bag it was desperately cold. With anorak hoods tight round our cheeks we walked fast on snow that froze our feet. We hadn't eaten since breakfast the day before.

We had walked for half an hour before realising that we'd been woken in the cave not by the light of a coming dawn, but by the ghostly glow of a full moon shining on the white mountainsides. It was still the middle of the night. We had to survive another three hours till daybreak. The prospect was so ghastly that we couldn't bring ourselves to acknowledge the mistake we'd made. In silence, we resumed our stumbling journey.

Then the dogs attacked, They came from all sides, howling and snarling. My stomach knotted. Icy fear rooted us to the spot. Only the anaesthetic of exhaustion stood in the way of unbridled terror. One wrong move and we'd be torn to bits.

'Are they wolves?' asked Dick.

'Could be' I replied, uncertain.

I was convinced that if one of them managed to bite us, the others would finish us off. There seemed to be five or six, and they were all big; black evil shadows against the snow. We were surrounded.

'Walk slowly and close and we'll look like a big animal,' I suggested.

In the darkness I could see twisted mouths and bared teeth coming to within our arms' reach then pulling away. The violence was deafening. We walked on, slowly, till they pulled away.

204

Their howling echoed along the valley long after they left us. We found another cave that sheltered us from the still falling snow till morning, when we started walking once again. An hour brought us to habitation: a small stone mill-house where five Tibetan men revived us with *tsampa* and salt tea and a toasting fire of dried dung.

During a violent wind-driven hailstorm that afternoon we bounced down the 4,794-metre Kambo La pass. Lhasa lay a day away. Day 27 was warm and sunny. We rode by a rushing river up a broad green-floored valley. Two men bobbed across the water in a skin coracle. The river braided into streams split by clean shingle banks and sunlit ripples reflected light on the flanks of cows munching rich green meadow grass. We passed a giant Buddha carved into a rock wall, and then, in the far distance we caught sight of two hillocks, one topped by a shining white rectangular building: the Potala Palace.

Half an hour later we were cycling beneath those serene sloping walls, brilliant white under a clear evening sky. It was 6.30 pm. The streets through the old part of Lhasa were busy with bicycles and carts, teeth-pullers, cloth-sellers, light and shade, cooking smells and a confusing tide of Tibetans and Chinese. 'Mao-suits' mixed with skin-coats, Tibetan women heavily dressed in jade and brass and silver jewellery lounged with fierce-looking Khambas, their long black hair top-knotted with red wool. How much Lhasa must have changed since the Chinese came. Only the solid, stone buildings looked uncorrupted. It was such a relief for us to be safe; and the sense of wonder at reaching this hidden city — a place which had defied all corners till the 20th century — left us bewildered. It was difficult to know where to look next.

From the gilded roofs of the Jokhang Temple the view northwards is blocked by high brown peaks. Beyond those peaks, the Tibetan Plateau assumes a new scale of desolation. The distance to Golmud, the next town on our route, was, we estimated, 1,330 kilometres. We left Lhasa on the evening of Day 30, riding through the outskirts full of a new confidence. But we took a wrong road and, trapped in a barrack-like school, were obliged to exit from the 'Forbidden City' via the back-wall of a boys' urinal.

Helpful winds blew us through the next morning. Yaks dotted the valley floor like shaggy black haystacks. We crossed a watershed. Dick timed us as we raced down the backslope and found we were passing a kilometre post every minute. Sixty kph at 4,900 metres. We were flying.

At a road-halt called Damsung we were served with a steaming green beverage in which floated a huge sugar crystal and two dark ovaloid nuts. 'Bollock tea' as it became known, was deliciously refreshing. Supper that night was taken 90 kilometres up the road in a nomad's tent where we were served cold rice and yak yoghurt laced with tiny pieces of dark yak meat and some slimy worm-like things. They refused to take the money we offered. We set off into a bitter twilight while thunder grumbled in the black mountains. Ten kilometres down the road we found a farm-camp where a crochety old woman let us sleep on animal skins in a store full of yak dung.

These brief stops in tents and tea houses were oases of tranquillity in a landscape of extraordinary desolation. With the wind behind us we crossed a high, open grassy moorland, the snow-peaks receding behind us. Apart from the occasional nomad's tent, the plateau was featureless but prey to baffling winds, like an ocean in the doldrums. The days became harder and harder. Our map sometimes imagined places that turned out not to exist, or it marked towns which revealed themselves as a single building, sometimes derelict. On Day 32 we rode for 122 kilometres through blasting gales to reach a place call Nagqu, only to find by late afternoon that no such place existed. We had to ride another 90 kilometres and cross two more passes that evening before reaching shelter in Amdo. Looking for the truck-drivers' barracks in the dark, a sudden storm of sand and snow pinned us to the ground. Too tired to help him, I heard Dick bawling abuse at the sheer hatefulness of the night. Stumbling through flooded trenches, we reached a three-metre wall. We lifted the bikes over, handing them to each other; a comradely gesture. By the safety of the huts I sat down, unable to speak. Dick found us a room.

So unpredictable was the weather that our eyes flicked constantly from horizon to horizon. A stack of black clouds could spread like a stain across the sky then just as quickly be spirited away. Blizzards would ambush us from side valleys, and the wild wind could throw us along like leaves in a full gale or reduce us to walking pace. It became harder to hide the fear of being caught out without food or shelter.

On the morning we had to tackle the highest pass on the plateau — the Tanggula — we sat by the doorway of a *chai* house watching snow pour down the valley. We were numb with cold. I scribbled in my notebook: 'If we're wearing *all* our clothes in a tea-house, what the hell's going to happen on top of a 17,000-foot pass?'. At 1 pm, there was a gap in the weather, and we stepped reluctantly outside. Hail and snow rattled on our jackets; water from the road soaked our feet. We rode upwards, persevering merely to survive; to get the job done. Then the storm was blown away, leaving an icy wind cutting from a blue sky. We stopped and tore off our frozen shoes and socks, pulling our thermal gloves over our feet and massaging the life painfully back into our toes. After 45 kilometres of climbing we saw prayer flags and whooped for joy. But the plateau played another of its tricks: the Tanggula was 40 kilometres further on.

It took another four days to reach Golmud; four days of wind and snow and struggle highlighted by dramatic windows in the weather through which the Tibetan Plateau presented itself in its awesome vastness, and encounters with isolated road-camps. We passed carcasses of dead yaks, and with each new day of hard-won progress I found it easier to slip into far-off fantasies. 'For the first time on this trip' said Dick 'this has all got beyond a joke.' One evening we came to a place called Tongtayho, a collection of cement huts set on a barren, stony plain. Animal bones lay all about. A mad-looking woman with cross-eyes and horrible white stuff on her forehead came from a door and laughed hideously at us. Another crazily cackling girl and her friend with wide staring eyes and thick matted hair came to stare too. They fed us and gave us a bed.

We climbed a pass called the Fohohshan in snow falling so thickly that we hadn't known we'd been cycling uphill until we reached a sign saying we were at 5,010 metres. And on the way down the other side, beside a river gorged with thick red muddy water, we came to a stone shelter where two kind old ladies fed us sweet bread and showed off their transistor radio by tuning in to 'My Music' so we could listen to Denis Norden and Frank Muir jesting on the BBC World Service. It was oddly comforting to hear their familiar voices so far from home. We slept that night in a tent, sharing a bed with four road-workers. On the next day, we climbed another 5,000-metre pass then crossed a sandpaper-coloured desert whose horizons were defined by mountains so small they looked unreachable. The sky was huge and threatened us with snow all afternoon. We came on a lonely building. In it were two young men whose duty it was to man some weather recording equipment. They had a tiny puppy which bit ankles. One of them came from Xian; the other from Chengdu. They were a very long way from home.

Across the plain the snow came. We were hanging on, from hour to hour. At the far side of the plain the hills began again. We came to an eerie collection of mostly broken buildings called Budonquan deserted but for a *chai* house. A man with a laughing moon-face made us hot food and cleared a shelf on which we could sleep. That smiling man of Budonquan brought us back to life. It snowed for most of the night. The next morning it was so cold that we started cycling with our sleeping bags wrapped around our bodies beneath our jackets.

We climbed slowly through snowy mountains and over the last pass of the high plateau — the Kunlun at 4,767 metres — then dropped down through interlocking spurs of dark mountainside to join a valley which in turn fed us into a narrow gorge. Still losing height we wound downwards while the river gained momentum and the gorge sides grew till they stepped up to the sky in towering brown cliffs. The air was warming with every kilometre. We were moving from the high, cold southern part of the Tibetan Plateau, to the lower, less cold northern part known as the Qaidam Pendi. We reached the town of Golmud that night, and celebrated by having our first wash for eight days and by eating a meal. Since Bangladesh, we had cycled 3,700 kilometres; we had now covered two-thirds of the total distance to the Centre of the Earth, and we knew from maps that the difficult part of the journey was now over.

All the maps marked the Silk Road as a broad band of red running diagonally through the Gobi Desert. We expected smooth tarmac, heavy motor traffic, roadside eat-halts and small hotels. We expected in essence, to be safe. We spent the next day oiling the bikes, and as a gesture of committment to our final sprint-for-the-finish we whittled a few more grams from our equipment by enlisting the help of a wrinkled old man in a workshop, who drilled three holes in our Campagnolo spanner.

Three days of hard riding took us a further 527 kilometres over mostly dirt tracks that cross the sand-dunes, salt pans and mountains of the northern plateau. The last pass on the plateau is the Dangjin La. From here we plummetted downwards for hundreds of metres into the Gobi Desert; out of the fridge and into the fire.

Beyond Dunhuang, there's a place called Liuyuan. The Silk Road runs through Liuyuan, on its way from Ansi towards Hami, Turfan and Urumqi. We rode into Liuyuan on Day 43, hot, confident, happy in the knowledge that just a few days of fast pedalling over tarmac separated us from our goal. At the time, it did seem strange that nobody in Liuyuan seemed to know where the Silk Road was. We found it, eight kilometres outside the town, a vague dust and gravel track fading into the distant haze and dust of the desert. We were stunned. It wasn't fair: just when we thought we were home and dry, we now had to face a problem bigger even than the Plateau we'd just crossed. I sat down on the stones, and stared, not wanting to believe it. Dick wandered around the junction, speechless. A phrase from a book written by Mildred Cable and Francesca French, two of the great Gobi travellers of the forties, just would not leave me. 'The desert which lies between Ansi and Hami', they had written, 'is a howling wilderness . . .'

So, we'd arrived a hundred years too late. The Silk Road, once the greatest trade route in the world, was dead, killed by a railway built in the 1950s. Where camel caravans loaded with silks, bronze mirrors, furs and gunpowder had once rested and slept on their arduous desert trek, we were now to discover roofless ruins and shrinking oases. For food and water we would have to rely on the occasional passing truck. The gravel on the first few kilometres of the Silk Road was so soft and deep that we had to push the bicycles. In two hours we managed to cover ten kilometres. We had one thousand kilometres to go.

On the second day, we rode further into the chain of bare rocky mountains that bar the way to the Taklamakan Basin, reputed to be the hottest desert in the world. We followed a gorge, dry-throated, our snow-goggles now fitted with side-pieces made from surgical tape to protect our eyes from the glare and the dust. Stung by centuries of burning sun, the rocks of the narrow defile just beyond Xing Xing Xia lay like cinders across the desert floor. An upward glance through the lancing rays revealed revetments, watch-towers and fortifications built to defend this once critical border outpost. Mildred Cable remembered garrisons of over a thousand troops. Among the ruins we found a solitary eating house, where a man told us that the next water lay 170 kilometres away. We drank until we couldn't manage another mouthful. Through the gorge was the Taklamakan Basin. This was the blackest dare of all. What if there were no trucks?

We checked the water bottles for leaks, lifted ourselves onto the saddles and began. The track twisted down through the rocky valley, emerging onto a hummocky plain. It was not quite impossible to ride the bicycles, and we made 30 kilometres in three hours.

'Trucks!' There was a dust-cloud in the distance. Two trucks slid and bounced towards us. We waved them down. The drivers let us swig rapaciously from their green metal canteens. That evening, we laid the sleeping bags on the gravel. Westwards, a burning sunset was being sucked into the sand and the rock as the day quietly released its grip on the landscape. Many travellers must have laid their weary bodies on this desert's warm stones, but few of them would have been using bicycles for windbreaks. All sense of time and place are lost in the peace and quiet of a desert at dusk. Dick was kneeling over our map, squinting close in the disappearing light. 'Fifty miles; there's not another person closer to us than fifty miles', he kept saying.

With each hour a little more ground was gained. Two or three trucks passed us each day. Sometimes we found it best to leave the track and ride along the baked crust of the desert floor, but mostly we wrestled the bikes along deep ruts and corrugations.

Two days after leaving Liuyuan we came to the oasis town of Hami, and were arrested. It was late at night, and the police chief's pyjamas were hanging out below his uniform trousers. It was, he said, illegal to ride bicycles across the Gobi Desert. However, if we left town quickly, he would forget the matter. We raced on into the night, climbing into the Pafrhku Shan mountains next day. We were heading into a particularly remote precinct of the Gobi. Once, we saw three camels, and another time, hours from the nearest settlement, we met a gang of men building a wall. They fed us on noodles, which we ate from their enamel washing bowls. Each day we nibbled a little more off the journey, and each day the urgency to finish increased. Nothing, but nothing, was going to stop us now.

High in the Pafrhku Shan a sand-storm tried to blow us from the mountain as we lay in our sleeping bags, and for a day we fought a wind strong enough to knock us from the bikes. We had to shout to hear each other. We became more desperate; more careless. Twice we had punctures from riding into rocks. After leaving it on the ground, Dick had to backtrack six kilometres into the wind to fetch our precious compass. From 2,000 metres on the Pafrhku Shan, the road dropped to below sea level in the Turfan Depression. When we reached the oasis town of Turfan itself, we were told that we were lucky it had been a cool day: just 38°C. We raced uphill for 183 kilometres to Urumqi, arriving in the city during the evening rush hour — a bewildering maelstrom of human activity after our days in the desert. We spent two days preparing ourselves for the final dash to the Centre of the Earth. We reckoned we could make it in three days. We left town early in the morning.

About 130 kilometres beyond Urumqi, Dick shouted: 'Don't look behind but we're being followed.' It was the police again. They took us to the Public Security Bureau headquarters. We were questioned and searched. In the darkness of the men's toilet we hid the US Defence map and the BBC's tape recorder under our clothing. They took away our passports and bicycles and the next day we were protestingly bundled into a van with bars on the windows. The van took us back to Urumqi.

Four days of interviews ended in us signing a 'confession' and paying fines of 100 *yuan* each. This cleared the way for us to make an official application to finish our journey. Riding the bikes was not allowed, but as a special concession, we were going to be allowed to finish our journey by light aircraft and truck, accompanied by a Chinese guide, Mr Chang Le. At a point close to the Centre of the Earth, we would be allowed to ride the bicycles for a 'symbolic kilometre'.

We flew to an airstrip at an oil town called Karamay, and next day reached Hoxtolgay, an oasis town sitting in the lee of the mountains along which runs the border with Russia. Outside the town, the truck got stuck in a sandy trench. The driver refused to risk his vehicle any further along the bumpy track. Latitude 46°16.8'N longitude 86°40.2'E was still 50 kilometres away. 'Now' said Chang 'you make your bicycle ride. One hour.' We lifted the bikes from the back of the van. Chang looked worried; perhaps he knew. It was 2 pm. We would not see him again for 17 hours. We rode as if our lives depended on it. The track was alternately sand and deep gravel; the bikes bucked and kicked. Pedals thrashed as they never had before. Here the desert was slightly undulating, tan-coloured, sizzling like a freshly fried pappadum. At 20 kilometres we came to a place called Hsia-tzu-chieh, and asked the way. We were looking for a small road that crossed the north of the Dzungarei Desert. None of the tracks we came across seemed to tie in with our map, and with every mistake we made, precious time ticked away. We knew that Chang would have to start a search for us by nightfall. By dawn the next day half the Chinese army would be on the warpath. The map said we should head east from the village, but all the tracks we tried drew us inexorably south-east. By 5 pm, with just 5 critical hours of daylight remaining, we had to admit that we were lost.

For a few moments, hopes drowned in the nausea of defeat. We backtracked. Tried again. And at 7.30 pm we found a rough track heading east. There were still 20 kilometres to go. We pounded the bikes mercilessly. Now there was no time to avoid riding over rocks and the bikes bounced across the desert with dry shrieking chains; powered by an all-consuming final desperation to snatch our goal before events overtook us.

A plume of dust rose on the desert behind us. The gap was closing. We were nearly there. We stopped while shaky fingers traced lines on the US air map and took compass bearings on the two bluffs. 'The Centre of the Earth' was 300 paces southwards. We started across the sand, counting.